AMERICAN INDIANS

DEVELOPMENTS, POLICIES AND RESEARCH

VOLUME 1

AMERICAN INDIANS: DEVELOPMENTS, POLICIES AND RESEARCH

Additional books in this series can be found on Nova's website under the Series tab.

Additional e-books in this series can be found on Nova's website under the e-books tab.

AMERICAN INDIANS

DEVELOPMENTS, POLICIES AND RESEARCH

VOLUME 1

ALBERT O. HUGHES

AND

ERIC A. SANDERS

EDITORS

nova
publishers
New York

Library of Congress Cataloging-in-Publication Data

ISBN 978-1-61122-351-4

ISSN: 2167-9916

Published by Nova Science Publishers, Inc. ✛ *New York*

CONTENTS

PREFACE

This book presents current research on new developments and policies in the American Indian population in the United States. Topics discussed in this compilation include a brief history of federal Indian education programs, the students served by these programs and their funding; the Indian Education Formula Grant Program of the Elementary and Secondary Education Act; the Indian Child Welfare Act (ICWA); addressing child hunger and obesity in Indian country; unique factors that may affect economic activity on tribal lands; gaming on newly acquired lands and the Indian Gaming Regulatory Act (IGRA); and Indian reserved water rights under the Winters Doctrine.

Chapter 1 - The federal government provides elementary and secondary education and educational assistance to Indian children, either directly through federally-funded schools or indirectly through educational assistance to public schools. Direct education is provided by the Bureau of Indian Education (BIE) in the U.S. Department of the Interior, through elementary and secondary schools funded by the BIE. Educational assistance to public schools is provided chiefly through programs of the U.S. Department of Education (ED). The student population served by federal Indian education programs consists of members (or descendants of members) of Indian tribes, not American Indians/Alaska Natives (AI/ANs), as identified by race/ethnicity. Most of this Indian education population attends public schools. Most federal data on Indian students are based on race/ethnicity, however, which complicates analysis of results for the population served by federal Indian education programs. The BIE was originally part of the Bureau of Indian Affairs (BIA) in the Interior Department. The BIA began the current system of direct Indian education in the decades following the Civil War, with congressional approval and funding. The system developed gradually to its current structure. In the late nineteenth century, the BIA began placing a few students in public schools, a trend that accelerated after about 1910. At present, 90% or more of the Indian student population attends public schools. The BIE-funded education system for Indian students includes 169 schools (and 14 "peripheral dormitories" for students attending public schools nearby). Schools and dorms may be operated by the BIE itself or by tribes and tribal organizations. A number of BIE programs provide funding and services, supplemented by set-asides for BIE schools from ED programs. Federal funding for Indian students in public schools flows to school districts chiefly through ED programs, with a small addition from a single BIE program. BIE and public schools are subject to the standards and accountability provisions in the Elementary and Secondary Education Act (ESEA), as amended by the No Child Left Behind Act (NCLB, P.L. 107-110), although not all such provisions apply to BIE schools. Authorization for most ESEA programs ended in FY2007. The 112th Congress is likely to consider reauthorization of the ESEA and may amend BIE and BIA educational provisions in Title 25 U.S. Code. Among the issues that may be raised are the academic outcomes of Indian students in public and BIE schools, the incorporation of native language instruction, the development of academic standards and assessments by Indian tribes, the conditions of BIE school facilities, and appropriate participation of Indian tribes in public school education.

Chapter 2 - The Title VII-A formula grant program, authorized by the Indian Education Act of the Elementary and Secondary Education Act (ESEA) as amended by the No Child Left Behind Act (NCLB; P.L. 107-110), is one of the current federal programs targeted to raising the educational achievement of Indian children. The Title VII-A Indian Education formula grant program is intended to provide supplementary funding for the education of Indian children. The program is intended to help Indian students meet state academic and content standards in an environment that values their culturally related academic needs. For purposes of the program, an Indian student is defined as a member or child or grandchild of a member of a federally recognized tribe, state-recognized tribe, or terminated tribe; an individual considered by the Secretary of the Interior to be an Indian; an Eskimo, Aleut, or other Alaska Native; or a member of an organized Indian group that received a grant under the program before October 20, 1994. Local educational agencies (LEAs), Indian tribes, and Bureau of Indian Education (BIE)-funded schools are eligible for funding. To be eligible, LEAs must meet one of the following criteria: serve a minimum of 10 Indian students; have an enrollment of at least 25% Indian students; be located in Alaska, California, or Oklahoma; or be located on or in proximity to a reservation. An Indian tribe that represents a minimum of 50% of the LEA's Indian enrollment is eligible in lieu of the LEA if the eligible LEA does not establish an Indian Parent Committee. The Indian Parent Committee contributes to and approves the LEA's plan for using grant funds. Grants are awarded by formula based on the enrollment of eligible Indian students and the average per pupil expenditure (APPE). In FY2010, it is estimated that the 1,265 grantees received an average of $220 per Indian student enrolled. The program's FY2010 appropriation was $104 million. Grantees, 90% of which are LEAs, have served 448,000-481,000 Indian students each year since FY1999. Since FY1999, LEAs in three states—Alaska, Arizona, and Oklahoma—have received almost half (45%) of the funding. LEAs in 12 states have not received any funding since at least FY2002. The 112th Congress may consider several issues related to the Title VII-A Indian education formula grant program and Indian education more generally as it considers reauthorization of the ESEA. The various definitions of Indian student used to determine eligibility for programs that support the education of Indian students complicates administration and makes program success difficult to measure. The educational outcomes of Indian children have continued to lag behind those of other American children. Many stakeholders believe the program is underfunded as measured by the program's original 1972 statutory goals, the educational achievement gaps, and the need for culturally relevant education.

Chapter 3 - From the 19th century to the passage of the Indian Child Welfare Act (ICWA) in 1978, the federal government, states, and private adoption agencies sought to remove Indian children from their tribes and families in order to "civilize" the children or provide them with better lives. Congress passed the ICWA to end this practice and the high rate at which Indian children were being removed from their homes and placed with non-Indians. One survey reported that 25%-35% of all Indian children were being separated from their families and placed in foster homes, adoptive homes, or institutions. The House Committee on Interior and Insular Affairs termed the disparity between placement rates for Indians and non-Indians "shocking." The committee concluded that many non-Indian social workers who recommended removal of Indian children from their families and communities were ignorant of Indian cultural values and social norms, and biased against typical Indian family life. This bias too often resulted in finding neglect or abandonment when there was none. The committee noted also that the decision to take Indian children from their natural homes was frequently carried out without due process of law and that most cases did not go through adjudication because parents voluntarily waived their parental rights in the face of coercion from the state. Accordingly, Congress passed the ICWA to establish standards for removing Indian children from their homes, prioritizing placement of Indian children with extended family members and other Indians, and giving tribes a recognized role in the placement of Indian children by, among other things, recognizing tribal court jurisdiction over Indian child placements and adoptions. In addition, the ICWA includes important procedural protections for Indian parents, custodians, and tribes to provide due process of law.

Chapter 4 - American Indian (AI) and Alaska Native (AN) children have approximately twice the levels of food insecurity, obesity, and Type II diabetes, relative to the averages for all U.S. children of similar ages. Those living on or near reservations or other tribal lands (often referred to as Indian Country) have historically been particularly disadvantaged. Section 141 of the Healthy, Hunger-Free Kids Act of 2010 (HHFKA) requires that the Department of Agriculture (USDA) provide a report to Congress on USDA programs that serve AI children living in Indian Country and may reduce these risks. This report describes how USDA nutrition programs serve children in Indian Country and how provisions of HHFKA and other recent initiatives might improve those services. The major USDA programs that serve children and families in Indian Country include the National School Lunch Program (NSLP); the Supplemental Nutrition Assistance Program (SNAP); the Special Supplemental Nutrition Program for Women, Infants, and Children (WIC); the Food Distribution Program on Indian Reservations (FDPIR); the Child and Adult Care Food Program (CACFP); and the Summer Food Service Program (SFSP). NSLP offers lunches free or at a reduced price to school children from low-income families. SNAP offers food assistance to low-income households in the form of debit cards that can be used to purchase food items at authorized retailers. WIC provides food packages to pregnant and postpartum women, infants, and children up to age 5 to meet their special nutritional needs as well as nutrition education, breastfeeding promotion and support, and referrals to health care and social service providers. The FDPIR provides USDA food packages to low-income AIs/ANs living in Indian Country who do not participate in SNAP. CACFP provides reimbursement for meals served to low- income children in child care settings. SFSP offers meals to children when schools are out. WIC and FDPIR are frequently administered by tribes themselves, whereas NSLP, SNAP, CACFP, and SFSP are administered by the States in which the reservations are located. Based on data from the March 2009 Current Population Survey, the NSLP has the widest reach; about 550,000 children identified as AI/AN alone received free or reduced-price school lunches in an average month in 2008, and 328,000 children who identified as AI/AN and white. SNAP also serves a large number of AI/AN individuals; for example, it served 540,000 people who identified as AI/AN alone and 260,000 who identified as AI/AN and white in an average month in 2008. During an average month in 2008, WIC served approximately 126,000 individuals identified as AI/AN alone, and 85,000 who identified as AI/AN and white. FDPIR, which is available only to households living in Indian

Country, served about 80,000 individuals per month in fiscal year 2011, based on administrative data. Specific data on the number of AI/AN children served in CACFP and SFSP are unavailable. Several provisions of HHFKA would help USDA improve the nutritional quality of meals served to children in Indian Country or increase access to program benefits. The law required updating nutrition standards for USDA-subsidized meals in schools and child care settings. The USDA proposed rule for nutrition standards and menu planning in the NSLP and School Breakfast Program would be an important step in reducing risk of obesity and type II diabetes; for example, the new standards include restrictions on the fat content of milk and requirements to increase offerings of fruits, vegetables, and whole grains. The new law will also improve access to school meals by allowing schools in low-income areas more options for serving free meals to all students without requiring parent applications, which could improve food security among children on reservations. USDA is one of the agencies sponsoring *Let's Move! In Indian Country*, a public/private initiative to provide technical assistance and social marketing materials to parents, schools, and communities in Indian Country to encourage healthy eating and physical activity.

Chapter 5 - Indian tribes are among the most economically distressed groups in the United States. In 2008, the U.S. Census Bureau reported that the poverty rate among American Indian and Alaska Natives was almost twice as high as the population as a whole—27 percent compared with 15 percent. Residents of tribal lands often lack basic infrastructure, such as water and sewer systems, and sufficient technology infrastructure. Without such infrastructure, tribal communities often find it difficult to compete successfully in the economic mainstream. This testimony statement summarizes GAO's observations on (1) five broad categories of unique issues that may create uncertainty and therefore affect economic activity in Indian country and (2) tribes' use of special gaming and small business contracting provisions. It is based on prior GAO reports. This testimony statement contains no new recommendations.

Chapter 6 - The Indian Gaming Regulatory Act (IGRA) (P.L. 100-497) generally prohibits gaming on lands acquired for Indians in trust by the Secretary of the Interior (SOI or Secretary) after October 17, 1988. The exceptions, however, raise the possibility of Indian gaming proposals for locations presently unconnected with an Indian tribe. Among the exceptions are land: (1) acquired after the SOI determines acquisition to be in the best interest of the tribe and not detrimental to the local community and the governor of the state concurs; (2) acquired for tribes that had no reservation on the date of enactment of IGRA; (3) acquired as part of a land claim settlement; (4) acquired as part of an initial reservation for a newly recognized tribe; and (5) acquired as part of the restoration of lands for a tribe restored to federal recognition. During the latter half of 2010, the Department of the Interior (DOI) conducted a series of consultation sessions with Indian tribes focusing on whether the implementing regulation should be revised. The regulation was issued on May 20, 2008; it specifies the standards to be satisfied by tribes seeking to conduct gaming on lands acquired after October 17, 1988. The regulation includes limiting definitions of some of the statutory terms and considerable specificity in the documentation required for tribal applications. On June 13, 2011, DOI determined the regulation to be satisfactory and withdrew earlier departmental guidance, which had been issued before the regulation had become final. The guidance addressed how DOI handled tribal applications for off-reservation land acquisitions for gaming. It had elaborate requirements for a tribe to satisfy with respect to applications for gaming facilities not within commutable distances from the tribe's reservation. In the 111th

Congress, two bills were enacted with gaming prohibitions in connection with land-into-trust acquisitions: (1) Section 2601 (h)(4)(A) of P.L. 111-11, which prohibits class II and class III gaming on land which the provision transfers to be held in trust for the Washoe Tribe; and (2) P.L. 111-323, which prohibits gaming on federal land transferred to the Hoh Tribe. Legislation in the 112th Congress includes S. 771, the Tribal Gaming Eligibility Act, which requires tribes to satisfy new standards before newly acquired lands may be found to be eligible for IGRA gaming on the basis of a land claim settlement, an initial reservation, or restoration of lands. There is also a bill, S. 1424, which would set new standards for taking off-reservation land into trust for gaming. Other bills providing for federal recognition of tribal status or taking land into trust include explicit provisions relating to gaming. Among them are S. 121 8/H.R. 27, the Lumbee Recognition Act; H.R. 475, the Fountainhead Property Land Transfer Act; H.R. 783/S. 379, the Thomasina E. Jordan Indian Tribes of Virginia Recognition Act; S. 675/H.R. 1250, the Native Hawaiian Government Reorganization Act; H.R. 1991, the Cocopah Lands Act; S. 617, the Elko Motocross and Tribal Conveyance Act, which transfers land into trust for the Te-moak Tribe of Western Shoshone Indians of Nevada; S. 908, which provides for the addition of certain real property to the reservation of the Siletz Tribe; and H.R. 2938, the Gila Bend Indian Lands Replacement Clarification Act.

Chapter 7 - Although the federal government has authority to regulate water, it typically defers to the states to allocate water resources within the state. The federal government maintains certain federal water rights, though, which exist separate from state law. In particular, federal reserved water rights often arise in questions of water allocation related to federal lands, including Indian reservations. Indian reserved water rights were first recognized by the U.S. Supreme Court in *Winters v. United States* in 1908. Under the *Winters* doctrine, when Congress reserves land (i.e., for an Indian reservation), Congress also reserves water sufficient to fulfill the purpose of the reservation. As the need for water grows with the development of new industries and growing populations, the tension arising from the allocation of scarce water resources highlights the difficulties that often surround reserved water rights, particularly in the western states. Western states generally follow some form of the prior appropriation system of water allocation. The prior appropriation system allocates water to users based on the order in which water rights were properly acquired. Because Indian reserved water rights date back to the government's reservation of the land for the Indians, these water rights often pre-date other water users' claims. Although the prior appropriation system's reliance on seniority provides a degree of certainty to water allocation, Indian reserved water rights may not have been quantified at the time of reservation. Because *Winters* did not dictate a formula to determine the quantity of water reserved, courts apply different standards to quantify tribal reserved water rights. As a result, other water users may not know whether, or the extent to which, Indian reserved water rights have priority. Because of these uncertainties, Indian reserved water rights are often litigated or negotiated in settlements and related legislation. This report will examine the creation of Indian reserved water rights under the *Winters* doctrine. It will analyze the scope of the doctrine, including the purposes for which the water right may be claimed and the sources from which the water may be drawn. It will also discuss various quantification standards that courts have used in attempting to clarify Indian reserved water rights. Finally, it will examine the effect of the McCarran Amendment, through which Congress extended jurisdiction to state courts to hear disputes involving Indian reserved water rights.

In: American Indians. Volume 1
Editors: Albert O. Hughes and Eric A. Sanders

ISBN: 978-1-61122-351-4
© 2012 Nova Science Publishers, Inc.

Chapter 1

FEDERAL INDIAN ELEMENTARY-SECONDARY EDUCATION PROGRAMS: BACKGROUND AND ISSUES[*]

Cassandria Dortch

SUMMARY

The federal government provides elementary and secondary education and educational assistance to Indian children, either directly through federally-funded schools or indirectly through educational assistance to public schools. Direct education is provided by the Bureau of Indian Education (BIE) in the U.S. Department of the Interior, through elementary and secondary schools funded by the BIE. Educational assistance to public schools is provided chiefly through programs of the U.S. Department of Education (ED). The student population served by federal Indian education programs consists of members (or descendants of members) of Indian tribes, not American Indians/Alaska Natives (AI/ANs), as identified by race/ethnicity. Most of this Indian education population attends public schools. Most federal data on Indian students are based on race/ethnicity, however, which complicates analysis of results for the population served by federal Indian education programs.

The BIE was originally part of the Bureau of Indian Affairs (BIA) in the Interior Department. The BIA began the current system of direct Indian education in the decades following the Civil War, with congressional approval and funding. The system developed gradually to its current structure. In the late nineteenth century, the BIA began placing a few students in public schools, a trend that accelerated after about 1910. At present, 90% or more of the Indian student population attends public schools.

The BIE-funded education system for Indian students includes 169 schools (and 14 "peripheral dormitories" for students attending public schools nearby). Schools and dorms may be operated by the BIE itself or by tribes and tribal organizations. A number of BIE programs provide funding and services, supplemented by set-asides for BIE schools from ED programs. Federal funding for Indian students in public schools flows to school districts

---

[*] This is an edited, reformatted and augmented version of the Congressional Research Service Publication, CRS Report for Congress RL34205, dated May 23, 2011.

chiefly through ED programs, with a small addition from a single BIE program. BIE and public schools are subject to the standards and accountability provisions in the Elementary and Secondary Education Act (ESEA), as amended by the No Child Left Behind Act (NCLB, P.L. 107-110), although not all such provisions apply to BIE schools.

Authorization for most ESEA programs ended in FY2007. The 112th Congress is likely to consider reauthorization of the ESEA and may amend BIE and BIA educational provisions in Title 25 U.S. Code. Among the issues that may be raised are the academic outcomes of Indian students in public and BIE schools, the incorporation of native language instruction, the development of academic standards and assessments by Indian tribes, the conditions of BIE school facilities, and appropriate participation of Indian tribes in public school education.

INTRODUCTION

The federal government provides elementary and secondary education and educational assistance to Indian[1] children, either directly through federally funded schools or indirectly through educational assistance to public schools. Direct education is provided by the Bureau of Indian Education (BIE)[2] in the U.S. Department of the Interior (Interior), through elementary and secondary schools funded primarily by the BIE. Approximately half of federal educational assistance to public schools is provided through programs of the U.S. Department of Education (ED). Other programs are administered by the BIE and other federal agencies.

Federal provision of educational services and assistance to Indian children is based not on race/ethnicity but on their membership in, eligibility for membership in, or familial relationship to members of Indian tribes, which are political entities. Federal Indian education programs are intended to serve Indian children who are members of, or, depending on the program, are at least second-degree descendants of members of, one of the 564 federally recognized Indian tribes certain other Indian tribes and groups.[3] The federal government considers its Indian education programs to be based on its trust relationship with Indian tribes, a responsibility derived from federal statutes, treaties, court decisions, executive actions, and the Constitution (which assigns authority over federal-Indian relations to Congress).[4] Despite this trust relationship, Indian education programs are discretionary and not an entitlement like Medicare.

Indian children, as enrollees in public education, are also eligible for the federal government's general programs of educational assistance, but such programs are not Indian education programs and will not be discussed in this report.

This report provides a brief history of federal Indian education programs, a discussion of students served by these programs, an overview of the programs and their funding, a discussion of the application to BIE schools of key provisions of the Elementary and Secondary Education Act, as amended by the No Child Left Behind Act (P.L. 107-110), and brief discussions of selected issues in Indian education.

BRIEF HISTORY OF FEDERAL INDIAN EDUCATION ACTIVITIES

U.S. government concern with the education of Indians began with the Continental Congress, which in 1775 appropriated funds to pay expenses of 10 Indian students at Dartmouth College.[5] Through the rest of the 18th century, the 19th century, and much of the 20th century, Congress's concern was for the *civilization* of the Indians, meaning their instruction in Euro-American agricultural methods, vocational skills, and habits, as well as in literacy, mathematics, and Christianity. The aim was to change Indians' cultural patterns into Euro-American ones—in a word, to assimilate them.[6]

From the Revolution until after the Civil War, the federal government provided for Indian education either by directly funding teachers or schools on a tribe-by-tribe basis pursuant to treaty provisions or by funding religious and other charitable groups to establish schools where they saw fit. The first Indian treaty providing for any form of education for a tribe—in this case, vocational—was in 1794.[7] The first treaty providing for academic instruction for a tribe was in 1803.[8] Altogether over 150 treaties with individual tribes provided for instructors, teachers, or schools, whether vocational, academic, or both, either permanently or for a limited period of time.[9] The first U.S. statute authorizing appropriations to "promote civilization" among Indian tribes was the Indian Trade and Intercourse Act of 1793,[10] but the Civilization Act of 1819 was the first authorization and appropriation specifically for instruction of Indian children near frontier settlements in reading, writing, and arithmetic.[11] Civilization Act funds were expended through contracts with missionary and benevolent societies. Besides treaty schools and "mission" schools, some additional schools were initiated and funded directly by Indian tribes. The state of New York also operated schools for its Indian tribes. The total of such treaty, mission, tribal, and New York schools reached into the hundreds by the Civil War.[12]

After the Civil War, the U.S. government began to create a federal Indian school system, with schools not only funded but also constructed and operated by the Bureau of Indian Affairs (BIA)[13] with central policies and oversight.[14] In 1869, the Board of Indian Commissioners—a federally appointed board that jointly controlled with Interior the disbursement of certain funds for Indians[15]—recommended the establishment of government schools and teachers.[16] In 1870, Congress passed the first *general* appropriation for Indian schools not provided for under treaties.[17] The initial appropriation was $100,000, but both the amount appropriated and the number of schools operated by the BIA rose swiftly thereafter.[18] The BIA created both boarding and day schools, including off-reservation industrial boarding schools on the model of the Carlisle Indian Industrial School (established in 1879).[19] Most BIA students attended on- or off- reservation boarding schools.[20] BIA schools were chiefly elementary and vocational schools.[21]

An organizational structure for BIA education began with a Medical and Education Division during 1873-1881, appointment of a superintendent of education in 1883, and creation of an education division in 1884.[22] The education of Alaska Native children, however, along with that of other Alaskan children, was assigned in 1885 to Interior's Office of Education, not the BIA.[23] Mission, tribal,[24] and New York state schools continued to operate, and the proportion of school- age Indian children attending a BIA, mission, tribal, or New York school rose slowly.[25]

A major long-term shift in federal Indian education policy, from federal schools to public schools, began in FY1 890-FY1 891 when the Commissioner of Indian Affairs, using his general authority in Indian affairs, contracted with a few local public school districts to educate nearby Indian children for whose schooling the BIA was responsible.[26] The BIA after 1910 pushed to move Indian children to nearby public schools and to close BIA schools.[27] Congress provided some appropriations to pay public schools for Indian students, although they were not always sufficient and moreover were not paid where state law entitled Indian students to public education.[28]

By 1920, more Indian students were in public schools than BIA schools.[29] **Figure 1** displays the changing number of Indian students in federal, public, and other schools from 1900 to 1975. The shift to public schools accompanied the increase in the percentage of Indian youths attending any school, which rose from 40% in 1900 to 60% in 1930.[30] Comparable data are no longer available.

In 1921, Congress passed the Snyder Act[31] in order to authorize all programs the BIA was then carrying out. Most BIA programs at the time, including education, lacked authorizing legislation. The Snyder Act continues to provide broad and permanent authorization for federal Indian programs.

In 1934, to simplify the reimbursement of public schools for educating Indian students, Congress passed the Johnson-O'Malley (JOM) Act,[32] authorizing the BIA to contract with the states, except Oklahoma, and the territories for the education of Indians (and other services to Indians).[33]

In the 1920s and 1930s, the BIA began expanding some of its own schools' grade levels to secondary education. Under the impetus of the Meriam Report and New Deal leadership, the BIA also began to shift its students toward its local day schools instead of its boarding schools, and, to some extent, to move its curriculum from solely Euro-American subjects to include Indian culture and vocational education.[34] In addition in 1931, responsibility for Alaska Native education was transferred to the BIA.[35]

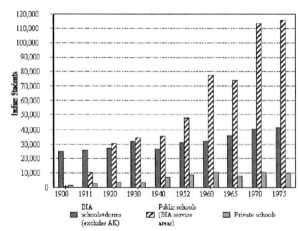

Source: U.S. Department of the Interior, Bureau of Indian Affairs, *Report on BIA Education.* Final Review Draft (Washington: Bureau of Indian Affairs, 1988), Tables 1 and 8, pp. 15, 27.

Notes: BIA data include students in peripheral dormitories but exclude students in Alaska BIA schools. Public school data are for Indian students living in BIA administrative or service areas.

Figure 1. Number of Indian Students Enrolled in BIA, Public, and Private Schools, 1900- 1975.

The first major non-Interior federal funding for Indian education in the 20th century began in 1953, when the Federal Assistance for Local Educational Agencies Affected by Federal Activities program,[36] now known as Impact Aid, was amended to cover Indian children eligible for BIA schools.[37] Impact Aid pays public school districts to help fund the education of children in "federally impacted areas." Further changes to the Impact Aid law in 1958 and the 1970s increased the funding that was allocated according to the number of children on Indian lands.[38] Congressional appropriations for Impact Aid increased as the JOM funding decreased. By FY1981, Impact Aid funding for Indian students amounted to $147 million,[39] while JOM funding the previous year was only $28.1 million.[40]

In 1966 Congress added further non-Interior funding for Indian education by amending the Elementary and Secondary Education Act (ESEA) of 1965,[41] the major act authorizing federal education aid to public school districts, to add set-asides for BIA schools to the program of grants to help educate students from low-income families; school library resources, textbook, and instructional materials; and supplementary educational centers and services.[42]

A congressional study of Indian education in the 1960s[43] that was highly critical of federal Indian education programs led to further expansion of federal non-Interior assistance for Indian education, embodied in the Indian Education Act of 1972, now known as ESEA Title VII.[44] The Indian Education Act established the Office of Indian Education (OIE) within the Department of Health, Education and Welfare and authorized OIE to make grants to local educational agencies (LEAs) with Indian children and eventually to BIA schools.[45] The OIE was the first organization outside of Interior (since Interior's birth in 1849) that was created expressly to oversee a federal Indian education program.

Federal Indian education policy also began to move toward greater Indian control of federal Indian education programs, in both BIA and public schools. In 1966, the BIA signed its first contract with an Indian group to operate a BIA-funded school (the Rough Rock Demonstration School on the Navajo Reservation).[46] In 1975, through enactment of the Indian Self- Determination and Education Assistance Act (ISDEAA),[47] Congress authorized all Indian tribes and tribal organizations, such as tribal school boards, to contract to operate their BIA schools. Three years later, in Title XI, Part B, of the Education Amendments of 1978, Congress required the BIA "to facilitate Indian control of Indian affairs in all matters relating to education."[48] This act created statutory standards and administrative and funding requirements for the BIA school system and separated control of BIA schools from BIA area and agency officers by creating a BIA Office of Indian Education Programs (OIEP) and assigning it supervision of all BIA education personnel.[49] Ten years later, the Tribally Controlled Schools Act (TCSA) of 1988[50] authorized grants to tribes and tribal organizations to operate their BIA schools, in addition to self- determination contracts. These laws provide that grants and self-determination contracts be for the same amounts of funding as the BIA would have expended on operation of the same schools.[51] Finally, the Improving America's Schools Act of 1994 (P.L. 103-382, Section 9112(b)) authorized Indian tribes to apply for a grant in lieu of one or more LEAs under the ESEA Title VII formula grant program under certain circumstances.

Indian control in public schools received an initial boost from the 1972 Indian Education Act. The ESEA Title VII requires that public school districts applying for its new grants prove adequate participation by Indian parents and tribal communities in program development, operation, and evaluation.[52] The 1972 Indian Education Act also amended the

Impact Aid program to mandate Indian parents' consultation in school programs funded by Impact Aid.[53] In 1975, the ISDEAA added to the JOM a requirement that public school districts with JOM contracts have either a majority-Indian school board or an Indian parent committee that has approved the JOM program.[54]

The number of schools in the BIA school system has shrunk over the years, through administrative consolidation and congressional closures. For example, all BIA-funded schools in Alaska were transferred to the state of Alaska between 1966 and 1985, removing an estimated 120 schools from BIA responsibility.[55] The number of BIA-funded schools and dormitories stood at 233 in 1930[56] and 277 in 1965,[57] but fell to 227 in 1982 and to 180 in 1986 before rising to 185 by 1994;[58] it currently stands at 183.[59] Since the 1990s, Congress has limited both the number of BIA schools and the grade structure of the schools.[60] The number of Indian students educated at BIA schools has for the last 20 years fluctuated between about 39,000 and 48,000.[61] In 2006, as noted above, the Secretary of the Interior separated the BIA education programs in the Office of Indian Education Programs from the rest of the BIA and placed them in a new Bureau of Indian Education (BIE) under the Assistant Secretary–Indian Affairs.[62]

STUDENTS SERVED BY FEDERAL INDIAN EDUCATION PROGRAMS

It is commonly estimated that BIE schools serve roughly 10% of Indian students, public schools serve roughly 90%, and private schools serve 1% or less. These general percentages, however, are not certain. Data on Indian students come from differing programs and sources. Different federal Indian education programs serve different, though overlapping, sets of Indian students. Their student data also differ (and overlap).

Although different federal Indian education programs have different eligibility criteria, none of the eligibility criteria are based solely on race/ethnicity. Eligibility is based on the political status of the groups of which the students are members or descendants of members.

The BIE school system, for instance, serves students who are members of federally recognized Indian tribes, or at least one-fourth degree Indian blood descendants of members of such tribes, and who reside on or near a federal Indian reservation or are eligible to attend a BIE off- reservation boarding school.[63] Many Indian tribes allow less than one-fourth degree of tribal or Indian blood for membership, so many BIE Indian students have less than one-fourth Indian blood. Separately, the BIE's JOM program, according to its regulations, serves students in public schools who are at least one-quarter degree Indian blood and recognized by BIA as eligible for BIA services.[64]

ED programs under the ESEA Title VII, on the other hand, serve a broader set of students, including not only those who are (1) BIE-eligible but also those who are (2) members (or one- quarter blood descendants of members) of two types of non-federally recognized tribes, state- recognized tribes and tribes whose federal recognition was terminated after 1940; (3) members of an organized Indian group that received a grant under the ED Indian Education formula grant program as it was in effect before the passage of the Improving America's Schools Act of 1 994;[65] (4) Eskimos, Aleuts, or other Alaska Natives; or (5) individuals considered to be Indian by the Secretary of the Interior, for any purpose.[66] Both public school districts and BIE schools are eligible for the ESEA Title VII, so data on the ESEA Title VII beneficiaries include BIE students as well as public school Indian students. Public school districts must have a minimum number or percentage of ESEA Title VII-eligible Indian students to receive a grant. The ESEA Title VII grants are administered by the OIE, so the OIE is the source of data on the ESEA Title VII students.

Another major ED program, the Impact Aid program, funds public schools whose students reside on "Indian lands" and other federally-connected children.[67] The students residing on Indian lands for whom Impact Aid is provided need not, however, be Indian.

Student data based on race/ethnicity does not match data from any of the aforementioned programs. Not all students identified as American Indian/Alaska Native (AI/AN) are members or descendants of members of politically recognized Indian tribes, and not all members of such tribes may identify as AI/AN. For example, ED's National Center for Education Statistics (NCES), which collects and analyzes student and school data and produces the National Assessment of Educational Progress (NAEP),[68] publishes reports on AI/AN students' characteristics and academic achievements. NCES data are based on race/ethnicity (except data on BIE students), so the data will include students who identify as AI/AN even though they are not members of tribes and do not fall into the eligibility categories of federal Indian education programs. NCES's race/ethnicity-based AI/AN student population is not the same as the student population served by federal Indian education programs. The two populations overlap to a very great extent, but the degree of overlap has not been determined. NCES data based on race/ethnicity, then, cannot be assumed to accurately represent the Indian student population served by federal Indian programs.

STATUS OF INDIAN AND AMERICAN INDIAN/ALASKA NATIVE EDUCATION

Although there is no source for the status of Indian educational achievement nationally, the educational environment and achievements of BIE students and AI/AN students is reported.

BIE Schools and Students

The BIE funds a system consisting of elementary and secondary schools, which provide free education to eligible Indian students, and "peripheral dormitories" (discussed below).[69] The BIE system is administered by a director and headquarters offices in Washington, DC, and Albuquerque, NM, and 22 education line offices (ELOs) across Indian Country. ELOs provide leadership, technical support, and instructional support for the schools and peripheral dorms.[70]

The BIE-funded school system includes day and boarding schools and peripheral dormitories. The majority of BIE-funded schools are day schools, which offer elementary or secondary classes or combinations thereof and are located on Indian reservations. BIE boarding schools house students in dorms on campus and also offer elementary or secondary classes, or combinations of both levels, and are located both on and off reservations. The most common combinations of grade levels offered in BIE schools are K-8, K-12, K-6, 9-12, and

7-12.[71] Peripheral dormitories house students who attend nearby public or BIE schools; these dorms are also located both on and off reservations.

Elementary and secondary schools funded by the BIE may be operated either directly by the BIE or by tribes and tribal organizations through grants or contracts authorized under the Tribally Controlled Schools Act (TCSA) of 1988 or the Indian Self-Determination and Education Assistance Act (ISDEAA) of 1975. (See the discussion of these two acts in "Statutory Authority for BIE Elementary and Secondary Schools," below). In addition, two schools, the Turtle Mountain Elementary and Middle schools in North Dakota, are operated by a cooperative agreement between a public school district and the BIE.[72] Also, there is at least one joint charter school/tribally operated school—Bahweting Anishnabe School in Michigan.

BIE funds 169 schools and 14 peripheral dorms. **Table 1** shows the number of BIE-funded schools and peripheral dorms, by type of operator. The majority of BIE-funded schools are tribally operated, and the number of tribally operated schools continues to rise.[73]

The total number of BIE schools and peripheral dorms and the class structure of each school have been limited by Congress since the mid-1990s. Through annual appropriation acts, Congress has since 1994 prohibited the BIE from funding schools that were not in the BIE system as of September 1, 1996, and has since 1996 prohibited use of BIE funds to expand a school's grade structure beyond the grades in place as of October 1, 1995.[74] Congress was concerned that adding new BIE schools or expanding existing schools would, in circumstances of limited financial resources, "diminish funding for schools currently in the system."[75]

Only Indian children attend the BIE school system, with few exceptions. In SY2010-2011, BIE-funded schools and peripheral dorms served approximately 41,000 Indian students representing over 250 tribes in 23 states.[76] **Table 2** shows the student count in BIE day and boarding schools and peripheral dormitories in SY2010-2011.

BIE-funded schools and peripheral dorms are generally small. The average size of BIE-funded schools was 235 students in SY20 10-2011,[77] compared to 516 students for public elementary and secondary schools in SY2007-2008.[78] In SY20 10-2011, 21% of BIE-funded schools had 100 or fewer children in attendance.[79]

Table 1. Number of BIE-Funded Schools and Peripheral Dormitories, SY2010-2011

Schools and Peripheral Dormitories	Tribally Operated	BIE-Operated	Total
Total	126	57	183
Elementary/Secondary Schools	113	56	169
Day schools	88	29	117
Boarding schools	25	27	52
Peripheral Dormitories	13	1	14

Source: U.S. Department of the Interior, Indian Affairs, *Budget Justifications Fiscal Year 2012* (hereafter referred to as the *FY2012 Budget*) and Department of the Interior, Bureau of Indian Education, *National Directory*, updated March 2009.

Table 2. Number of Students in BIE-Funded Schools and Dormitories, SY2010-2011

Schools and Peripheral Dormitories	Total
Total	41,178
Elementary/Secondary Schools	39,671
Day schools	24,278
Boarding schools	15,394
Peripheral Dormitories	1,507

Source: *FY2012 Budget*, pp. Appendix 2-2–2-7 and Department of the Interior, Bureau of Indian Education, *National Directory*, updated March 2009.

Note: Student counts are based on the three-year average daily membership, which counts students attendance during the entire year.

BIE schools and dormitories are not evenly distributed across the country. In SY20 10-2011, almost 72% of BIE schools and dormitories and just over 75% of BIE students were located in 4 of the 23 states: Arizona (29% of students), New Mexico (22%), South Dakota (16%), and North Dakota (8%). **Table 3** shows the distribution of BIE schools and students across the 23 states. There are no BIE schools or students in Alaska, a circumstance directed by Congress (see "Brief History of Federal Indian Education Activities," above).[80]

One measure of a school system's quality and the academic achievement of students is the percentage of schools that make adequate yearly progress (AYP). AYP is a measure of the percentage of students in a school that reach academic proficiency or a higher level of achievement compared to established targets (For a broader discussion of AYP, see the subsequent section entitled "Adequate Yearly Progress"). According to the BIE, 25% of BIE schools made AYP in SY2007-2008, and 33% made AYP in SY2008-2009.[81] In SY2008-2009, 66% of all public schools made AYP.[82]

Another measure of educational achievement is the average score of students on the National Assessment of Educational Progress (NAEP) reading and mathematics assessments.[83] **Table 4** indicates that, on average, students in BIE schools score below students in public schools with statistical significance, except 8th grade English language learners on the reading NAEP assessment. For example, on the 4th grade NAEP reading assessment BIE school students scored an average of 181 while public school students scored an average of 220, which is significantly higher.

Public Schools and AI/AN Students

There were over 48 million public school students enrolled in kindergarten through 12th grade in 2008, and 417,000 (0.9%) were AI/ANs.[84] In 2006, almost half (49.5%) of AI/AN students lived in the 13 western states of Alaska, Arizona, California, Colorado, Hawaii, Idaho, Montana, Nevada, New Mexico, Oregon, Utah, Washington, and Wyoming.[85] A greater than average proportion of AI/AN students live in poverty and require language development services and services for students with disabilities. At the elementary level in

2008, 28% of AI/AN students were enrolled in high-poverty elementary schools,[86] and 15% of secondary AI/AN students were enrolled in high-poverty secondary schools.[87] An estimated 65,000 AI/AN children ages 5–17 spoke a language other than English at home, and 12,000 AI/AN children ages 5–17 spoke English with difficulty.[88] A greater percentage (14%) of AI/AN students received services under the Individuals with Disabilities Education Act (IDEA) than all children (9%) in 2006.[89] In 2008, 14.6% of AI/AN 16- through 24-year-olds were not enrolled in high school and had not earned a high school credential, compared to 8.0% of all 16- through 24-year-olds.[90]

The educational achievement of AI/AN students in public schools can be deduced from the percentage of students scoring at or above proficient on the NAEP. **Table 4** presents results of the 2009 NAEP by race/ethnicity for students in grades 4 and 8. A lower percentage of AI/AN students score at or above proficient compared to all students—the difference is greater than 10 percentage points for reading and math in grades 4 and 8. For example, 20% of AI/AN 4th graders scored at or above proficient in reading compared to 33% of all 4th graders. A higher percentage of AI/AN students scored at or above proficient compared to black or Hispanic students on the 4th and 8th grade reading assessments and 8th grade math assessment.

Table 3. BIE Schools and Peripheral Dormitories and Students: Number and Percent, by State, SY2010-2011, in Descending Order of the Number of Students

	State	Schools and Dorms		Students	
		Number	Percent	Number	Percent
1	Arizona	54	29.5	11,750	28.5
2	New Mexico	44	24.0	9,108	22.1
3	South Dakota	22	12.0	6,559	15.9
4	North Dakota	11	6.0	3,367	8.2
5	Mississippi	8	4.0	1,848	4.5
6	Washington	8	4.0	1,525	3.7
7	Oklahoma	5	2.7	1,221	3.0
8	North Carolina	1	0.5	1,004	2.4
9	Wisconsin	3	1.6	811	2.0
10	Minnesota	4	2.2	629	1.5
11	California	2	1.1	489	1.2
12	Montana	3	1.6	425	1.0
13	Michigan	2	1.1	400	1.0
14	Oregon	1	0.5	315	0.8
15	Florida	2	1.1	276	0.7
16	Maine	3	1.6	265	0.6
17	Utah	2	1.1	256	0.6
18	Wyoming	1	0.5	214	0.5
19	Iowa	1	0.5	191	0.5
20	Idaho	2	1.1	180	0.4
21	Nevada	2	1.1	93	0.2
22	Kansas	1	0.5	85	0.2
23	Louisiana	1	0.5	84	0.2
	Total	**183**	**100**	**41,178**	**100.0**

Source: *FY20 12 Budget*, p. Appendix 2-2–2-7.

Note: Student counts are based on the three-year average daily membership, which counts students attendance during the entire year.

Table 4. Average Scores in NAEP Reading and Math, by Type of School and Select Student Characteristics: 2009

Type of School and Student Characteristics	Average NAEP Score			
	Grade 4 Reading	Grade 8 Reading	Grade 4 Math	Grade 8 Math
BIE schools				
Overall	181*	229*	207*	248*
Eligible for National School Lunch Program [a]	181 *	228*	207*	247*
Students with disabilities [b]	147*	197*	191*	224*
English language learners [c]	169*	216	200*	237*
Public schools				
Overall	220	262	239	282
Eligible for National School Lunch Program	206	249	228	266
Students with disabilities	187	226	219	246
English language learners	188	219	218	243

Source: U.S. Department of Education, Institute of Education Sciences, National Center for Education Statistics, National Assessment of Educational Progress (NAEP) Data Explorer, available at http://nces.ed.gov /nationsreportcard/naep data/.

Notes: * Significantly different (p < .05) from public schools.

a. The National School Lunch Program (NSLP), also known as the free/reduced-price lunch program, is a federally assisted meal program that provides low-cost or free lunches to eligible students. Free or reduced- price lunches are offered to those students whose family incomes are at or below 185% of the poverty level.

b. Students with disabilities are defined by the Individuals with Disabilities Education Act (IDEA; 20 U.S.C., Chapter 33). The students with disabilities exclude those with 504 Plans under the Rehabilitation Act.

c. English language learners (ELLs), also known as limited English proficient (LEP) students, are defined by the Elementary and Secondary Education Act (ESEA; 20 U.S.C., Chapter 70).

FEDERAL INDIAN EDUCATION PROGRAMS AND SERVICES

Federal Indian education programs serve Indian elementary and secondary students in both public schools and BIE system schools. Except for one BIE program, public schools do not receive BIE funding. Public schools instead receive most of their federal assistance for Indian education through the U.S. Department of Education (ED). BIE-funded schools, on the other hand, receive funding both from the BIE and from ED. The BIE estimates that it provides about 74% of BIE-funded schools' overall funding, and ED provides most of the remainder.[91] This section of the report profiles first the BIE programs and second those ED programs that provide significant funding for Indian education.

Statutory Authority for BIE Elementary and Secondary Schools

Currently, BIE-funded schools, dorms, and programs are administered under a number of statutes. The key statutes are summarized here.

Table 5. Percentage of Students at or Above Proficient, by Assessment, Grade, and Race/Ethnicity: 2009

Race/Ethnicity[a]	Reading		Math	
	Grade 4	Grade 8	Grade 4	Grade 8
Total	33	32	39	34
White	42	41	51	44
Black	16	14	16	12
Hispanic	17	17	22	17
Asian/Pacific Islander	49	45	60	54
American Indian/ Alaska Native	20	21	21	18

Source: S. Aud, W. Hussar, M. Planty, T. Snyder, K. Bianco, M. Fox, L. Frohlich, J. Kemp, L. Drake, *The Condition of Education 2010* (NCES 2010-028), National Center for Education Statistics, Institute of Education Sciences, U.S. Department of Education, Washington, DC, 2010, pp. 175, 181.

Notes: Achievement levels define what students should know and be able to do: "Basic" indicates partial mastery of fundamental skills, "Proficient" indicates demonstrated competency over challenging subject matter, and "Advanced" indicates superior performance. The percentage of students at or above Proficient includes students at the Proficient and the Advanced achievement levels.

a.   Race categories exclude persons of Hispanic ethnicity.

Snyder Act of 1921[92]

This act provides a broad and permanent authorization for federal Indian programs, including for "[g]eneral support and civilization, including education." The act was passed because Congress had never enacted specific statutory authorizations for most BIA activities, including BIA schools. Congress had instead made detailed annual appropriations for BIA activities. Authority for Indian appropriations in the House had been assigned to the Indian Affairs Committee after 1885 (and in the Senate to its Indian Affairs Committee after 1899). Rules changes in the House in 1920, however, moved Indian appropriations authority to the Appropriations Committee, making Indian appropriations vulnerable to procedural objections because they lacked authorizing acts. The Snyder Act was passed in order to authorize all the activities the BIA was then carrying out. The act's broad language, however, may be read as authorizing—though not requiring— nearly any Indian program, including education, for which Congress enacts appropriations.

Indian Self-Determination and Education Assistance Act of 1975 (ISDEAA)[93]

ISDEAA, as amended, provides for tribal administration of certain federal Indian programs, including BIA and BIE programs. The act allows tribes to assume some control over the management of BIE-funded education programs by negotiating "self-determination contracts" with BIE for tribal management of specific schools or dorms. Under a self-determination contract, BIE transfers to tribal control the funds it would have spent for the contracted school or dorm, so the tribe may operate it. Tribes or tribal organizations may contract to operate one or more schools.[94]

Education Amendments Act of 1978[95]

This act declares federal policy on Indian education and establishes requirements and guidelines for the BIE-funded elementary and secondary school system. As amended, the act covers academic accreditation and standards, a funding allocation formula, BIE powers and functions, criteria for boarding and peripheral dorms, personnel hiring and firing, the role of school boards, facilities standards, a facilities construction priority system, and school closure rules, among other topics. It also authorizes several BIE grant programs, including administrative cost grants for tribally operated schools (described below), early childhood development program grants (also described below), and grants and technical assistance for tribal departments of education.

Tribally Controlled Schools Act (TCSA) of 1988[96]

TCSA added grants as another means, besides ISDEAA contracts, by which Indian tribes and tribal organizations could operate BIE-funded schools. The act requires that each grant include all funds that BIE would have allocated to the school for operation, administrative cost grants, transportation, maintenance, and ED programs. Because ISDEAA contracts were found to be a more cumbersome means of Indian control of schools, most tribally operated schools are grant schools.[97] As of March 2009, approximately two-thirds of BIE schools and dormitories were funded by TCSA grants.[98]

BIE Programs

Funding for and operation of BIE-funded schools are carried out through a number of different programs. The major BIE funding programs are "forward-funded"—that is, the BIE programs' appropriations for a *fiscal* year are used to fund the *school* year that begins during that fiscal year. [99]

Indian School Equalization Program (ISEP)

The Indian School Equalization Program (ISEP) is the formula-based program through which Congressional appropriations for BIE-funded schools' academic (and, if applicable, residential) operating costs are allocated among the schools. Before allocation under the funding formula, part of ISEP funds are set aside for program adjustments, contingencies, and appeals. In recent years, program adjustments have funded safety and security projects, behavior intervention programs, targeted education projects to increase academic achievement, police services, and parental participation projects. The targeted education project since SY2005-2006 has been the FOCUS program, which supports at-risk students in schools that are close to making adequate yearly progress (AYP) by providing for technical assistance on effective teaching practices and data-driven instructional decision-making.[100]

The ISEP formula, although authorized under the Education Amendments of 1978,[101] is specified not in statute but in federal regulations. The formula is based on a count of student "average daily membership" (ADM) that is weighted to take into account schools' grade levels and residential- living status (e.g., in boarding schools or peripheral dorms) and is then supplemented with weights or adjustments for gifted and talented students, language development needs, supplemental education programs, and a school's size. These weighted figures are called "weighted student units" (WSUs). Total WSUs are calculated for each school, by school year. A three-year WSU average is calculated for each school and nationally. Each school receives a portion of the ISEP appropriation that is the same proportion that the school's three-year WSU average is to the national three-year average WSU.[102]

Student Transportation

To transport its students, both day and boarding, the BIE funds an extensive student transportation system. Student transportation funds provide for buses, fuel, maintenance, and bus driver salaries and training, as well as certain commercial transportation costs for some boarding school students. Because of largely rural and often remote school locations, many unimproved and dirt roads, and the long distances from children's homes to schools, transportation of BIE students can be expensive. Student transportation funds are distributed on a formula basis, using commercial transportation costs and the number of bus miles driven (with an additional weight for unimproved roads).[103]

Early Childhood Development

BIE's early childhood development program funds the agency's Family and Child Education (FACE) grants to tribes and tribal organizations for services for pre-school Indian students and their parents.[104] FACE programs include early childhood education for children under six years old, and parenting skills and adult education for their parents to improve their employment opportunities. The grants are distributed by formula among applicant tribes and organizations who meet the minimum tribal size of 500 members. In FY2006 FACE programs were being carried out at 38 BIE funded schools.[105]

Tribal Grant Support Costs (Administrative Cost Grants)

Tribal grant support costs,[106] formerly known as administrative cost grants, pay administrative and indirect costs for tribally operated BIE-funded schools. Administrative costs for BIE-operated schools are funded through BIE program management appropriations. By providing assistance for direct and indirect administrative costs that may not be covered by ISEP or other BIE funds, administrative cost grants are intended to encourage tribes to take control of their schools. These are formula grants based on an "administrative cost percentage rate" for each school, with a minimum grant of $200,000.[107]

Facilities Operations

This program funds the operation of educational facilities at all BIE-funded schools and dorms. Operating expenses may include utilities, supplies, equipment, custodians, trash removal, maintenance of school grounds, minor repairs, and other services, as well as monitoring for fires and intrusions.[108] This is not a forward-funded program. These funds are available at the beginning of the fiscal year for a period of 24 months.

Education Program Enhancements

Education Program Enhancements receive a line item in the appropriations request. This program allows the BIE to target improvements to its educational programs through special studies, projects, and other activities. Funding in recent years has been used to improve reading and math achievement at particular schools, leadership training, professional development, and mentoring programs and to hire content-area experts. The BIE has been expanding its BIE Reads and Math Counts initiatives into additional grade levels and schools since SY2007-2008. BIE Reads is designed to improve reading outcomes among students reading below grade level. Math Counts supports schools with the lowest student performance in math.

Residential Education Placement Program

The Residential Education Placement program ensures that eligible Indian students with disabilities or social or emotional needs receive an appropriate education in the least restrictive environment and as close to home as possible. Services include physical and occupational therapy, counseling, and alcohol and substance abuse treatment. In SY2008-2009, the BIE served 59 institutionalized students.[109]

Juvenile Detention Education

The Juvenile Detention Education program supports educational services for children in 24 BIA-funded detention facilities.

Education Department Set-Asides

The BIE receives funding from the Education Department under set-asides in the Elementary and Secondary Education Act (ESEA), the Individuals with Disabilities Education Act (IDEA), and other acts, and allocates the funds to its schools. More detailed discussion of the sources of ED funding for BIE is provided in "U.S. Department of Education (ED) Indian Programs," below.

BIE Assistance to Public Schools

There is one program by which the BIE provides assistance to tribes, tribal organizations, states, and LEAs for Indian students attending public schools. There are instances in which the BIE provides funding to public school districts.

Tuition Assistance

The BIE pays tuition to Sevier Public Schools, UT, for out-of-state Indian students living in a nearby BIE peripheral dormitory while attending Sevier.[110]

Johnson O'Malley Program

The Johnson O'Malley (JOM) program provides supplementary financial assistance, through contracts, to meet the unique and specialized educational needs of eligible Indian students in public schools and non-sectarian private schools. Eligible Indian students, according to BIE regulations, are students in public schools who are at least one-quarter degree Indian blood and recognized by the BIA as eligible for BIA services.[111] BIE contracts with tribes and tribal organizations to distribute funds to schools or other programs providing JOM services, and it also contracts directly with states and public school districts for JOM programs. Most JOM funds are distributed through tribal contractors—88% as of FY2011.[112] Prospective contractors must have education plans that have been approved by an Indian education committee made up of parents of Indian students. Funds are to be used for supplemental programs, such as tutoring, other academic support, books, supplies, Native language classes, cultural activities, summer education programs, after-school activities, or a variety of other education-related needs. JOM funds may be used for general school operations only when a public school district cannot meet state educational standards or requirements without them, and enrollment in the district is at least 70% eligible Indian students.[113]

Enacted in 1934, the Johnson O'Malley Act authorized the Secretary of the Interior to contract directly with states, local governments (such as school districts), colleges, and private entities "for the education, medical attention, agricultural assistance, and social welfare, including relief of distress, of Indians in such State."[114] Education eventually came to be the chief area of JOM contracting. After enactment of Impact Aid gave public school districts a separate and much larger source of federal funding for Indian students (see "Brief History of Federal Indian Education Activities," above), Indian groups argued that JOM funds should be used only for Indian students and not for districts' general operating costs. The BIA amended its regulations in 1974 to restrict school districts' use of JOM funds to supplementary programs purely for Indian students (the same regulations also made it clear that Indian tribes were eligible for JOM contracts).[115] In 1985, Congress enacted a statute limiting JOM contracts to supplementary educational services for Indian students.[116]

By statute, JOM funds are distributed to contractors by formula, based on a count of Indian students and average per-pupil operating costs. Student counts for allocating funds have been effectively frozen since FY1995. The House and Senate reports, accompanying the Department of the Interior and Related Agencies Appropriations Act, 1995 (P.L. 103-332), instructed the BIA to transfer JOM allocations to tribal priority allocations (TPA) along with certain funds for housing improvement in an effort to stabilize funding for tribes and provide them additional control and flexibility in the use of the funds.[117] The intention was to include the JOM funds in each tribe's recurring base funding. Based upon public comment and the appropriations reports, the BIA decided to use the FY1995 JOM allocations based on the FY1995 student counts to establish JOM base funding for each of the tribal contractors, excluding tribal organizations.[118] There is a statutory prohibition on changing a tribe's base funding.[119] This transfer to TPA has resulted in what is commonly referred to as the *JOM freeze*. In FY2005, JOM served about 272,000 students in 33 states.[120]

BIE School Facilities Repair and Construction

The BIA funds repair, improvement, and construction activities for BIE schools and school facilities. Activities may include replacing all facilities on an existing BIE school campus, replacing individual buildings, or making major and minor repairs and improvements. Included in the education construction program is improvement and repair of BIE employee housing units. Construction may be administered either by the BIA or by tribes under the ISDEAA or the TCSA. In order to prioritize projects and guide expenditures, the BIA maintains an aggregate Facilities Condition Index (FCI), a Replacement School Construction Priority list, a Five Year Deferred Maintenance and Capital Improvement Plan, an Asset Management Plan, a list of necessary emergency repairs, and a list of deficiencies with respect to the Americans with Disabilities Act (ADA; 42 U.S.C. § 12101 et seq.), Uniform Federal Accessibility Standards (UFAS; 42 U.S.C. § 4151-4157), Environmental Protection Agency (EPA), National Fire Protection Association (NFPA), and other requirements.

Table 6. Appropriations for BIE Elementary-Secondary Education Programs and BIA Education Construction, Compared with BIA Totals, FY2003-FY2010 (current dollars in thousands)

	FY2003[a]	FY2004	FY2005	FY2006	FY2007	FY2008	FY2009	FY2009 ARRA[b]	FY2010
BIA Operation of Indian Programs (OIP)	1,845,246	1,893,291	1,926,091	1,962,190	1,988,223	2,047,809	2,128,630	176,000	2,335,965
BIE Elementary-Secondary Education	533,292	542,353	536,505	542,420	549,293	577,863	600,881	—	622,609
Percent of OIP	*29%*	*29%*	*28%*	*28%*	*28%*	*28%*	*28%*	—	*27%*
Elementary/Secondary (Forward-Funded)	445,072	452,874	449,721	457,750	458,310	479,895	499,470	—	518,702
ISEP Formula Funds	347,204	349,919	348,073	350,062	351,817	358,341	375,000	—	391,699
ISEP Program Adjustments	670	659	1,145	5,116	7,533	3,205	3,266	—	3,338
Student Transportation	37,262	38,116	39,444	42,738	42,833	47,844	50,500	—	52,808
Early Childhood Development	15,164	15,604	15,355	15,281	12,067	15,024	15,223	—	15,374
Tribal Grant Support Costs[c]	44,772	48,576	45,704	44,553	44,060	43,373	43,373	—	43,373
Education Program Enhancements	—	—	—	—	—	12,108	12,108	—	12,110
Elementary/Secondary Programs	76,128	77,557	76,218	75,887	72,390	74,621	75,126	—	77,379
Facilities Operation	55,423	57,106	55,976	55,812	56,047	56,504	56,972	—	59,410
Residential Education Placement Program[d]	3,797	3,785	3,732	3,704	3,713	3,715	3,737	—	3,760
Juvenile Detention Education	—	—	—	—	630	620	620	—	620
Johnson-O'Malley Program	16,908	16,666	16,510	16,371	12,000	13,782	13,797	—	13,589
Education Program Management	12,092	11,922	10,566	8,783	18,593	23,347	26,285	—	26,528
All BIA Construction	345,988	346,827	319,129	271,582	271,823	203,754	217,688	314,000	225,000
Education Construction[e]	293,795	294,954	263,372	206,787	204,956	142,935	128,837	292,311	112,994
Percent of All BIA Construction	*85%*	*85%*	*83%*	*76%*	*75%*	*70%*	*59%*	*93%*	*50%*
Replacement School Construction	124,409	139,612	105,550	64,530	83,891	46,716	22,405	141,634	5,964
Replacement Facility Construction	—	—	—	—	26,873	9,748	17,013	—	17,013
Employee Housing Repair	3,100	3,081	3,038	1,971	1,973	1,942	4,445	—	4,451
Education Facilities Improvement and Repair	163,306	146,335	142,531	140,286	92,219	84,529	84,974	150,677	85,566
Tribal School Construction Demonstration Program	2,980	5,926	12,253	—	—	—	—	—	—
All BIA Appropriations	2,257,244	2,306,401	2,295,702	2,274,270	2,308,304	2,291,279	2,376,131	500,000	2,619,560
Total: BIE Elementary-Secondary Education and Education Construction	827,087	837,307	799,877	749,207	754,249	720,798	729,718	292,311	735,603
Percent of All BIA Appropriations	*37%*	*36%*	*35%*	*33%*	*33%*	*31%*	*31%*	*58%*	*28%*

Source: "Annual comprehensive budget table," in U.S. Department of the Interior, Bureau of Indian Affairs, *Budget Justifications and Performance Information, Fiscal Years 2005-2012.*

Notes: In this table, "BIA" includes all Indian programs under the Assistant Secretary–Indian Affairs in the Department of the Interior. Totals for BIE elementary-secondary education were calculated by CRS. N/A = not applicable.

Abbreviations:

BIA—Bureau of Indian Affairs

BIE—Bureau of Indian Education

ISEP—Indian School Equalization Program

OIP—BIA Operation of Indian Programs (includes all BIA and BIE programs except construction, miscellaneous payments, land and water rights settlements, and loan guarantees)

a. FY2003 BIA data have been rearranged from BIA's budget structure at that time to BIA's current budget structure.

b. FY2009 ARRA funds were appropriated by the American Recovery and Reinvestment Act of 2009 (ARRA; P.L. 111-5).

c. Tribal grant support costs were previously entitled *Administrative Cost Grants.*

d. The Residential Education Placement Program was formerly called the *Institutionalized Disabled Program.*

e. Education construction includes a small amount of funds for BIA postsecondary education institutions.

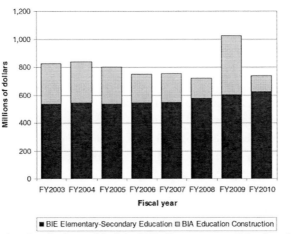

Source: "Annual comprehensive budget table," in U.S. Department of the Interior, Bureau of Indian
Affairs, *Budget Justifications and Performance Information, Fiscal Years 2005-2012*.

Notes: BIA Education Construction includes a small amount of funds for BIA postsecondary
institutions. The American Recovery and Reinvestment Act of 2009 (P.L. 111-5) appropriated
$292 million for replacement school construction and facilities improvement and repair.

Figure 2. Appropriations for BIE Operations and BIA Education Construction, FY2003-FY2010.

Indian Affairs Elementary and Secondary Education Appropriations

Indian Affairs (the budgetary combination of BIA and BIE functions) appropriations for
elementary and secondary education are divided between program funds, expended through
the BIE, and construction and related spending carried out through the BIA. **Table 6** shows
detailed appropriations for BIE programs and BIA education construction for FY2003-
FY2010.[121]

Appropriations for BIE elementary-secondary programs have remained relatively stable,
rising 17% over the eight-year period, from $533.3 million in FY2003 to $622.6 million in
FY2010.[122] As a proportion of BIA's Operation of Indian Programs (OIP) budget, BIE
elementary-secondary program funding has consistently stood at just below 30% of OIP
appropriations. Total BIA spending on elementary-secondary education, however, has fallen
11% over the same period, from $827.1 million to $735.6 million, and has shrunk from 37%
of total BIA appropriations to 28%. As illustrated in **Figure 2** and with the exception of
FY2009, changes in BIA education construction appropriations account for the reduction;
current appropriations for education construction have fallen 62%, from $293.8 million in
FY2003 to $113.0 million in FY2010.

U.S. Department of Education (ED) Indian Programs

The U.S. Department of Education (ED) provides funding specifically for Indian
elementary and secondary education to both public and BIE schools. About three-quarters of
this Indian education-specific funding goes to public schools and related organizations (see
Table 7 below).

ED's assistance specifically for Indian education is not to be confused with its general assistance to elementary and secondary education nationwide. Indian students benefit from ED's *general* assistance as they attend public schools. This section covers ED Indian assistance—that is, assistance statutorily specified for Indians or allotted according to the number of Indians—not general ED assistance that may also benefit Indian students.

ED Indian education funding to public and BIE schools flows through a number of programs, most authorized under the Elementary and Secondary Education Act (ESEA) or the Individuals with Disabilities Education Act (IDEA), although other acts also authorize Indian education assistance. Some general ED programs have set-asides for BIE schools, while other programs either may be intended solely for Indian students, may specifically include Indian and non-Indian students, or may mention Indian students as a target of the assistance. In many instances, BIE schools are included in the definition of local educational agency (LEA) in the ESEA[123] and IDEA,[124] so many ED programs may provide funding to BIE schools even when the programs have no BIE set-aside or other specific provision for BIE schools, but these programs are not discussed here. Tribes and tribal organizations are also eligible to apply for certain programs.

Major ED Indian programs are profiled below, divided between set-aside programs for BIE schools and all other programs. See **Table 7** below for a list of all ED programs for Indian elementary and secondary education.

ED Set-Asides for BIE System Schools

ED funds that are set aside for BIE schools are administered and allocated by the BIE. See **Table 7** for the amount of funds under each ED program.

ESEA Title I-A Grants to Local Educational Agencies

Title I, Part A, of the ESEA[125] authorizes formula grants to LEAs for the education of disadvantaged children. ESEA Title I-A grants go to LEAs to serve pupils in schools with relatively large numbers or percentages of children from low-income families, and are used to provide supplementary education services, as either schoolwide programs or targeted assistance to the lowest-achieving students. Section 1121 of the ESEA sets aside 1% of Title I-A appropriations for Interior and the outlying areas. Interior funds are for BIE schools and for out- of-state Indian students being educated in public schools under BIE contracts (e.g., students in peripheral dorms). The portion of the 1% provided to Interior is the amount determined by the Secretary of Education to be needed to meet the special educational needs of the Indian students (in recent years it has been approximately 70% of the total set-aside).[126]

ESEA Title II-A Improving Teacher Quality State Grants

Title II, Part A, Subpart 1, of the ESEA[127] authorizes grants to states for the recruitment, retention, and professional development of highly qualified teachers and principals in elementary and secondary schools. Section 2111 (b)(1)(A)(ii) of the ESEA sets aside 0.5% of appropriations for programs in BIE schools.

ESEA Title IV-B 21st Century Community Learning Centers

Title IV, Part B, of the ESEA[128] authorizes formula grants to states for activities that provide learning opportunities for school-aged children during non-school hours. States award competitive subgrants to LEAs and community organizations for before- and after-school activities that will advance student academic achievement. Section 4202(a)(3) of the ESEA sets aside no more than 1% of Title IV-B appropriations for the BIE and the outlying areas. The portion of the 1% that goes to the BIE is determined by the Secretary of Education.

IDEA Part B Special Education Grants to States

Part B of the IDEA[129] authorizes formula grants to states to help them provide a free appropriate public education to children with disabilities. States make subgrants to LEAs. Funds may be used for salaries of teachers or other special-education personnel, education materials, transportation, occupational therapy, or other special-education services. Section 611 (b)(2) of the IDEA reserves 1.226% of state-grant appropriations for Interior. Each appropriations act since the Departments of Labor, Health and Human Services, and Education, and Related Agencies Appropriations Act, 2006 (P.L. 109-149) has limited the Interior set-aside to the prior year set-aside amount increased for inflation.[130] As a consequence in FY2010, the Interior set-aside is now 0.800%. Section 611(h) of the IDEA directs the Secretary of the Interior to allocate 80% of the funds to BIE schools for special education for children aged 5-21 and 20% to tribes and tribal organizations on reservations with BIE schools for early identification of children with disabilities aged 3-5, parent training, and provision of direct services.

ED Indian Education Programs for Public Schools

ED programs (or portions of programs) that are specifically for Indian students or based on numbers of Indian students are discussed below. In some of these programs, funding may go to BIE schools in addition to public schools.

Impact Aid

Impact Aid, Title VIII of the ESEA,[131] provides financial assistance to school districts whose tax revenues are significantly reduced, or whose student enrollments are significantly increased, because of the impacts of federal property ownership or federal activities. Among such impacts are having a significant number of children enrolled who reside on "Indian lands,"[132] which is defined as Indian trust and restricted lands,[133] lands conveyed to Alaska Native entities under the Alaska Native Claims Settlement Act of 1971,[134] public lands designated for Indian use, and certain lands used for low-rent housing. [135] Impact Aid funds are distributed by formula directly to LEAs and are used for basic operating costs, special education, and facilities construction and maintenance. There is no requirement that the funds be used specifically or preferentially for the education of Indian students. There is, however, a requirement that Indian children participate on an equal basis with non-Indian children in all of the educational programs and activities provided by the LEA, including but not limited to those funded by Impact Aid. ED indicates that about 114,000 students residing on Indian lands were used to determine formula allocations under Impact Aid for FY2010.[136] The amount of Impact Aid funding going to LEAs based on the number of children residing on Indian lands makes it the largest ED Indian education program. A few BIE schools receive Impact Aid funding.

Indian Education Programs

Title VII, Part A, of the ESEA[137] authorizes formula grants to eligible LEAs, BIE schools, and (in certain circumstances) Indian tribes for supplementary education programs to assist Indian students in meeting challenging state standards. The supplementary programs can include tutoring, after-school programs, dropout prevention, early childhood and family programs, culturally related activities, and many other activities. For an LEA to be eligible, at least 10 Indian students must be enrolled or at least 25% of its total enrollment must be Indians (exempted from these requirements are LEAs in Alaska, California, and Oklahoma and LEAs located on or near an Indian reservation). An LEA's application must be approved by a local Indian education committee of parents, teachers, and secondary students.[138]

The Indian Education programs also authorize several competitive grant programs. One provides demonstration grants to develop innovative services and programs to improve Indian students' educational opportunities and achievement. LEAs, colleges, tribes and tribal organizations, and BIE schools are eligible for these grants. Another competitive program provides for professional development grants to colleges, or tribes or LEAs in consortium with colleges, to train Indian individuals as teachers or other professionals. In addition, the Indian Education programs authorize national programs for in-service training for teachers of Indian children, fellowships for Indian students, initiatives for gifted and talented Indian students, grants to tribes for education administrative planning and development, initiatives to improve the educational opportunities for adult Indians, and also the National Advisory Council on Indian Education, which advises the Secretary of Education and Congress on Indian education.

Alaska Native Education Equity

Title VII, Part C, of the ESEA[139] authorizes competitive grants to Alaska Native organizations, educational entities with Native experience, and cultural and community organizations for supplemental education programs that address the educational needs of Alaska Native students, parents, and teachers. Grants may be used for development of curricula and educational materials, student enrichment in science and math, professional development, family literacy, home preschool instruction, cultural exchange, dropout prevention, and other programs.

ED Indian Education Funding

ED Indian education funding goes primarily to public schools and related organizations. With the exception of FY2009, less than a quarter of ED Indian education funds is transferred to BIE schools (see **Table 7**, below). FY2009 funding was augmented by additional appropriations from the American Recovery and Reinvestment Act of 2009 (ARRA; P.L. 111-5). For most ED Indian education programs, the funding pattern during FY2003-FY2010 showed an increase from FY2003 to FY2004, a smaller increase from FY2004 to FY2005, a decline from FY2005 to FY2006, and an increase from FY2006 to FY2009, excluding funding from ARRA. Some programs received an increase in FY2010 above the FY2009 annual appropriations while other programs received a decrease in funding compared to the FY2009 levels.

Table 7. Estimated Funding for Department of Education's Indian Elementary-Secondary Education Programs, in Descending Order of FY2010 Funding: FY2003-FY2010 (dollars in thousands)

Education Department (ED) Programs	FY2003	FY2004	FY2005	FY2006	FY2007	FY2008	FY2009	FY2009 ARRA[a]	FY2010
ED Funds for Indian Education	**679,978**	**730,490**	**738,001**	**719,317**	**724,257**	**740,373**	**788,225**	**71,698**	**786,992**
Percent of Total ED Programs	*76%*	*77%*	*77%*	*77%*	*77%*	*76%*	*77%*	*42%*	*77%*
ESEA Title VIII Impact Aid[b]	502,737	551,457	559,457	545,454	550,691	567,039	612,120	71,698	605,887
ESEA Title VIII Impact Aid - Basic Support	472,111	495,861	503,166	515,813	520,436	528,558	573,448	—	575,969
ESEA Title VIII Impact Aid - Disabilities	21,685	21,393	21,222	20,731	21,345	20,972	21,163	—	21,163
ESEA Title VIII Impact Aid – Construction	8,942	34,203	35,069	8,910	8,910	17,509	17,509	71,698	8,755
ESEA Title VII-A Indian Education[b]	121,573	120,856	119,889	118,690	118,690	119,564	122,282	—	127,282
ESEA Title VII-A-1 Indian Education - LEA Grants	96,502	95,933	95,166	95,331	95,331	96,613	99,331	—	104,331
ESEA Title VII-A-2 Indian Education - Special Programs	19,870	19,753	19,595	19,399	19,399	19,060	19,060	—	19,060
ESEA Title VII-A-3 Indian Education - National Programs	5,201	5,170	5,129	3,960	3,960	3,891	3,891	—	3,891
ESEA Title VII-C Alaska Native Education Equity	30,798	33,302	34,224	33,908	33,907	33,315	33,315	—	33,315
Carl D. Perkins Vocational and Technical Education Act Title I-D Native American Program	14,903	14,938	14,929	14,780	14,780	14,511	14,511	—	14,511
ESEA Title III-A-1 English Language Acquisition	5,000	5,000	5,000	5,000	5,000	4,990	5,000	—	5,000
ESEA Title I-B-3 Even Start	4,968	4,938	4,502	1,485	1,189	954	997	—	997
ED Fund Set-Asides for the BIE	**209,109**	**219,076**	**220,706**	**217,111**	**222,079**	**228,676**	**235,300**	**98,758**	**229,009**
Percent of Total ED Programs	*24%*	*23%*	*23%*	*23%*	*23%*	*24%*	*23%*	*58%*	*23%*
ESEA Title I-A Grants to Local Educational Agencies	81,886	90,093	91,322	88,423	91,754	96,688	101,126	72,314	100,671
ESEA Title II-A Improving Teacher Quality State Grants	14,581	14,577	14,510	14,635	14,365	14,603	14,665	—	14,665
ESEA Title IV-B 21st Century Community Learning Centers	7,145	7,317	7,565	7,323	7,129	8,070	8,163	—	8,433

Table 7. (Continued)

Education Department (ED) Programs	FY2003	FY2004	FY2005	FY2006	FY2007	FY2008	FY2009	FY2009 ARRA[a]	FY2010
IDEA Part C Grants for Infants and Families with Disabilities	5,360	5,486	5,442	5,388	5,388	5,388	5,623	—	5,623
ESEA Title I, Sec. 1003 School Improvement Grants	—	—	—	—	877	3,322	3,793	20,870	3,682
ESEA Title VI-A- 1 State Assessment Grants	1,900	1,950	2,000	2,000	2,000	2,000	2,000	—	2,000
ESEA Title II-D Educational Technology State Grants	5,115	5,085	3,646	2,001	2,001	1,966	1,984	4,875	735
McKinney-Vento Homeless Assistance Act Title VII-B Homeless Children and Youth	546	596	625	619	619	641	654	700	654
ESEA Title VI-B Rural Education	418	420	427	422	422	430	430	—	437
ESEA Title I-B-4 Literacy through School Libraries	62	99	98	97	195	96	96	—	96
ESEA Title IV-A Safe and Drug-Free Schools	4,750	4,750	4,750	4,750	4,750	4,750	4,750	—	—
ESEA Title I-B Reading First	4,968	5,120	5,208	5,146	5,146	1,965	—	—	—
ESEA Title I-F Comprehensive School Reform	1,918	1,966	1,567	—	—	—	—	—	—
Total ED Indian Elementary- Secondary Education Programs	**889,087**	**949,566**	**958,706**	**936,428**	**946,336**	**969,049**	**1,023,525**	**170,457**	**1,016,001**

Source: U.S. Department of Education, Budget Service, unpublished tables, transmitted on various dates, 2003-2011. The most recent table was transmitted January 6, 2011.

Notes: Columns may not sum to totals due to rounding.

Abbreviations:

ED—U.S. Department of Education

ESEA—Elementary and Secondary Education Act

IDEA—Individuals with Disabilities Education Act

LEA—Local educational agency (school district)

a. FY2009 ARRA funds were appropriated by the American Recovery and Reinvestment Act of 2009 (ARRA; P.L. 111-5).

b. Some grants are awarded to BIE schools.

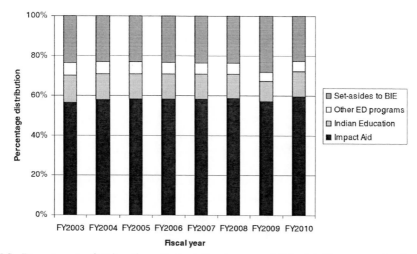

Source: U.S. Department of Education, Budget Service, unpublished tables, transmitted on various dates, 2003- 2011. The most recent table was transmitted January 6, 2011.

Figure 3. Distribution of ED Funding for Indian Education Programs, FY2003-FY2010.

Impact Aid is the largest single ED Indian education program, as **Figure 3** illustrates. The second largest program is the Indian Education program, especially its formula grants to LEAs. Other ED programs—focused on Alaska Natives, career and technical education, early childhood education, and English language acquisition—account for about 6% of the ED funding provided for Indian education.

In excess of 20% of ED Indian education funding comes from set-asides. Set-asides for the BIE are authorized chiefly under ESEA and IDEA. The two largest set-asides for BIE schools come from the LEA grant program for disadvantaged children under Title I, Part A, of ESEA, and the special education grants to states under Part B of IDEA. Together these two set-asides account for about 80% of ED Indian education funds set aside for the BIE.

BIE SCHOOLS UNDER THE NO CHILD LEFT BEHIND ACT

Amendments to the ESEA by the No Child Left Behind Act (NCLB) significantly expanded ESEA's requirements of schools receiving assistance under ESEA Title I-A. Some key provisions of the ESEA, as amended by NCLB, concern accountability of public school systems and individual public schools for improving academic outcomes of students. Accountability requirements included in Title I-A of the ESEA require states to implement content and performance standards and assessments aligned with these standards for reading/language arts, mathematics, and science for multiple grades. The results of these assessments are used to make complex annual adequate yearly progress (AYP) determinations for each public school and LEA. A series of increasingly substantial consequences must be applied to schools and LEAs that fail to meet the AYP standards for two consecutive years or more. Accountability requirements also extend to virtually all public school teachers and aides with respect to their qualifications.

BIE-funded schools are generally subject to the key provisions of the ESEA, with some specific exceptions, described below. BIE-funded schools are not subject to the jurisdiction of SEAs but rather to that of the BIE.[140] Many ESEA statutory and regulatory requirements may be waived by the Secretary of Education, and Indian tribes as well as SEAs and LEAs may request waivers from the Secretary.[141]

Standards-Based Assessments

Annual assessments of students must be implemented by the SEA and be based on the state's "challenging student academic achievement standards,"[142] but the choice of assessments to be used in BIE-funded schools depends on how the school is accredited. As of March 2011, 9% of the BIE schools were state accredited, 89% were regionally accredited, and 1% were in the process of being accredited. [143] State-accredited BIE schools must use either the state's assessments or other appropriate assessments approved by the Secretary of the Interior. BIE schools accredited by a regional accreditation agency must use appropriate assessments, approved by the Secretary of the Interior, that meet NCLB requirements and are consistent with assessments used by other schools in the state or region. Finally, BIE schools accredited by a tribal accreditation agency or a tribal education department must use the tribal agency's or division's assessments if the Secretary of the Interior ensures that the assessments meet NCLB requirements. [144] BIE regulations require that each BIE school use the state assessment system and standards of the state in which the school is located.[145]

Adequate Yearly Progress

States, LEAs, and schools must develop an accountability system to ensure that the state, LEAs, and schools meet AYP, as measured by standards-based assessments and other academic indicators.[146] Each state defines AYP for its LEAs and schools, subject to approval by the Secretary of Education. [147] The Secretary of the Interior must define AYP using negotiated rulemaking, taking into account BIE schools' unique needs and circumstances, and the definition must be consistent with the NCLB; and the Secretary of the Interior may use the definition established by the state where the BIE-funded school is located. [148] In either case a tribe or tribal school board may seek a waiver of all or part of the Secretary of the Interior's definition and use its own alternative AYP definition, unless the Secretary of Education determines the alternative definition does not meet NCLB requirements.[149] The Secretary of the Interior, with the Secretary of Education if the former requests, must provide technical assistance to a tribe or tribal school board seeking to develop an alternative AYP definition.[150] Current regulations require that schools use the state definition of AYP.

Teachers and Paraprofessionals

NCLB requires states and LEAs to ensure that teachers are highly qualified, and that school paraprofessionals meet certain qualification requirements.[151] BIE-funded schools are subject to this requirement as well. The BIE uses qualification requirements that are at least equivalent to those of the licensing and certification authorities of the state in which the position is located.[152]

School Improvement, Corrective Action, and Restructuring

NCLB requires states to identify schools that fail to meet AYP standards for two consecutive years for school improvement. Being designated for school improvement carries with it the requirement to develop or revise a school plan designed to result in the improvement of the school. LEAs are required to provide schools within their jurisdictions with technical assistance in the design and implementation of school improvement plans. Responsibility for development of the school plan is assigned to the BIE for BIE-operated schools and to the school board for BIE-funded contract and grant schools.[153] The BIE provides technical assistance to all BIE schools.[154] In general, students attending a school that has been identified for improvement must be provided with public school choice—the option to attend other public schools that make AYP. BIE schools, however, are not required to provide public school choice.

If a Title I-A school fails to meet AYP standards for a third year, students from low-income families must be offered the opportunity to receive instruction from a supplemental educational services (SES) provider of their choice. BIE schools are not required to provide the opportunity for SES. One or more additional "corrective actions," such as implementing a new curriculum, must be taken with respect to Title I-A schools that fail to meet AYP for a fourth year. Those that fail to meet AYP standards for a fifth year must develop a "restructuring" plan, involving such actions as reopening as a charter school. If a school fails to make AYP for a subsequent year, the school must implement its restructuring plan. Responsibility for all corrective actions and restructuring is assigned to the BIE for BIE-operated schools and to the school board for BIE-funded contract and grant schools.[155]

Procedures analogous to those for schools apply to LEAs that receive Title I-A grants and fail to meet AYP requirements. BIE schools, however, are not subject to the procedures for LEAs.[156]

The BIE is required to report annually to the Secretary of Education and Congress on BIE schools identified for school improvement. The report is to include an analysis of whether sufficient resources were available to enable such schools to achieve AYP.[157]

BIE-Funded Schools Accreditation Sanctions

Title X, Part D of NCLB amended one of the major BIE education laws, the Education Amendments of 1978 (see "Statutory Authority for BIE Elementary and Secondary Schools," above), to subject BIE-funded schools that are neither accredited nor candidates for accreditation, by certain accrediting agencies, to actions similar to the ESEA's accountability actions.[158] Parallels include school plans, technical assistance, parental notification, school choice options to transfer to other BIE-funded schools or public schools (with transportation provided), staff or administrative changes, tribal option to take over BIE-operated schools, and school operation by an outside contractor.[159] These sanctions must be waived, however, if the school's failure to become accredited, or to be a candidate for accreditation, is due to certain circumstances beyond the school board's control, such as a significant decline in financial resources; a natural disaster; or the poor condition of the school's facilities, vehicles, or other property.[160]

ISSUES IN INDIAN EDUCATION

Some of the issues of concern with regard to Indian education pertain to the academic outcomes of Indian students, the use of native language instruction, the conditions of BIE school facilities, and NCLB provisions in the ESEA that affect both public and BIE schools. Congress is currently considering the reauthorization of NCLB.

Academic Achievement and Outcomes

There are significant gaps in educational outcomes for Indian students in BIE schools and AI/AN students in public schools compared to other students. As noted in the ESEA, "it is the policy of the United States to fulfill the federal government's unique and continuing trust relationship with and responsibility to the Indian people for the education of Indian children."[161] Title 25 of the U.S. Code also refers to "the federal responsibility for and assistance to education of Indian children."[162] According to the BIE, 25% of BIE schools made AYP in SY2007-2008, and 33% made AYP in SY2008-2009.[163] In SY2008-2009, 66% of all public schools made AYP.[164] **Table 4** indicates that public school students score a statistically significant 20 points higher than BIE school students overall on the NAEP 4th and 8th grade reading and math assessments. **Table 5** indicates that a smaller percentage of AI/AN students in public schools score at or above proficient compared to all students on the NAEP 4th and 8th grade reading and math assessments, and there is a greater than 20 percentage-point gap between AI/AN students and Asian/Pacific Islander students, the racial/ethnic group with the highest academic achievement.

Since SY2005-2006, the BIE has tried to raise academic achievement through targeted initiatives such as BIE Reads, Math Counts, and the FOCUS on Student Achievement Project. The percentage of schools making AYP increased from SY2007-2008 to SY2008-2009.

Enactment of NCLB has focused public schools on the academic achievement of economically disadvantaged students, LEP students, students with disabilities, and students in major racial and ethnic groups. The percentage of AI/AN students scoring at or above proficient on the NAEP 4th and 8th grade reading assessments and NAEP 4th grade math assessments has not significantly changed since 2005 in the aggregate of public schools, BIE schools, Department of Defense schools, and private schools.[165] However, the percentage of AI/AN students scoring at or above proficient on the NAEP 8th grade math assessments has increased from 14% in 2005 to 16% in 2007 and 18% in 2009 in aggregate for public schools, BIE schools, Department of Defense schools, and private schools.[166]

Native Language Instruction

There have been consistent calls to increase the use of native language instruction to increase cultural relevance and improve overall academic performance. One argument contends that language, culture, and identity are intertwined and thus are important to the tribal identity. While NCLB and other federal laws support native language instruction, native language proficiency is not part of the NCLB accountability provisions and thus may not be prioritized.

There is not consensus in the research literature regarding the relative effectiveness of native language instruction. One commonly cited review of research studies with control groups, for instance, suggests that bilingual instruction in some instances was found to improve English reading proficiency in comparison to English immersion, but in other instances it had no impact. This review focused principally on studies conducted prior to 1996 and examining instruction for Spanish-speaking elementary school children, and many of the studies have limitations. The one study of Indian native language students included in the review found no significant difference in English reading outcomes between bilingual and English-immersion instruction.[167]

The Obama Administration in its March 13, 2010, *Blueprint for Reform: The Reauthorization of the Elementary and Secondary Education Act* proposed expanding the use of funds under the ESEA Title III-A Indian education programs for native language immersion and restoration.[168] The National Indian Education Association encourages incorporating native language instruction, assessments, and teacher qualifications into ESEA Titles I and III for public and BIE schools.[169] The challenges of native language instruction are the multitude of native languages that may be spoken in a single classroom, developing and maintaining qualified instructors, and developing and maintaining assessments.

There are federal programs that support native language acquisition:

- Title III of the ESEA, which funds English language acquisition, language enhancement, and academic achievement programs for English language learners (ELLs), provides a 0.5 percent or $5,000,000 set-aside for projects operated predominately for Native American, Alaska Native, Native Hawaiian, or Native American Pacific Islander children. The Title III projects may use funds to help children learn and study Native American languages, except that an outcome shall be increased English proficiency.

- The Native American Language Preservation and Maintenance program (42 USC 2991b-3) supports the revitalization of Native American languages and funds Indian tribes, community-based Indian organizations, Native American organizations, Alaska Native villages, public and nonprofit agencies serving Native Hawaiians, and tribally controlled colleges, among other entities, to ensure the survival and continuing vitality of these languages and the cultures of native peoples for future generations.[170]

- The special Indian Education program for the Improvement of Educational Opportunities for Indian Children (ESEA Title VII-A-2) allows funds to be used for bilingual and bicultural projects.

BIE School Issues

BIE school-specific issues include legislative recognition, definitions of AYP for BIE schools, construction and repair of BIE schools, and issues of crime and substance use.

Legislative Oversight and Recognition

On occasion, new educational programs do not include tribes, the BIE, or BIE schools as eligible entities for funding. In other instances, BIE schools may be eligible for funding but may be unable to meet non-federal matching requirements unless waivers are permitted. Some individual BIE schools may not have the capacity or expertise to operate certain projects without BIE support or technical assistance. It is unclear whether the omission is intentional or unintentional, but the result limits potential funding to BIE schools and excludes BIE schools from certain new statutes. Examples include the following:

- Neither BIE schools nor the BIE, acting in the capacity of a state educational agency, are generally eligible for ESEA programs that fund states unless the program provides a specific set-aside for BIE schools or defines a state to include the BIE.[171]
- The State Fiscal Stabilization Fund (SFSF), enacted by the ARRA, did not provide a set-aside for BIE schools and did not include the BIE as an eligible entity. ARRA appropriated $53.6 billion to support early childhood, elementary, secondary, and postsecondary education; the Race to the Top Fund; and the Innovation Fund.
- The proposed Early Learning Challenge Fund would fund states to develop, maintain, or expand systems of high-quality early learning and development. As proposed by the Supporting State Systems of Early Learning Act (S. 470), introduced on March 3, 2011, Indian tribes and states would be eligible but the BIE would not.
- The Gaining Early Awareness and Readiness for Undergraduate Programs (GEAR UP; 20 U.S.C. 1070a–21 et seq.) funds states and partnerships of LEAs and institutions of higher education to assist eligible low-income students, including students with disabilities, in obtaining a secondary school diploma (or its recognized equivalent) and to prepare for and succeed in postsecondary education. Although the BIE is not eligible for a state grant, individual BIE schools may apply within a partnership.

Definitions of AYP for BIE Schools

As noted above, under the ESEA as amended by NCLB, the Secretary of the Interior defines AYP for BIE schools. Under the negotiated-rulemaking process required by NCLB, the Secretary of the Interior defined AYP for each BIE school as that of the state in which the school is located.[172] A tribe or BIE school board, however, may seek a waiver and an alternative AYP definition.[173] As noted above, the Interior Department and ED (if requested) are required to provide technical assistance to applicants seeking alternative AYP definitions.

As of September 2008, the BIE had received three requests for alternative AYP definitions, from two tribes (the Navajo Nation and the Miccosukee Tribe) and a group of tribally operated schools in North Dakota and South Dakota called the Oceti Sakowin Education Consortium (OSEC).[174] The three applicants reported that they had received insufficient technical assistance from Interior and ED, and a study by the U.S. Government

Accountability Office (GAO) recommended that BIE (with ED) provide prompt technical assistance to applicants; create guidelines and provide training to tribes, tribal school boards, and ELOs; and establish internal processes and timelines to ensure timely responses to requests for technical assistance. [175] Interior agreed with GAO's recommendations and has taken some of the steps, according to GAO.[176] As of August 2010, the BIE was still working with OSEC to develop an alternative AYP definition.[177]

On August 6, 2010, the BIE announced that it is developing a single set of standards and assessments for all BIE schools.[178] A single set of standards and assessments will allow the BIE to compare outcomes and quality across its school system. The BIE announcement also included an intention to consider the unique educational needs of Indian students, which may lead to a curriculum that addresses Indian cultures and languages.

BIA School Construction and Repair

BIE school facilities are characterized by a very large number of old facilities with a high rate of deficiencies, higher than that for public schools.[179] Some facilities are dangerously deteriorated.[180] Before FY2000, the BIA determined that more than 120 schools were in poor condition, and in FY20 11 63 schools were in poor condition. [181] BIA retains responsibility for BIE school construction, including replacement of all of a school's facilities, replacement of individual facilities at schools, improvement and repair of existing school facilities, and repair of education employee housing. Schools and school facilities are replaced or repaired according to several BIA priority lists. A five-year plan for facility improvement and repair ranks projects according to health and safety needs, resource protection, mission criticality, the Facilities Condition Index (FCI), the Asset Priority Index (API), and the Bureau's Asset Management Plan (AMP). The latest replacement school construction priority list was published in 2004, and some of the projects still await funding as of the end of FY20 10.[182]

NCLB required that Interior establish a negotiated rulemaking committee to report on BIE schools' needs for school and school facilities replacement and repair, and to develop formulas to distribute funds to address these needs.[183] In 2006, the BIA initiated the process to establish a negotiated rulemaking committee and announced members of the committee on December 11, 2009.[184] The committee held its sixth meeting in April 2011.

On December 31, 2009, the BIA estimated that the costs to replace, repair, construct, and improve existing facilities in poor condition, excluding facilities in fair or good condition, would be $1.3 billion.[185] Total appropriations, including appropriations from the American Recovery and Reinvestment Act (ARRA; P.L. 111-5) for BIA school construction, improvement, and repair in FY2009 and FY20 10 were $525 million.

Violence, Crime, and Alcohol and Drug Use

Tribal representatives have indicated that violence and alcohol and drug use are serious community issues that affect students and their ability to learn. A high incidence of substance abuse in Indian country communities contributes to or is symptomatic of high levels of depression, domestic violence, suicide, disease, death, and other situations that are not conducive to learning. The BIE does not have a dedicated funding stream to address these issues on school campuses.

A February 2010 evaluation of violence prevention policies and measures at BIE schools by Interior's Office of Inspector General (OIG) found areas of concern for potential violence and deficiencies in the policies and procedures for preventing and managing incidents.[186] The

OIG evaluation cited 2004 statistics about Indian country communities indicating that the violent crime rate is two to three times greater than the national average and that 75% of gang members were school age. According to the OIG evaluation, in recent years 6% of public high school students carried a weapon on campus, whereas 37% of BIE middle school students reported the same. A 2003 National Household Survey on Drug Abuse report revealed that AI/AN youth ages 12 to 17 have higher rates of illicit drug use and binge drinking than other racial/ethnic groups.[187] The OIG evaluation found that many BIE schools had open campuses—little or no fencing, inadequate security access procedures, and flawed camera surveillance systems. The OIG recommended that the BIA and BIE

- establish safety policies and accurate incident tracking systems,[188]
- evaluate campus safety and security,
- correct weaknesses or require tribal operators to correct weaknesses,
- address safety as a criterion for tribes to maintain operating grants and contracts, and
- implement staff training to prevent and manage incidents.

According to the BIE Assistant Deputy Director for Administration on August 6, 2010, the BIE has begun addressing the OIG's recommendations.[189] The BIE is providing training on anger management, bullying prevention, suicide prevention, drug abuse resistance, emergency preparedness, and continuity of operations to BIE and tribal school staff. Online training is provided on the subjects of drug abuse and awareness and the H1N1 flu virus.[190] The BIE is also working with schools to start developing safety policies. Finally, the BIE has proposed using FY2010 ISEP Program Adjustments to improve external and internal physical security measures and provide security training for employees at 10 schools and two dormitories.

Public School Indian Education Issues

Indian education issues affecting public schools include the JOM freeze and the participation of Indian parents and tribes. Other issues raised for schools with Indian students may overlap with NCLB issues for all students.

Johnson O'Malley Program Freeze

As a result of the 1995 freeze, the BIE no longer systematically collects data about the numbers of students served by projects, the needs of those students, the services provided, or the outcomes realized. The freeze allows pre-1995 contractors to receive funding based on their 1995 student count regardless of the number of students actually served. The freeze included each tribe's 1995 JOM allocation into its base funding tribal priority allocation (TPA). TPA allows tribes flexibility in the management and use of funds for various programs and services. Tribes that receive JOM funding through TPA are dependent on this as a fairly stable source of funding.

Indian Control of Indian Education

The participation and influence of Indian parents and tribes in the education of Indian students has increased over time. The JOM and Indian Education formula grant programs require consultation with an Indian parent committee. Passage of ISDEAA has enabled tribes to operate BIE schools. There is interest in increasing the role of Indian tribes in an effort to increase student achievement and cultural relevance of education. Increasing the role of tribes in public schools may confront sovereignty, accountability, collective bargaining, and property ownership issues and will impact non-Indian students in public schools. For instance, the Tribal Education Departments National Assembly, Co. has proposed allowing tribal education departments (TEDs) to operate public schools, particularly public schools on or near reservations and public schools with large enrollments of tribal children.[191] Secretary of Education Arne Duncan indicated that ED would "pursue a pilot program to enhance the role of tribal education agencies and tribes in the education of their members on an experimental basis ... [as] part of our proposal to reauthorize the Elementary and Secondary Act."[192] The BIE was authorized to make grants to TEDs by the Augustus F. Hawkins-Robert T. Stafford Elementary and Secondary School Improvement Amendments of 1988 (P.L. 100-297; 25 U.S.C. § 2020). ED grants to tribes for education administrative planning and development (20 U.S.C. § 7455) were originally authorized by the Improving America's Schools Act of 1994 (P.L. 103-382).

End Notes

[1] In this report, the term "Indian" means American Indians and Alaska Natives (the latter term includes the American Indians, Eskimos (Inuit and Yupik), and Aleuts of Alaska).

[2] The BIE was formerly the Office of Indian Education Programs (OIEP) in the Bureau of Indian Affairs (BIA). In 2006, the Secretary of the Interior moved the OIEP out of the BIA and made it an agency equivalent to the BIA, renaming it the BIE. Both bureaus are under the Assistant Secretary - Indian Affairs. For education programs, this report uses "BIE" for current information and programs and "BIA" for historical periods.

[3] The list of federally recognized tribal entities is published annually in the *Federal Register*. The most recent list is U.S. Department of the Interior, Bureau of Indian Affairs, "Indian Entities Recognized and Eligible To Receive Services From the United States Bureau of Indian Affairs," 75 *Federal Register* 60810-60814, October 1, 2010.

[4] Decisions of the U.S. Supreme Court have characterized the role of the federal government with respect to Indian tribes as involving a trust relationship. Having identified the trust relationship, the Court has upheld congressional power to provide special treatment for Indians, declaring that "[a]s long as the special treatment can be tied rationally to the fulfillment of Congress' unique obligation toward the Indians, such legislative judgments will not be disturbed" (Morton v. Mancari, 417 U.S. 535, 555 (1974)). However, the Court has never interpreted the trust relationship to require any definite action on the part of Congress. When called upon to decide whether an administrative agency has breached its trust obligation or when called upon to enforce the trust obligation against an agency of the Executive Branch, moreover, the Court confines its review to whether the agency has a trust obligation imposed upon it by statute. See, for example, United States v. Mitchell, 463 U.S. 206 (1983).

[5] Worthington Chauncey Ford, ed., *Journals of the Continental Congress, 1774-1789, Vol. II, 1775, May 10-September 20* (Washington: GPO, 1905), pp. 176-177. Congress's stated intent was to keep the students from returning to their homes in British Canada.

[6] Francis Paul Prucha, *The Great Father: The United States Government and the American Indians* (Lincoln: University of Nebraska Press, 1984), pp. 135-136.

[7] Treaty with the Oneida, Etc., Art. III, December 2, 1794, 7 Stat. 47, 48. The United States agreed not only to construct gristmills and sawmills for the Oneida, Tuscarora, and Stockbridge tribes but also to send persons to instruct the tribes in their use. See also Alice C. Fletcher, *Indian Education and Civilization*, U.S. Bureau of Education Special Report, Sen. Ex. Doc. 95, 48th Cong., 2nd sess. (Washington: GPO, 1888), p. 162.

[8] Treaty with the Kaskaskia, Art. 3d, August 13, 1803, 7 Stat. 78, 79.

[9] Nell Jessup Newton, ed.-in-chief, *Cohen's Handbook of Federal Indian Law 2005 Edition* (Newark, NJ: LexisNexis Matthew Bender, 2005), p. 1356. Congress ended treaty-making with Indian tribes in 1871.

[10] Sec. 9, Act of March 1, 1793, Chap. 19, 2nd Cong., 2nd sess., 1 Stat. 329, 331. As civilizing factors, the section specifically authorizes domestic animals, farming equipment, goods, money, and resident agents, but not teachers or schools.

[11] Act of March 3, 1819, Chap. 85, 15th Cong., 2nd sess., 3 Stat. 516. Previous appropriations for Indian affairs would have funded education only for children of tribes that signed treaties providing for education.

[12] Fletcher, *Indian Education and Civilization*, p. 197.

[13] The Bureau of Indian Affairs (BIA), which housed the former Office of Indian Education Programs (OIEP), was responsible for Indian education programs. In 2006, the Secretary of the Interior moved the OIEP out of the BIA and made it an agency equivalent to the BIA, renaming it the Bureau of Indian Education (BIE). Both bureaus are under the Assistant Secretary–Indian Affairs. For education programs, this report uses "BIE" for current information and programs and "BIA" for historical periods.

[14] Szasz, Margaret Connell, and Ryan, Carmelita, "American Indian Education," in Wilcomb E. Washburn, vol. ed., *Handbook of North American Indians, Vol. 4, Indian-White Relations* (Washington: Smithsonian, 1988), p. 290.

[15] The Board of Commissioners was created by the April 10, 1869, act (16 Stat. 40).

[16] Fletcher, *Indian Education and Civilization*, p. 167.

[17] An Act Making Appropriations for the Current and Contingent Expenses of the Indian Department ..., Act of July 15, 1870, Chap. 296, 41st Cong., 2nd sess., 16 Stat. 335, 359. See also U.S. American Indian Policy Review Commission, Task Force Five: Indian Education, *Report on Indian Education*, Committee Print (Washington: GPO, 1976), p. 69.

[18] Paul Stuart, *Nations Within a Nation: Historical Statistics of American Indians* (New York: Greenwood Press, 1987), pp. 135, 165.

[19] Founded by Army Captain Richard H. Pratt on an unused Army base in Carlisle, PA, the school's model of educating Indian students in an off-reservation manual labor boarding school, away from students' families and cultures, became well-known. Pratt, its first superintendent, publicized the school and its emphasis on assimilation. Carlisle was funded through Indian appropriations bills and private donations. It closed in 1918. See Szasz and Ryan, "American Indian Education," pp. 290-291.

[20] Prucha, *Great Father*, pp. 815-816.

[21] Szasz and Ryan, "American Indian Education," pp. 290-294.

[22] Edward E. Hill, comp., *Guide to Records in the National Archives of the United States Relating to American Indians* (Washington: National Archives and Records Service, 1981), p. 24. See also Szasz and Ryan, "American Indian Education," pp. 290, 293.

[23] Hill, *Guide to Records*, p. 112; and Szasz and Ryan, "American Indian Education," p. 297. Authorization for Alaska Native education was in §13, Act of May 17, 1884, Chap.53, 48th Cong. 1st sess., 23 Stat. 24, 27-28.

[24] After 1870, most tribal schools were in Oklahoma, operated by one of the "Five Civilized Tribes" (Cherokee, Chickasaw, Choctaw, Creek, and Seminole), as they were then called.

[25] Szasz and Ryan, "American Indian Education," p. 291.

[26] U.S. Department of the Interior, Office of Indian Affairs, *Annual Report of the Commissioner of Indian Affairs [Fiscal Year 1890-1891]* (Washington: GPO, 1891), p. 71.

[27] Prucha, *Great Father*, pp. 823-825.

[28] Prucha, *Great Father*, pp. 824-825.

[29] U.S. Department of the Interior, Bureau of Indian Affairs, *Report on BIA Education: Excellence in Indian Education Through the Effective Schools Process.* Final Review Draft (Washington: The Department, 1988), Table 1, p. 15.

[30] Marlita A. Reddy, ed., *Statistical Record of Native North Americans* (Detroit: Gale Research, 1993), p. 141. The percentages are of Indians aged 5 to 20 and are based on Census data. Szasz and Ryan state, "In 1928 almost 90 percent of all Indian children were enrolled in some school" ("American Indian Education," p. 294). The discrepancy in percentages may be related to differing age ranges and differing definitions of the Indian population.

[31] Act of November 2, 1921, 42 Stat. 208, as amended; 25 U.S.C. § 13.

[32] P.L. 73-167, Act of April 16, 1934, 48 Stat. 596, as amended; 25 U.S.C. § 452-457.

[33] Szasz and Ryan, "American Indian Education," p. 295.

[34] Szasz and Ryan, "American Indian Education," pp. 294-295; Prucha, *Great Father*, pp. 836-839, 977-983; and Margaret Connell Szasz, "W. Carson Ryan: From the Meriam Report to the Indian New Deal," in *Education and the American Indian: The Road to Self-Determination Since 1928*, 2nd ed. (Albuquerque: University of New Mexico Press, 1977), pp. 16-36. The Meriam Report was an influential study of federal Indian affairs undertaken by the Institute for Government Research (Lewis A. Meriam, ed., *The Problem of Indian Administration* (Baltimore: Johns Hopkins Press, 1928)).

[35] Szasz and Ryan, "American Indian Education," p. 297.

[36] P.L. 81-874, Act of September 30, 1950, 64 Stat. 1100, as amended; currently codified as Title VIII of the Elementary and Secondary Education Act (ESEA).

[37] P.L. 83-248, Act of August 8, 1953, 67 Stat. 530.

[38] Larry LaCounte, *Tribal Perspective of the Impact Aid Program* (Washington: National Indian Policy Center, 1993), pp. 3-5.

[39] U.S. Congress, Senate Select Committee on Indian Affairs, *Indian Education Oversight*, hearings, May 18-19, 1982, 97th Cong., 2nd sess. (Washington: GPO, 1983), p. 433.

[40] U.S. Department of Education, National Center for Education Statistics, *Digest of Education Statistics 2006*, NCES 2007-0 17 (Washington: GPO, 2007), p. 536.

[41] P.L. 89-10, Act of April 11, 1965, 79 Stat. 27, as amended.

[42] Sec. 102, Elementary and Secondary Education Amendments of 1966, P.L. 89-750, Act of Nov 3, 1966, 80 Stat 1191.

[43] U.S. Congress, Senate Labor and Public Welfare Committee, Special Subcommittee on Indian Education, *Indian Education: A National Tragedy, A National Challenge* (Washington: GPO, 1969).

[44] Title IV of the Education Amendments Act of 1972, P.L. 92-318, Act of June 23, 1972, 86 Stat. 235, 334, as amended; currently codified as ESEA Title VII-A.

[45] The OIE was transferred to the new Department of Education in 1980.

[46] Prucha, *Great Father*, p. 1102.

[47] P.L. 93-638, Act of January 4, 1975, 88 Stat. 2203, as amended; 25 U.S.C. § 450 *et seq.*

[48] P.L. 95-561, Title XI, Part B, Act of November 1, 1978, 92 Stat. 2143, 2316, as amended; currently codified at 25 U.S.C., Chap. 22. The quote is from §1130 of the original act (now § 1131 of the amended act).

[49] Prucha, *Great Father*, p. 1146.

[50] P.L. 100-297, Title V, Act of April 28, 1988, 102 Stat. 130, 385, as amended; 25 U.S.C., Chap. 27.

[51] Provisions are currently codified at 25 U.S.C. § 2007 and 25 U.S.C. § 2503.

[52] Sec. 421(a) of the 1972 act; currently codified at ESEA § 7114(c)(4).

[53] P.L. 92-318, §41 1(a),(c)(2), 86 Stat. 334-339; currently codified, as amended, at ESEA § 8004. See also Szasz and Ryan, "American Indian Education," p. 298.

[54] 25 U.S.C. § 456.

[55] U.S. Congress, House Committee on Appropriations, *Department of the Interior and Related Agencies Appropriations for 1994*, hearings, part 8, 103rd Cong., 1st sess. (Washington: GPO, 1993), p. 168.

[56] U.S. Department of the Interior, Bureau of Indian Affairs, *Report on BIA Education: Excellence in Indian Education Through the Effective Schools Process*. Final Review Draft (Washington: The Department, 1988), p. 17.

[57] U.S. Department of the Interior, Bureau of Indian Affairs, Branch of Education, *Fiscal Year 1965 Statistics Concerning Indian Education* (Haskell, Kansas: Haskell Institute Publications Service, 1966), p. 15.

[58] U.S. Department of the Interior, Bureau of Indian Affairs, Office of Indian Education Programs, *Fiscal Year 1995 Annual Education Report* (Washington: The Bureau, no date), p. vi.

[59] U.S. Department of the Interior, Indian Affairs, *Budget Justifications Fiscal Year 2012* (hereafter referred to as the *FY2012 Budget*). p. IA-EDU-6.

[60] The limitations are in the annual BIA appropriations acts.

[61] *FY1995 Annual Education Report* and *Budget Justifications FY2008–FY2012, loc.cit.*

[62] U.S. Department of the Interior, Indian Affairs, *Budget Justifications Fiscal Year 2008*, pp. IA-EDUC-5 to -6

[63] 25 U.S.C. § 2007(f). "One-fourth degree" is the equivalent of one "full-blood" grandparent out of four.

[64] 25 C.F.R. 273.12.

[65] P.L. 103-382, Act of October 20, 1994, 108 Stat. 3518.

[66] ESEA § 7151(3).

[67] 25 U.S.C. § 7703(a)(1).

[68] NAEP is often known as "the nation's report card."

[69] BIE also funds post-secondary institutions and programs not discussed in this report. A small number of BIE-funded elementary-secondary schools also receive funding as public schools from their states.

[70] *FY2012 Budget*, p. IA-EDU-5 and Department of the Interior, Bureau of Indian Education, *National Directory*, updated March 2009. BIE plans for reorganization of ELOs had elicited tribal opposition, which included court injunctions in 2006 halting reorganization in New Mexico and North and South Dakota. Settlements in 2007 changed the number of ELOs and the school assignments of some ELOs.

[71] Department of the Interior, Bureau of Indian Education, *National Directory*, updated March 2009.

[72] For a history of the schools, see http://www.belcourt.k12.nd.us/education/components/scrap book/default. php?sectiondetailid=1258.

[73] *FY2012 Budget*, p. IA-EDUC-19.

[74] See Interior Department and Further Continuing Appropriations, Fiscal Year 2010 (P.L. 111-88), Act of October 30, 2009, 123 Stat. 2919.

[75] U.S. Congress, Senate Appropriations Committee, *Department of the Interior and Related Agencies Appropriations Bill, 1995*, report to accompany H.R. 4602, 103rd Cong., 2nd sess., S.Rept. 103-294 (Washington: GPO, 1994), p. 58.

[76] *FY2012 Budget*, pp. IA-EDU-3, 4, and 6.

[77] Excludes BIE peripheral dorms. CRS calculation based on the FY2012 Budget, pp. Appendix 2-2–2-7. Adding in students in BIE peripheral dorms raises the average size to 259 students.

[78] U.S. Department of Education, National Center for Education Statistics, *Digest of Education Statistics 2005*, NCES 2006-030 (Washington: GPO, 2006), Table 87.

[79] U.S. Department of Education, National Center for Education Statistics, *Status and Trends in the Education of American Indians and Alaska Natives*, NCES 2005-108 (Washington: GPO, 2005), p. 32.

[80] Annual appropriation acts for the Department of the Interior regularly include an administrative provision prohibiting BIA expenditures to support operation of schools in Alaska (except through the Johnson-O'Malley program); see, for example, P.L. 110-161 (121 Stat. 2113).

[81] *FY2012 Budget*, p. IA-EDU-10.

[82] U.S. Department of Education, Justifications of Appropriation Estimates to the Congress, Fiscal Year 2012.

[83] The NAEP, directed by the U.S. Department of Education, is the largest nationally representative and continuing assessment of what America's students know and can do in various subject areas. Since NAEP assessments are administered uniformly across the nation, NAEP results serve as a common metric.

[84] S. Aud, W. Hussar, M. Planty, T. Snyder, K. Bianco, M. Fox, L. Frohlich, J. Kemp, L. Drake, *The Condition of Education 2010* (NCES 20 10-028), National Center for Education Statistics, Institute of Education Sciences, U.S. Department of Education, Washington, DC, 2010.

[85] J.F. DeVoe, and K.E. Darling-Churchill, *Status and Trends in the Education of American Indians and Alaska Natives: 2008* (NCES 2008-084), National Center for Education Statistics, Institute of Education Sciences, U.S. Department of Education, Washington, DC, 2008.

[86] High-poverty schools are those where 76%-100% of students are eligible for free or reduced-price lunch (FRPL) through the National School Lunch Program (NSLP). Twenty percent of public elementary schools and 9 percent of public secondary schools in the United States are high poverty using this definition.

[87] S. Aud, W. Hussar, M. Planty, T. Snyder, K. Bianco, M. Fox, L. Frohlich, J. Kemp, L. Drake, *The Condition of Education 2010* (NCES 20 10-028), National Center for Education Statistics, Institute of Education Sciences, U.S. Department of Education, Washington, DC, 2010.

[88] Ibid.

[89] J.F. DeVoe, and K.E. Darling-Churchill, *Status and Trends in the Education of American Indians and Alaska Natives: 2008* (NCES 2008-084), National Center for Education Statistics, Institute of Education Sciences, U.S. Department of Education, Washington, DC, 2008.

[90] S. Aud, W. Hussar, M. Planty, T. Snyder, K. Bianco, M. Fox, L. Frohlich, J. Kemp, L. Drake, *The Condition of Education 2010* (NCES 20 10-028), National Center for Education Statistics, Institute of Education Sciences, U.S. Department of Education, Washington, DC, 2010.

[91] *FY2012 Budget*, p. IA-EDU-5.

[92] Act of November 2, 1921, 42 Stat. 208, as amended; 25 U.S.C. § 13.

[93] P.L. 93-638, act of January 4, 1975, 88 Stat. 2203, as amended; 25 U.S.C. § 450 et seq.

[94] ISDEAA's Title IV, "Tribal Self-Governance," §§401-408 (25 U.S.C. § 458aa-458hh), authorizes "self-governance compacts" with tribes under which a tribe may operate multiple BIA programs under a single compact, but BIE's formula funding for schools is excluded from these compacts (§403(b)(4)(B); 25 U.S.C. § 458cc(b)(4)(B)).

[95] P.L. 95-561, Title XI, Part B, Act of November 1, 1978, 92 Stat. 2143, 2316, as amended by §1042 of the Native American Education Improvement Act of 2001, which was Title X, Part D, of the No Child Left Behind Act, P.L. 107- 110, Act of January 8, 2002, 115 Stat. 2007, as further amended; 25 U.S.C., Chap. 22 (25 U.S.C. §2000 *et seq.*).

[96] P.L. 100-297, Title V, Act of April 28, 1988, 102 Stat. 130, 385, as amended; 25 U.S.C., Chap. 27.

[97] *Cohen's Handbook of Federal Indian Law 2005 Edition*, p. 1361.

[98] *FY2012 Budget* and Department of the Interior, Bureau of Indian Education, *National Directory*, updated March 2009.

[99] Federal fiscal years (FY) begin on October 1 and end on the following September 30. School years (SY) begin on July 1 (three-quarters of the way through the fiscal year) and end the following June 30. Hence, BIE appropriations for *FY2012* (October 1, 2011-September 30, 2012) will be used to fund *SY2012-2013* (July 1, 2012-September 30, 2013).

[100] Title I-A of the Elementary and Secondary Education Act (ESEA) includes accountability requirements that require states to implement content and performance standards and assessments aligned with standards for reading/language arts and mathematics for multiple grades. The results of these assessments are used to determine whether each public school and local educational agency (LEA) makes annual adequate yearly progress (AYP). A series of increasingly substantial consequences must be applied to schools and LEAs that fail to meet the AYP standards for two consecutive years or more.

[101] 25 U.S.C. § 2007.

[102] 25 C.F.R. Part 39, Subparts A-C.

[103] *FY2012 Budget*, pp. IA-EDU-18, and 25 C.F.R. Part 39, Subpart G.

[104] 25 U.S.C. § 2019.

[105] *FY2012 Budget*, pp. IA-EDU-22.

[106] 25 U.S.C. § 2008.

[107] *FY2012 Budget*, pp. IA-EDU-22 to -23, and 25 C.F.R. Part 39, Subpart J.

[108] *FY2012 Budget*, p. IA-EDU-24.

[109] U.S. Department of the Interior, Indian Affairs, *Budget Justifications Fiscal Year 2011*. p. IA-EDU-21.

[110] *FY2012 Budget*, p. Appendix 2-7.

[111] 25 C.F.R. 273.12.

[112] *FY2012 Budget*, p. IA-EDU-25.

[113] 25 C.F.R. Part 273.13.

[114] P.L. 73-167, Act of April 16, 1934, Chap. 147, 73rd Cong., 48 Stat. 596, as amended; 25 U.S.C. § 452-457. The quote is from § 1 (25 U.S.C. § 452).

[115] 39 Fed.Reg. 30114-30116 (August 21, 1974). See also Prucha, *Great Father*, pp. 1143-1144.

[116] P.L. 99-190, § 101(d) (Title I), Act of December 19, 1985, 99 Stat. 1185, 1235.

[117] U.S. Congress, House Committee on Appropriations, *Department of the Interior and Related Agencies Appropriations Bill, 1995*, Report to accompany H.R. 4602, 103rd Cong., 2nd sess., June 17, 1994, H.Rept. 103-551, pp. 54-55 and U.S. Congress, Senate Committee on Appropriations, *Department of the Interior and Related Agencies Appropriations Bill, 1995*, Report to accompany H.R. 4602, 103rd Cong., 2nd sess., June 28, 1994, S.Rept. 103-294, p. 55.

[118] U.S. Department of the Interior, Bureau of Indian Affairs, "Tribal Consultation of Indian Education Topics," 60 *Federal Register* 53932, October 18, 1995.

[119] 25 U.S.C § 450j-1(b)(2).

[120] U.S. Department of the Interior, Bureau of Indian Affairs, *Budget Justifications and Performance Information, Fiscal Year 2005* (Washington: The Department, 2004), p. BIA-58.

[121] For more information on BIA appropriations, see CRS Report R40685, *Interior, Environment, and Related Agencies: FY2010 Appropriations*, coordinated by Carol Hardy Vincent.

[122] Totals for the BIE elementary-secondary education program were calculated by CRS.

[123] ESEA, § 9101(26(C).

[124] IDEA, § 602(19)(C).

[125] For more information on the ED program, see CRS Report RL33731, *Education for the Disadvantaged: Reauthorization Issues for ESEA Title I-A Under the No Child Left Behind Act*.

[126] Calculated from "Fiscal Year 2001-2012 State Tables for the U.S. Department of Education: State Tables by Program," U.S. Department of Education, Budget Service, http://www.ed. gov/about/overview/budget/statetables/index.html.

[127] For more information on the ED program, see CRS Report RL3 1882, *Teacher Quality Enhancement Grants (Title II, Part A of the Higher Education Act): Overview and Reauthorization Issues*.

[128] For more information on the ED program, see CRS Report RL3 1240, *21st Century Community Learning Centers: Background and Funding*.

[129] For more information on the ED program, see CRS Report R40055, *The Individuals with Disabilities Education Act: Final Part B Regulations*, by Nancy Lee Jones and Ann Lordeman.

[130] The inflation index has been either as specified in section 619(d)(2)(B) of the IDEA or the percent change in the IDEA appropriations from the prior year.

[131] For more information on this ED program, see CRS Report RL34119, *Impact Aid for Public K-12 Education: Reauthorization Under the Elementary and Secondary Education Act*, by Rebecca R. Skinner and Richard N. Apling.

[132] ESEA, § 80 13(5), (7).

[133] Trust lands and restricted lands are not taxable by states or local governments, including LEAs. Trust lands are lands held by the federal government in trust for an Indian tribe or individual; restricted lands are lands held by an Indian tribe or individual subject to federal restrictions on alienation.

[134] P.L. 92-203, Act of December 18, 1971, 85 Stat. 688; 43 U.S.C. § 1601 *et seq.*

[135] ESEA § 80 13(5), (7).

[136] U.S. Department of Education, Fiscal Year 2012 Budget Request.

[137] ESEA, § 7111-7152.

[138] For more detailed information on the Indian Education formula grant program, see CRS Report R41598, *Indian Education Formula Grant Program of the Elementary and Secondary Education Act*, by Cassandria Dortch.

[139] ESEA, § 7301-7306.

[140] ESEA § 9101(26)(C) and ESEA § 9103. BIA-funded schools' definition as LEAs is limited by a minimum size requirement.

[141] ESEA § 9401. For discussion of waivers in the NCLB, see CRS Report RL3 1583, *K-12 Education: Special Forms of Flexibility in the Administration of Federal Aid Programs*, by Rebecca R. Skinner.

[142] ESEA §§ 1111(b)(3) and 1116(a)(1)(A).

[143] E-mail from the Bureau of Indian Education, Special Assistant to the Director, March 29, 2011.

[144] ESEA § 1111(m).

[145] 25 C.F.R. § 30.104.

[146] ESEA § 1111(b)(2).

[147] ESEA § 1111(b)(2)(C).

[148] ESEA § 1116(g)(1).

[149] ESEA § 1116(g)(1)(B).

[150] ESEA. § 1116(g)(1)(C).

[151] ESEA § 1119.

[152] 25 C.F.R. § 38.5.

[153] ESEA § 1116(g)(3)-(4).

[154] ESEA § 1116(g)(3).

[155] ESEA § 1116(g)(3)-(4).

[156] ESEA § 1116(b-c) and § 11 16(g)(2).

[157] ESEA § 16(g)(5).

[158] Native American Education Improvement Act of 2001, P.L. 107-110, Title X, Part D, § 1042, Act of January 8, 2002, 115 Stat. 1439, 2007, as amended; 25 U.S.C., Chap. 22, §§ 2000 *et seq.*

[159] 25 U.S.C. § 2001(b)(3), (7)-(8).

[160] 25 U.S.C. § 200 1(b)(8)(B).

[161] ESEA § 7101.

[162] 25 U.S.C. § 450(b)(2).

[163] *FY2012 Budget*, p. IA-EDU-10.

[164] U.S. Department of Education, Justifications of Appropriation Estimates to the Congress, Fiscal Year 2012.

[165] U.S. Department of Education, Institute of Education Sciences, National Center for Education Statistics, National Assessment of Educational Progress (NAEP), *2009 National Indian Education Studies Part I*, pp. 13.

[166] Ibid.

[167] Robert E Slavin and Alan Cheung, "A Synthesis of Research on Language of Reading Instruction for English Language Learners," *Review of Educational Research*, vol. 75, no. 2 (Summer 2005), pp. 247-284.

[168] For more information on the Blueprint, see CRS Report R41355, *Administration's Proposal to Reauthorize the Elementary and Secondary Education Act: Comparison to Current Law*, by Rebecca R. Skinner et al.

[169] National Indian Education Association, *Priorities for Improving the Elementary and Secondary Education Act (ESEA) for Native American Students*, Washington, DC, 2010.

[170] U. S. Department of Health and Human Services, Administration for Children and Families, Administration for Native Americans, *Native American Language Preservation and Maintenance* , HHS-201 1-ACF-ANA-NL-0 139, February 25, 2011, http://www.acf.hhs. gov/grants/open/foa/view/HHS-2011-ACF-ANA-NL-0139.

[171] The Advanced Placement Test Fee Program (ESEA Title I-G, Section 1704) and the School Dropout Prevention Initiative (ESEA Title I-H, Subpart 2) define "state" to include the BIA.

[172] 25 C.F.R. 30.104, promulgated April 28, 2005.

[173] ESEA, § 1116(g) (20 U.S.C. § 6316(g)).

[174] "Statement of Stanley R. Holder, Chief, Division of Performance and Accountability, Bureau of Indian Education, U.S. Department of the Interior," in U.S. Congress, House Education and Labor Committee, Subcommittee on Early Childhood, Elementary and Secondary Education, *Challenges Facing Bureau of Indian Education Schools in Improving Student Achievement*, hearings, 110th Cong., 2nd sess., September 9, 2008, Serial No. 110–108 (Washington: GPO, 2008), p. 18.

[175] U.S. Government Accountability Office (GAO), *Bureau of Indian Education Schools: Improving Interior's Assistance Would Help Some Tribal Groups Implement Academic Accountability Systems*, GAO-08-679 (Washington: GAO, June 2008), pp. 25-31.

[176] U.S. Government Accountability Office, *Bureau of Indian Education: Improving Interior's Assistance Would Aid Tribal Groups Developing Academic Accountability Systems*, GAO-08-1125T (Washington: GAO, September 9, 2008), p. [ii].

[177] U.S. Department of the Interior, Bureau of Indian Education, Statement of David Talayumptewa, Assistant Deputy Director for Administration, Before the House Committee on Natural Resources Field Hearing on Indian Education, August 6, 2010, http://natural resources.house.gov/UploadedFiles/Talayumptewa Testimony08.06.10.pdf.

[178] U.S. Department of the Interior, Bureau of Indian Education, Statement of David Talayumptewa, Assistant Deputy Director for Administration, Before the House Committee on Natural Resources Field Hearing on Indian Education, August 6, 2010, http://natural resources.house.gov/ UploadedFiles/ Talayumptewa Testimony08.06.10.pdf.

[179] See U.S. General Accounting Office, *BIA and DOD Schools: Student Achievement and Other Characteristics Often Differ from Public Schools'*, GAO-01-934 (Washington: GAO, September 2001), pp. 23-32; and GAO, *School Facilities: Reported Condition and Costs to Repair Schools Funded by Bureau of Indian Affairs*, GAO/HEHS-98-47 (Washington: GAO, December 1997). GAO reported that in 2000, BIA school administrators reported 65% of schools and 76% of peripheral dormitories had one or more buildings in inadequate condition, compared to 24% of public schools (GAO-01-934, p. 25).

[180] U.S. Department of the Interior, Office of Inspector General, *Bureau of Indian Affairs and Bureau of Indian Education: Schools in Need of Immediate Action*, C-IN-BIA-0008-2007 (Washington: DOI/IG, May 2007).

[181] *FY2012 Budget*, pp. IA-CON-SUM-9 and IA-CON-ED-9.

[182] U.S. Department of the Interior, Bureau of Indian Affairs, "Replacement School Construction Priority List as of FY 2004," 69 *Federal Register* 13870, March 24, 2004.

[183] 25 U.S.C. § 2005(a)(5).

[184] U.S. Department of the Interior, Bureau of Indian Affairs, "No Child Left Behind Act of 2001—Membership of the School Facilities and Construction Negotiated Rulemaking Committee," 74 *Federal Register* 65784-65786, December 11, 2009.

[185] "Indian Affairs Funded Schools in Poor Condition as Indicated by Facility Condition Index (FCI)," provided by the BIA to CRS in February 2010.

[186] U.S. Department of the Interior, Office of Inspector General, *Evaluation Report—School Violence Prevention*, Report No. NM-EV-BIE-0003-2008, Washington, DC, February 2010.

[187] U.S. Department of Health and Human Services, Substance Abuse and Mental Health Services Administration (SAMHSA), Office of Applied Studies, *National Household Survey on Drug Abuse: The NHSDA Report*, May 16, 2003, http://www.oas.samhsa.gov/2k3/AmIndians/AmIndians.pdf.

[188] The evaluation indicated that reporting of incidents in the Native American Student Information System (NASIS) is inconsistent and inaccurate.

[189] U.S. Department of the Interior, Bureau of Indian Education, Statement of David Talayumptewa, Assistant Deputy Director for Administration, Before the House Committee on Natural Resources Field Hearing on Indian Education, August 6, 2010, http://natural resources.house.gov/UploadedFiles/ TalayumptewaTestimony 08.06.10.pdf.

[190] Bureau of Indian Education, "Safe Schools Online Training Courses," http://www.bie.edu/idc/ groups/xbie/ documents/text/idc010830.pdf, retrieved May 18, 2011.

[191] Tribal Education Departments National Assembly, *The Elementary and Secondary Education Act Reauthorization Recommendations for Tribal Education Departments/Agencies*, Boulder, CO, February 11, 2011, http://www.tedna.org/ articles/esea_reauthorization_ recommendations.pdf.

[192] U. S. Department of Education, "Education in Indian Country: Prepared Remarks of U.S. Secretary of Education Arne Duncan at Town Hall/Listening Session with Tribal Officials," speech, December 15, 2010, http://www.ed.gov/news/speeches/education-indian-country-prepared-remarks-us-secretary-education-arne-duncan-town-hall.

In: American Indians. Volume 1
Editors: Albert O. Hughes and Eric A. Sanders

ISBN: 978-1-61122-351-4
© 2012 Nova Science Publishers, Inc.

Chapter 2

INDIAN EDUCATION FORMULA GRANT PROGRAM OF THE ELEMENTARY AND SECONDARY EDUCATION ACT[*]

Cassandria Dortch

SUMMARY

The Title VII-A formula grant program, authorized by the Indian Education Act of the Elementary and Secondary Education Act (ESEA) as amended by the No Child Left Behind Act (NCLB; P.L. 107-110), is one of the current federal programs targeted to raising the educational achievement of Indian children. The Title VII-A Indian Education formula grant program is intended to provide supplementary funding for the education of Indian children. The program is intended to help Indian students meet state academic and content standards in an environment that values their culturally related academic needs. For purposes of the program, an Indian student is defined as a member or child or grandchild of a member of a federally recognized tribe, state-recognized tribe, or terminated tribe; an individual considered by the Secretary of the Interior to be an Indian; an Eskimo, Aleut, or other Alaska Native; or a member of an organized Indian group that received a grant under the program before October 20, 1994.

Local educational agencies (LEAs), Indian tribes, and Bureau of Indian Education (BIE)-funded schools are eligible for funding. To be eligible, LEAs must meet one of the following criteria: serve a minimum of 10 Indian students; have an enrollment of at least 25% Indian students; be located in Alaska, California, or Oklahoma; or be located on or in proximity to a reservation. An Indian tribe that represents a minimum of 50% of the LEA's Indian enrollment is eligible in lieu of the LEA if the eligible LEA does not establish an Indian Parent Committee. The Indian Parent Committee contributes to and approves the LEA's plan for using grant funds.

---

[*] This is an edited, reformatted and augmented version of the Congressional Research Service Publication, CRS Report for Congress R41598, dated January 18, 2011.

Grants are awarded by formula based on the enrollment of eligible Indian students and the average per pupil expenditure (APPE). In FY2010, it is estimated that the 1,265 grantees received an average of $220 per Indian student enrolled. The program's FY2010 appropriation was $104 million. Grantees, 90% of which are LEAs, have served 448,000-481,000 Indian students each year since FY1999. Since FY1999, LEAs in three states—Alaska, Arizona, and Oklahoma—have received almost half (45%) of the funding. LEAs in 12 states have not received any funding since at least FY2002.

The 112th Congress may consider several issues related to the Title VII-A Indian education formula grant program and Indian education more generally as it considers reauthorization of the ESEA. The various definitions of Indian student used to determine eligibility for programs that support the education of Indian students complicates administration and makes program success difficult to measure. The educational outcomes of Indian children have continued to lag behind those of other American children. Many stakeholders believe the program is underfunded as measured by the program's original 1972 statutory goals, the educational achievement gaps, and the need for culturally relevant education.

INTRODUCTION

The Indian education formula grant program provides supplementary support for the education of Indian students in local educational agencies (LEAs), by tribes, and by the Bureau of Indian Education (BIE). The program was most recently reauthorized as Title VII-A of the Elementary and Secondary Education Act (ESEA) by the No Child Left Behind Act of 2001 (NCLB; P.L. 107-110). The NCLB authorized virtually all ESEA programs through FY2008. The 112th Congress may consider reauthorizing and amending the ESEA.

State and local governments have primary responsibility for the education of all students attending public schools. The BIE has primary responsibility for the education of students, who are predominantly Indian, in its school system. The ESEA Title VII-A program provides supplementary education assistance to help Indian students meet challenging state academic standards.

This report provides a brief history of the ESEA Title VII-A Indian education formula grant program to local educational agencies; describes the major provisions; analyzes data on the distribution of funds, grants, and Indian students served; and discusses selected issues. It does not address the special programs and national activities also authorized by the ESEA Title VII-A.

HISTORY OF THE INDIAN EDUCATION FORMULA GRANT PROGRAM

The ESEA Title VII-A Indian education formula grant program to local educational agencies was originally enacted as the Indian Education Act of 1972, Title IV of the Education Amendments of 1972 (P.L. 92-318). Passage of the Indian Education Act of 1972 was influenced by several reports and commissions during the 1960s, including the often-cited 1969 Senate report entitled *Indian Education: A National Tragedy–A National*

Challenge, also known as the Kennedy Commission Report.[1] The 1969 Senate report indicted the federal government for failing to meet its responsibility for the education of Indian students. The report also indicated that the existing Indian education programs for public schools had not improved the educational outcomes of Indian students. Two programs had been established in the first half of the 20th century to provide consistent support for the education of Indian students in public schools: the Johnson-O'Malley (JOM) Act[2] and the Financial Assistance for Local Educational Agencies Affected by Federal Activities program[3] (now known as the Impact Aid program[4]).

The Indian Education Act of 1972 amended the Impact Aid Program to add a new Title III entitled the *Indian Elementary and Secondary School Assistance Act* to support formula grants to LEAs for the "special educational needs" of Indian students. The Indian Education Act also authorized several special programs within Title VIII of the Elementary and Secondary Education Act (ESEA) to improve educational opportunities for Indian children, authorized two special programs within the Adult Education Act for Indians, established the Office of Indian Education within the Office of Education (now known as the U.S. Department of Education (ED)), established the National Advisory Council on Indian Education (NACIE) to advise the Commissioner (now known as the Secretary) of Education,[5] amended Title V-D of the Higher Education Act of 1965 to provide a 5% set-aside for teacher preparation programs that prepare teachers to serve children living on reservations, and amended the Bilingual Education Programs of the ESEA to allow nonprofit organizations and Indian tribal organizations that operate schools near reservations to apply as LEAs.

A program providing formula grants to LEAs for the education of Indian students has been reauthorized three times since 1972. Title V-C of the Augustus F. Hawkins-Robert T. Stafford Elementary and Secondary School Improvement Amendments of 1988 (Stafford Act; P.L. 100- 297) enacted the Indian Education Act of 1988 (25 U.S.C. § 2601 et seq.) to include financial assistance to LEAs for the education of Indian children, previously known as the Indian Elementary and Secondary School Assistance Act; enacted special programs to improve the education of Indian students, the teachers of Indian students, and adult Indians; and established the Office of Indian Education and NACIE. The Stafford Act repealed the Indian Elementary and Secondary School Assistance Act of 1972 (20 U.S.C. § 241aa et seq.) and repealed the establishment of the Office of Indian Education and NACIE as authorized under the Indian Education Act of 1972. Although the Indian Education Act of 1988 was authorized in Title 25 (Indians) of the U.S. Code, the programs were still administered by the Secretary of Education. The Improving America's Schools Act of 1994 (P.L. 103-382) repealed the Indian Education Act of 1988 and enacted Title IX of the ESEA (20 U.S.C. § 7811 et seq.) to provide for Indian education, including formula grants to LEAs. The No Child Left Behind Act of 2001 (P.L. 107- 110) moved the program from Title IX of the ESEA to Title VII of ESEA (20 U.S.C. § 7111 et seq.).

DESCRIPTION OF THE INDIAN EDUCATION FORMULA GRANT PROGRAM TO LEAS

The current Indian Education formula grant program to LEAs is intended to provide supplementary funding for the education of Indian children. The supporting policy is based on

- the special educational and culturally related academic needs of Indian students,
- the need for Indian parental involvement and influence,
- the need for Indian students to meet state academic performance standards, and
- "The United States['] ... unique and continuing trust relationship[6] with and responsibility to the Indian people for the education of Indian children."[7]

The following subsections describe the definition of an Indian student, the eligible grantees, the application process, and formula allocation in the Title VII-A Indian Education formula grant program. Major statutory changes are included for historical context.

Definition of Indian Student

For the purpose of the ESEA Title VII-A, an Indian is currently defined as

- a member, or descendent in the first or second degree of a member, of an Indian tribe or band, as membership is defined by the tribe or band, including terminated[8] or state-recognized tribes and bands;
- an individual considered by the Secretary of the Interior to be an Indian for any purpose;
- an Eskimo, Aleut, or other Alaska Native; or
- a member of an organized Indian group that received a grant under the program as in effect on October 20, 1994.[9]

This definition includes three groups of individuals that are not generally eligible for special programs and services provided by the United States to Indians because of their status as Indians.[10] The first are the children and grandchildren of members of federally recognized[11] or terminated tribes. The children and grandchildren may not identify themselves as Indians and may not meet tribal membership criteria. The Senate Indian Affairs Committee indicated that "the program was designed to serve students of Indian ancestry (parent or grandparent enrolled in a tribe), not just those Indian children who are enrolled in a federally or state-recognized tribe."[12]

The second are the members and children and grandchildren of members of state-recognized tribes. The federal government does not generally provide benefits to state-recognized tribes unless the tribe is also federally recognized. State criteria and processes for recognition may not meet federal standards. The 1972 program statute was purposely intended to include state- recognized tribes, off-reservation Indians, and terminated tribes because several reports indicated that Indians had a significant need for remedial education support, but "not necessarily because of any trust responsibility towards, or treaty obligation to, these Indians."[13]

The third group are members of an organized Indian group that received a grant under the program as in effect on October 20, 1994. On October 20, 1994, the term "Indian" was defined as above except that it also included a member or child or grandchild of a member of an "other organized group" of Indians and any individual determined to be an Indian under regulations promulgated by the Secretary after consultation with the NACIE. During the debate that preceded the 1994 reauthorization, NACIE recommended excluding "other organized groups," children and grandchildren of members, any Indian tribes or bands that were not self-governing, and some state-recognized tribes from the definition. [14] NACIE determined that the broader definition eroded the authority of the self-governing entities and distorted the definition to include individuals with no discernible tribal culture. [15] The 1994 reauthorization[16] excluded the term "other organized groups of Indians" from the definition of Indian but grandfathered in all of the members of those "other organized groups of Indians" that received grants prior to the reauthorization. The House Education and Labor Committee indicated that all students who were currently eligible or who would be eligible if in school should be eligible.[17]

Eligible Entities

Under the Title VII-A formula grant program, three types of entities—LEAs, Indian tribes, and Bureau of Indian Education (BIE)-funded schools—may be eligible for funding. The specific eligibility criteria differ by the type of entity.

LEAs that either serve a minimum of 10 Indian students or have an enrollment of at least 25% Indian students are eligible.[18] Since most LEAs serve more than 40 students, only the requirement to serve a minimum of 10 Indian students applies.[19] Although the LEA must apply for the grant, not all of the schools within the LEA must participate in the grant. Also, LEAs in Alaska, California, or Oklahoma or LEAs located on or in proximity to a reservation that serve a minimum of one Indian student are eligible.[20] The original 1972 act exempted LEAs in Alaska, California, and Oklahoma and LEAs on or near reservations from the minimum Indian student enrollment to "extend the benefits ... in isolated and sparsely settled areas, where the need for special services is often greatest, and to encourage increased enrollment [into public schools] on the part of Indians in these areas."[21] Finally, consortia of LEAs that individually meet the eligibility requirements are eligible. LEAs, such as a high school LEA and an elementary LEA serving the same area, may form a consortium to provide services more effectively.

An Indian tribe that represents a minimum of 50% of each LEA's Indian enrollment is eligible to apply for a grant in lieu of one LEA or multiple LEAs if the eligible LEAs do not establish an Indian Parent Committee (see the "Application Process" section for more information on the Indian Parent Committee).[22] Allowing tribes to be eligible entities was expected to strengthen the input and participation of tribal governments in the education of Indian children and to ensure the Title VII-A program services were available to more Indian students.[23] As of October 2010, there were 564 federally recognized tribal entities in the 34 states of Alabama, Alaska, Arizona, California, Colorado, Connecticut, Florida, Idaho, Indiana, Iowa, Kansas, Louisiana, Maine, Massachusetts, Michigan, Minnesota, Mississippi, Montana, Nebraska, Nevada, New Mexico, New York, North Carolina, North Dakota, Oregon, Rhode Island, South Carolina, South Dakota, Texas, Oklahoma, Utah, Washington, Wisconsin, Wyoming.[24]

BIE-funded schools are eligible in the same way as LEAs for Title VII-A formula awards.[25] BIE-funded schools may apply for Title VII-A awards individually or as consortia. In FY2010, the BIE school system served approximately 42,000 students from over 250 tribes in 183 schools and dormitories, which house Indian children who attend public schools, located in 23 states. In FY2010, there were 169 BIE-funded schools, excluding dormitories. It is commonly estimated that BIE-funded schools serve roughly 10% of Indian students, public schools serve roughly 90%, and private schools serve 1% or less.

Application Process

The first steps in applying for a one-year Title VII-A formula award are the LEAs, tribes, or BIE-funded schools properly documenting the enrollment of Indian students, assessing their unique educational and culturally related academic needs, and developing a program to meet those needs. The LEAs must also convene an Indian Parent Committee.[26]

Indian Parent Committee
Prior to passage of the Indian Education Act of 1972, momentum was building to increase Indian control over activities affecting Indians. As evidence, the 1969 Senate report recommended that Indian parents be afforded a measure of influence and control over the education of their children, whether they were in the Bureau of Indian Affairs (BIA)-funded[27] or the public school system. Also, President Nixon acknowledged in 1970 that all federal Indian programs should allow a measure of self-determination to end a "suffocating pattern of paternalism."[28]

The Indian Parent Committee required under the Title VII-A program supports the involvement of Indian parents in the education of their children in public schools. Under current statute, the Indian Parent Committee is composed of and selected by parents of Indian children in the LEA, at least one teacher in the LEA, and, if appropriate, at least one secondary school Indian student attending the LEA. While a majority of committee members must be parents of Indian children, the committee membership must include at least one LEA teacher and, if applicable, one secondary LEA student. The Indian Parent Committee is required to establish and abide by policies, procedures, and bylaws that are approved by the LEA. Besides contributing to the development of the LEA's plan and application for the Title VII-A grant, the Indian Parent Committee must approve the application and plans, in writing. In addition, the Indian Parent Committee has input into, but not control over,[29] the hiring of personnel supported by grant funding.[30]

Documentation of Indian Student Enrollment
All applicants must provide an accurate count of eligible Indian students to be served by the Title VII-A formula grant. With the exception of BIE-funded schools, applicants must document each eligible Indian student with a Title VII Student Eligibility Certification form (also known as Form ED506).[31] LEAs maintain a file of the eligibility forms.[32] BIE-funded schools that do not apply within a consortium and that do not count preschool/pre-kindergarten students may use either Form ED506 or total student enrollment[33] as reported to the BIE for the BIE formula grant education program.[34] Form ED506 requests

- the Indian student's name, date of birth, school, and grade;
- the name of the tribe;

- an indication of why the tribe is eligible;
- the name and enrollment number of the tribal member;
- the tribal member's relationship to the student;
- the name and address of the organization maintaining membership data; and
- the signature of the student's parent or legal guardian.

The membership number is not required, but proof of membership is. The Indian students must be counted and new forms collected within a 1-to-31 consecutive day period during the school year in which the Title VII-A application is submitted.[35] Indian Parent Committees are not allowed to review the forms.[36] Because of the historical contention regarding the definition and eligibility of Indian students, ED is required to annually audit a sample of grantees and their forms.[37] Students and LEAs that provide false information become ineligible for funding indefinitely.

Although LEAs and tribes are required to collect and maintain Form ED506 for each Indian student, the LEA, the Indian Parent Committee, tribal members, or all of the above may encourage students and their parents to submit forms. For instance, the Portland Public Schools in Oregon encourage networking among Indian parents and guardians who have already submitted forms to encourage new Indian students and their families to submit the form identifying the student as eligible.[38] Some tribes actively coordinate and encourage their members to ensure forms are submitted on behalf of their children and grandchildren.[39]

Types of Projects

Applicants must choose between implementing one of the following project types: comprehensive, school-wide, or integration of services.

A comprehensive project must be a supplementary program to meet the assessed academic, cultural, and linguistic needs of Indian students.[40] The project plan must be developed in consultation with teachers, Indian parents, and Indian secondary school students, if appropriate. Grantees that choose the comprehensive project option must develop a plan that meets the linguistic and cultural needs of its Indian students and is consistent with ESEA Title I-A plans, the state academic standards in particular.[41] The project must also include professional development to ensure teachers and staff are prepared to meet the needs of Indian students and the plan's objectives. Grantees may use funds to supplement the regular school program by providing services and activities such as early childhood and family programs, supporting the attainment of state academic achievement standards, educating individuals concerning substance abuse, or incorporating American Indian- and Alaska Native-specific content into the curriculum.[42] The project must include regular assessments of Indian students and dissemination of assessment results to the Indian Parent Committee and community at-large.

The school-wide project option allows recipients to consolidate funds under several federal, state, and local programs to upgrade the entire educational program of a school. In school-wide projects, funds may be used to improve the performance of *all* students in a school. To be eligible for a school-wide project, the percentage of low-income pupils served by the ESEA Title I-A-eligible school must be 40% or higher, and the school must be operating a school-wide program under Section 1114 of the ESEA.[43] With the Indian Parent Committee's approval, Title VII-A funding can be consolidated into the school-wide plan.

Supporters of the school-wide project option wanted to encourage program coordination[44] and to give schools the flexibility to integrate Indian students, language, and culture into the whole school.[45] The school-wide project option must meet the basic program objectives and fiscal accountability requirements of each consolidated federal, state, and local program.

A third option, the integration of services project, was authorized by the NCLB. Under this option, grantees are permitted to consolidate funds under one or more federal formula grant programs that provide educational and related services exclusively to Indian students and families.[46] In contrast to the school-wide project option, which allows consolidation of certain federal formula and discretionary grant education programs, the integrated services option allows consolidation of federal formula grant programs that provide educational and related services exclusively to Indian students and families. Few LEAs are eligible for this type of project since few LEAs receive funds from more than one formula grant program designated exclusively for Indian students and families. Grantees that choose the integration of services program for any portion of program funds must develop a single, comprehensive program with reduced administrative costs that is approved by all relevant federal agencies. The plan must be consistent with the Title VII-A Indian Education formula grant program and must be approved by the Indian Parent Committee. In response to an acceptable, formal plan, the Secretary of Education in cooperation with other federal agencies will allow the applicant to consolidate various formula grant programs. Each federal agency may waive any statutory provisions, regulations, policies, or procedures, as necessary, to enable implementation of the plan provided the waivers are not inconsistent with the programs' objectives. As of the FY2009 award cycle, only one school—a BIE-funded school—has chosen the integration of services option.[47]

Additional Application Requirements

Because Title VII-A projects are to be based on the assessed needs of Indian students, ED requires that applicants provide state assessment scores and proficiency rates, high school graduation rates, and data from other applicable assessments for American Indian/Alaska Native (AI/AN) students and all students. All applicants, whether LEAs, BIE schools, or tribes, are required to hold at least one public hearing to review their project plan and seek comments.[48] LEAs, and tribes applying in lieu of LEAs, are required to submit their application to their state educational agency (SEA) for comment before submitting it to ED.[49] This change, enacted in the 1994 reauthorization, was requested by ED, despite the objections of tribal interest groups, to foster coordinated efforts at the local, state, and federal level.[50] Through FY2009, only one SEA has commented on an application.[51] Finally, all grantees must annually share the community educational achievement data for Indian students served by the project and those not served by the project.

Formula Allocation and Grant Award Considerations

Eligible entities with approved applications are allocated a grant award based on a statutorily defined calculation that uses the number of eligible Indian students (NEIS) and an average per pupil expenditure (APPE).[52] The first step is determining a preliminary grant. The preliminary grant is the product of the enrollment of eligible Indian students and the APPE. The APPE is the greater of the state APPE (SAPPE) for public K-12 education or 80% of the national APPE (NAPPE).[53] For BIE schools, the APPE is based on the state in which the school is located.

Step 1: Preliminary Grant = (NEIS * SAPPE) or (NEIS * 0.8 * NAPPE), whichever is greater

If the program appropriations are "insufficient"[54] to provide the preliminary grant, the second step is determining the intermediate grant. The intermediate grant is calculated by proportionately (ratably) reducing the preliminary grants of all grantees such that their sum equals the program appropriations. Specifically, in Step 2 the amount for each grantee in Step 1 is divided by the total of these amounts for all eligible grantees in the nation, then multiplied by the available appropriation (APP). If not for the ratable reduction to account for appropriations, the end result of the formula would be to approximately double the available funding for every Indian student in an LEA.

Step 2: Intermediate Grant = (Preliminary Grant / $\sum$ Preliminary Grant) * APP

The final step of calculating grants under Title VII-A is an adjustment of the intermediate grant through application of the minimum grant threshold (MGT). The minimum grant threshold is either $3,000 or $4,000, at the discretion of the Secretary of Education.[55] The intermediate grant is adjusted upward for grantees serving small numbers of Indian students and downward for all other grantees in order to pay the costs of applying the minimum. Specifically, in the final step the amount for each grantee in Step 2 is adjusted by a factor to account for the application of the minimum grant threshold, given a fixed total appropriation level. The minimum grant threshold in FY2006 through FY2010 has been $4,000.

Step 3: Final Grant = (Intermediate Grant * MGT_ADJ) or (MGT), whichever is greater

Where:
APP = Appropriation
MGT = Minimum grant threshold
MGT_ADJ = minimum grant threshold adjustment (proportional decrease in grantees not benefitting from the minimum grant threshold)
NAPPE = 80% of national average per pupil expenditure
NEIS = Number of eligible Indian students
SAPPE = State average per pupil expenditure
$\sum$ = Sum (for all eligible grantees in the nation)

The final grants for the BIE-funded schools that are operated by the BIE are transferred by ED to the BIE for disbursement. The BIE withholds a 1.5% administrative fee before disbursing the remaining funds to the BIE-funded schools that are operated by the BIE. BIE-funded schools that are operated by tribes or tribal organizations, LEAs, and tribes receive their final grant amount directly from ED.

Grantees must meet the statute's supplement, not supplant and maintenance of effort provisions. Applicants must make an assurance that the Title VII-A funds will supplement the funds that would have otherwise been available to educate Indian students.[56] The maintenance of effort provision requires that the combination of state and local expenditures, computed on either a per student or aggregate expenditure basis, for the previous fiscal year were at least 90% of the second preceding fiscal year. Failure to meet the maintenance of effort provision results in a proportional reduction of the Title VII-A award unless ED grants a waiver due to exceptional or uncontrollable circumstances.[57] States cannot take into consideration an LEA's Title VII-A award in determining what the state will allocate to the LEA. [58]

There are additional award considerations. Grantees may use no more than 5% of their award on administration, unless a waiver is granted.[59] Because the Title VII-A awards are one-year grants, any funds not obligated during the year by grantees must be returned to ED unless a budget extension has been approved.

APPROPRIATIONS, AWARDS, AND STUDENTS

This section provides a historical look at ESEA Title VII-A appropriations, grant amounts and numbers, and numbers of students served from FY2001 to FY2010.[60] The section concludes with a detailed description of the estimated FY2010 grantees and awards.

Historical Analysis

Table 1 shows the formula grant program appropriations, distribution of funds, number of grants, and number of eligible students served, from FY2001 through FY2010. Funding increased from $93 million in FY2001 to $97 million in FY2002 before decreasing annually until FY2006, when the appropriations began to increase again. The FY2010 appropriation was $104 million. Since FY2001, LEAs and tribes have received approximately 93% of the annual appropriations. The remaining 7% of appropriations has been awarded to BIE-funded schools.

On average, the program has awarded 1,224 grants annually since FY2001. LEAs and tribes have received approximately 90% of the grants awarded. In FY2010, 21 tribes received grants. Since FY2001, Title VII-A has provided support to between 94 and 142 BIE-funded schools annually (see **Table 1**).

The number of Indian students served by the program has varied but has generally increased from 462,827 in FY2001 to an estimated 473,145 in FY2010. This represents a 2.2% increase in the number of Indian students served over the 10-year period. LEAs and tribes serve approximately 93% of the eligible students served (see **Table 1**).

The average award per eligible student remained flat from FY2003 to FY2009 at an average of $204 but increased to $220 in FY2010. LEAs that choose to consolidate their grant funds as part of a school-wide project, however, will have fewer funds per pupil as the funds will be distributed across all students (see **Table 1**).

The distribution of funds by state since FY1999 is in **Table A-1**. Award amounts and proportions for individual states have been fairly consistent since FY2002. Three states— Alaska, Arizona, and Oklahoma—have received almost half (45%) of the funding. California and New Mexico received the next highest proportion of funding at 6% and 8%, respectively.

Table 1. ESEA Title VII-A Indian Education Formula Grant Program Appropriations, Grants, Awards, and Students by Recipient Type: FY2001–2010

	FY2001	FY2002	FY2003	FY2004	FY2005	FY2006	FY2007	FY2008	FY2009	FY2010
Distribution of funds ($000)										
LEAs and tribes	85,489	90,146	89,954	90,308	88,453	89,297	88,611	89,497	91,386	97,299
BIE grant and contract schools	4,506	4,240	3,919	3,121	4,009	3,696	4,128	4,593	5,100	4,188
BIE operated schools	2,770	2,747	2,629	2,504	2,703	2,338	2,592	2,523	2,845	2,844
Total appropriation	92,765	97,133	96,502	95,933	95,165	95,331	95,331	96,613	99,331	104,331
Number of grants										
LEAs and tribes	1,079	1,078	1,076	1,072	1,144	1,101	1,112	1,130	1,122	1,147
BIE grant and contract schools	79	64	61	48	65	57	74	86	89	67
BIE operated schools	54	47	46	46	50	38	51	54	53	51
Total	1,212	1,189	1,183	1,166	1,261	1,196	1,237	1,270	1,264	1,265
Number of eligible students										
LEAs and tribes	422,897	418,472	435,968	429,719	445,799	437,769	439,007	439,786	432,884	439,247
BIE grant and contract schools	24,214	21,039	20,134	15,702	21,338	18,921	21,545	23,340	25,335	20,522
BIE operated schools	15,716	14,194	14,236	13,078	14,490	12,318	13,893	13,278	14,312	14,204
Total	462,827	453,705	470,338	458,499	481,627	469,008	474,445	476,404	472,531	473,973
Average award per eligible student ($)	200	209	205	209	198	203	201	203	210	220

Source: Table prepared by CRS based on FY2001 –FY2011 U.S. Department of Education (ED) budget requests and the Estimated FY2010 award slate provided by ED.

Twelve states—Connecticut, Delaware, the District of Columbia, Hawaii, Indiana, Kentucky, New Hampshire, Ohio, Pennsylvania, Rhode Island, Tennessee, and West Virginia—have not received any funding since FY2002 (see **Table A-1**). The LEAs in those states may have chosen not to apply or may not have sufficient numbers of eligible Indian students. There are no BIEfunded schools in the 12 states. Of the states that receive no funding, Connecticut, Indiana, and Rhode Island have at least one federally recognized Indian tribe,[61] while Delaware, Georgia, and Ohio have state-recognized tribes.[62]

FY2010 Grant Estimate Analysis

Figure 1 presents the number of Indian students enrolled by all FY2010 grantees. The inset graph of **Figure 1** shows that there are several grantees serving more than 1,000 Indian students, including the Public Schools of Robeson County in North Carolina serving 11,355 Indian students. The main graph in **Figure 1** focuses on the grantees serving no more than 1,000 Indian students. It demonstrates that the preponderance (84%) of grantees serve fewer than 560 Indian students, and most (68%) serve fewer than 320 Indian students. Twenty-eight grantees serve 20 or fewer Indian students, and six grantees serve fewer than 10 Indian students (not shown separately).

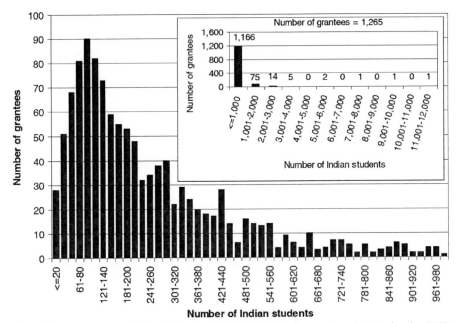

Source: These data were prepared by CRS using FY20 10 Preliminary Award Data for the ESEA Title VII-A Formula Grant Program as provided by the U.S. Department of Education (ED).

Notes: The inset graph shows the universe of FY20 10 grantees by the number of Indian students. The larger graph shows the FY20 10 grantees that enroll fewer than 1,001 Indian students by the number of Indian students. In other words, the larger graph provides an expanded view of the first column in the inset graph.

Figure 1. Profile of Number of Indian Students Enrolled at FY2010 Grantees. Number of grantees = 1,166.

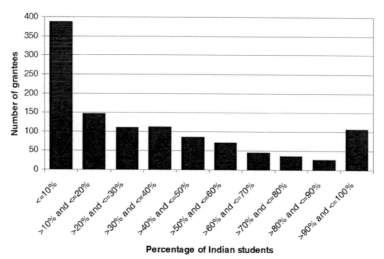

Percentage of Indian students

Source: This data was prepared by CRS using FY2010 Preliminary Award Data for the ESEA Title VII-A Formula Grant Program as provided by the U.S. Department of Education (ED).

Notes: The figure excludes 118 BIE-funded schools, most of which are not required to report total student enrollment, and 18 additional LEAs that did not report total enrollment.

Figure 2. Profile of Percentage of Indian Students Enrolled at FY2010 Grantees
Number of grantees = 1,129.

The BIE-funded grantees receiving FY2010 Title VII-A awards, not shown separately from the other grantees in **Figure 1**, serve between 10 and 2,106 Indian students. Most (80%) BIE-funded grantees serve between 86 and 622 Indian students. Only three of the BIE-funded entities—Pine Ridge School in South Dakota, Tuba City Boarding School in Arizona, and Choctaw Tribal School District in Mississippi—serve more than 1,000 students.

Figure 2 shows Indian students as a percentage of total student enrollment for each Title VII-A grantee. The figure excludes 118 BIE-funded schools, most of which are not required to report total student enrollment, and 18 additional LEAs that did not report total enrollment. One-third (34%) of non-BIE-funded grantees have an Indian student enrollment that is below 10% of the total enrollment. More than half (5 7%) of the grantees in **Figure 2** have an Indian student enrollment that is less than 30% of the total enrollment. Title VII-A requires LEAs either to serve at least 10 Indian students or to have an Indian student enrollment of at least 25%. It is evident that the requirement to serve at least 10 Indian students is the primary determinant of eligibility. A noticeable portion (9%) of the non-BIE-funded grantees enroll a student body that is more than 90% Indian students. Of the 106 grantees whose Indian student enrollment exceeds 90%, 16 are in Alaska, 26 are in Arizona, and 11 are in North Dakota.

Table 2 shows descriptive statistics of estimated awards granted in FY2010. The average award was $82,475. Six grantees received more than $1 million, with the highest award at $2,688,479. Most grantees (80%) received between $11,827 and $181,558. Nineteen grantees received the minimum award of $4,000. BIE-operated schools receive a smaller grant because the BIE keeps a 1.5% administrative fee from the funds awarded to BIE-operated schools. Also accounting for actual awards below the minimum in FY2010, ED adjusted the grant amount for one LEA to account for a formula error in prior years.

Table 2. Estimated FY2010 Award Profile
($4,000 minimum award)

Statistic	Number/Amount
Number of awards	1,265
Average award amount	$ 82,475
Median award amount	$ 41,874
Minimum award amount	$ 3,872
Maximum award amount	$ 2,688,479

Source: This data was prepared by CRS using FY20 10 Preliminary Award Data for the ESEA Title
    VII-A Formula Grant Program as provided by the U.S. Department of Education.
Notes: By statute and ED's decision, the minimum award, excluding the BIE administration, is $4,000,
    but one LEA required a negative adjustment for prior year awards.

Table B-1 presents the estimated total number of grants, amount received, number of Indian students enrolled, and award per Indian pupil for each state, excluding BIE-funded schools, and the amount received by BIE-funded schools in FY2010. **Table B-1** also shows the FY2008 state APPE, which is used to determine formula allocations. Formula allocations for BIE-funded schools use the state APPE for the state in which they are located. After applying the statutory formula, ED made several adjustments to the FY2010 award amounts to correct improper FY2008 allocations. The states that do not receive any funding from the program are not shown.

A review of **Table B-1** indicates that, on average, the grants supplement the state APPE by $220 for each Indian pupil. The average award per Indian pupil in BIE-operated schools ($200) and BIE grant and contract schools ($204) is below average ($220) because these schools are clustered in the states of Arizona, New Mexico, and South Dakota, which have below-average state APPE. New York received the highest average award per Indian pupil ($403), almost double (183%) the program average, but the state expends almost double the national average for all students ($17,824, or 171% of the state APPE).

The difference in the density of Indian students is evidenced in the difference in the number of grants and amounts received between various states. For instance, California received $6,386,727 for 98 grants, whereas New Mexico received $6,984,044 for 26 grants. On average, there are more Indian students enrolled in each of New Mexico's grantees than in each of California's grantees (see **Table B-1**).

POLICY ISSUES

Differing Definitions of Indian Students

The current definition of "Indian" for the Title VII-A program does not fully coincide with the definition used for other educational programs. The consequences of these differing definitions include

- possible confusion regarding participant eligibility for the various programs,
- the inability to determine the efficacy of programs using common measures,

- increased administrative and paperwork requirements and a greater need for auditing the eligibility of participants, and
- a disjointed federal Indian education policy that in some instances supports members of federally recognized tribes or members of federally recognized Indian tribes of specific ancestry and in other instances supports a broader group of individuals.

Broadening the Title VII-A definition could simplify the identification and administration of Title VII-A student eligibility, but it could also dilute the per pupil expenditures and reduce the significance of the political and trust relationship between tribes and the federal government. If individuals who are not members of federally recognized Indian tribes are eligible for the same federal services and programs as members of federally recognized Indian tribes, the political recognition as a federally recognized Indian tribe has diminished importance. Narrowing the definition could make currently eligible students ineligible and increase the expenditures per Indian pupil.

The Indian students eligible for services under the Title VII-A program differ from the Indian students eligible under most BIA education-related programs, BIE programs,[63] and the U.S. Department of the Interior set-asides under the ESEA and the Individuals with Disabilities Education Act (IDEA; 20 U.S.C., Chapter 33).[64] The Indian students eligible for services under the Title VII-A program also differ from the Native American children provided special services under the ESEA Title III program.[65] Likewise, the definition of "Indian" for the Title VII-A program does not coincide with the socially and culturally constructed racial definition of American Indian/Alaska Native (AI/AN) used by the U.S. Census Bureau (Census). With the exception of students attending BIE-funded schools, educational outcomes are measured using Census categories for race/ethnicity. There are no national educational statistics for members of federally recognized tribes.

BIA education-related, BIE, and the ESEA Title III programs provide benefits to members of federally recognized tribes, which are defined to include Alaska Native corporations.[66] Tribes may be federally recognized by an administrative U.S. Department of the Interior (Interior) process, [67] by Congress, or by the federal courts.[68] The Interior publishes the list of federally recognized tribes annually in the *Federal Register*. Interior's list of federally recognized tribes applies to all federal assistance programs that provide particular benefits exclusively for recognized tribes. In addition to federally recognized tribes, IDEA includes state-recognized tribes in its definition. The ESEA Title VII-A definition of "Indian" is broader than these definitions because it includes state-recognized tribes, the descendents of members of Indian tribes, and additional individuals who were eligible for the Title VII-A program in the past.

The definition of "Indian" for the Title VII-A program also does not coincide with the socially and culturally constructed racial definition of American Indian/Alaska Native (AI/AN) used by the Census. Census categorizes persons by self-reported race and ethnicity. One of the racial categories is American Indian/Alaska Native (AI/AN) for persons having origins in any of the original peoples of North America and South America (including Central America), and who maintain tribal affiliation or community attachment.[69] The categories were developed to provide a standard for data on race and ethnicity across federal agencies and to facilitate the enforcement of civil rights laws. "The categories represent a social-political construct designed for collecting data on the race and ethnicity of broad population groups in this country, and are not anthropologically or scientifically based."[70] Some students and their families may choose not to be identified as Indians for the purpose of Title VII-A funding, and some students who meet the Title VII-A definition of Indian may not identify themselves as AI/AN. The Census definition of the AI/AN category is used by ED in collecting data on race and ethnicity. In fact, most state and national data on student educational achievement outcomes are disaggregated for AI/AN students but seldom disaggregated for other definitions of "Indian."

In summary, the focus, oversight, and administration of programs may benefit from the elimination of discrepancies in the definitions of groups of individuals served. With any change of this sort, however, a redistribution of benefits occurs, and these potential effects also merit consideration.

Educational Outcomes

The Indian Education Act of 1972 was enacted, in part, to close the educational achievement gap between Indian students and other students, but there are significant gaps in educational outcomes for AI/ANs compared to other students. The 1969 Senate report[71] found that the prevalence of negative stereotypes of and discrimination against Indians in public school curricula and textbooks, among public school staff, and on public school boards had led to alienation of Indian students. Specifically, the 1969 Senate report provided evidence of high dropout rates and low English literacy skills among Indian students, particularly in public school systems. According to the report, between 1966 and 1970 BIA schools graduated 60% of 9th grade students compared to the national graduation rate of 74%. The BIA school graduates were two or more years behind non-Indian high school graduates of the time. The report determined that some of the poor academic outcomes were a consequence of low expectations of the BIA teachers and staff, unsatisfactory instructional practices, deficient guidance and counseling, a punitive school environment, little parental and community involvement, and a BIA organization that was not equipped to manage a school system.

In 2007, 36% of AI/AN students who were public high school graduates completed a core academic track compared with 52% of all students.[72] The 2008 status dropout rate (14.6%) for 16- through-24 year old AI/ANs in the United States was almost double (1.8 times) the national average of 8.0%.[73] One factor that may make education more culturally relevant for AI/AN students is that the number of AI/AN teachers instructing AI/AN students has increased, from 1% of Indian elementary students having an Indian teacher or principal in 1969 to 13% of 4th and 8th grade AI/AN students having an AI/AN teacher in 2007.[74]

According to the 2009 National Assessment of Educational Progress (NAEP),[75] AI/AN students are academically behind their peers. In 2009, a higher percentage of AI/AN 4th and 8th grade students scored below basic[76] on the NAEP reading and mathematics assessments than nonAI/AN students (**Figure 3**).[77] For example, on the 4th grade math assessment, 34% of AI/AN students scored below basic compared to 18% of non-AI/AN students. Also in 2009, a lower percentage of AI/AN 4th and 8th grade students scored at or above proficient[78] on the NAEP reading and mathematics assessments than non-AI/AN students (**Figure 4**).[79] On the 4th grade reading assessment, 20% of AI/AN students scored at or above proficient compared to 33% of non-AI/AN students.

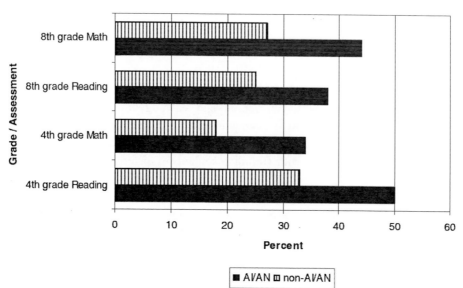

Source: U.S. Department of Education (ED), Institute of Education Sciences, *National Indian Education Study 2009: Part I, Performance of American Indian and Alaska Native Students at Grades 4 and 8 on NAEP 2009 Reading and Mathematics Assessments*, NCES 2010-462, Washington, DC, pp. 15 and 54.

Figure 3. Students Scoring Below Basic on 4th and 8th Grade Reading and Mathematics NAEP Assessments by Race/Ethnicity: 2009.

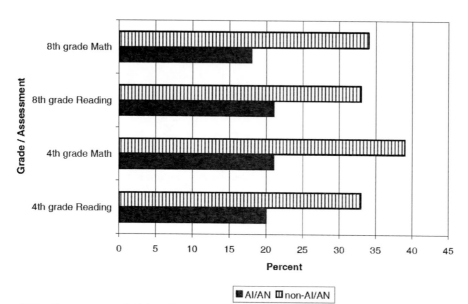

Source: U.S. Department of Education (ED), Institute of Education Sciences, *National Indian Education Study 2009: Part I, Performance of American Indian and Alaska Native Students at Grades 4 and 8 on NAEP 2009 Reading and Mathematics Assessments*, NCES 2010-462, Washington, DC, pp. 15 and 54.

Figure 4. Students Scoring At or Above Proficient on 4th and 8th Grade Reading and Mathematics NAEP Assessments by Race/Ethnicity: 2009.

Cultural vs. Academic Emphasis

Since the program's inception, there has been an issue about the role of Indian culture in the education of Indian students. There is a difference between providing supplemental academic services to Indian students to help them meet state academic standards and incorporating Indian culture into the curriculum and teaching strategies to more fully engage Indian students in an effort to improve academic outcomes. Incorporating culture in a school with a student body that is 80-100% Indian students may be very different from incorporating Indian culture into a large school with 10 Indian students of different Indian cultures scattered across multiple grades.

The 1969 Senate report recognized that the denigration of Indian students and disrespect for Indian culture contributed to poor academic outcomes. It also recommended that BIA and public school curricula should incorporate Indian language, history, and culture in a positive way. The 1972 formula grant program was intended to meet the "special educational needs" of Indian students in public schools. "Special educational needs" were not defined. In 1978, the act was revised to meet the "special educational and culturally related academic needs" of Indian students in public schools.[80] This revision was recommended by the NACIE and other tribal organizations.[81] NACIE advocated for more cultural components to counterbalance the "Puritan ethics" that were predominantly taught at the time.[82] The House Committee on Education and Labor indicated that the revision would be particularly important to Indian students in an urban setting or in a predominantly non-Indian school.[83] The House Committee also indicated that the change was not intended to diminish the importance of academic educational assistance. [84] The 1994 reauthorization added the expectation that Indian students meet state academic performance standards.[85] The 2001 reauthorization expanded the list of possible activities to include the incorporation of culturally responsive teaching and learning strategies, American Indian and Alaska Native specific curricula, and appropriately qualified tribal elders and seniors.[86]

Appropriations Level

Many stakeholders believe the program is underfunded. The average per Indian pupil expenditure in FY20 10 was $220. It may be debated whether supplemental funding of $220 per pupil is adequate to operate programs that are of sufficient size, scope, and quality to be effective. In its FY2005-FY2006 annual report, NACIE recommended increasing funding to $250 per Indian pupil.[87]

The original 1972 act provided that LEAs were entitled to a grant amount equal to the average per pupil expenditure multiplied by the number of eligible Indian students. The act also provided that "if the sums appropriated ... are not sufficient to pay in full the total amounts which all [LEAs] are eligible to receive ... [then] ... the maximum amounts ... shall be ratably reduced."[88] These provisions are used as an indicator that the original intention of the law was to double the state average per pupil expenditure ($10,431 in FY2008) for each Indian student served by the program.

Table A-1. Historical ESEA Title VII-A Indian Education Formula Grant Awards by State: FY1999–FY2010 ($000)

State	FY1999	FY2000	FY2001	FY2002	FY2003	FY2004	FY2005	FY2006	FY2007	FY2008	FY2009	FY2010
United States	62,000	62,000	92,765	97,133	96,502	95,933	95,165	95,331	95,331	96,613	99,331	104,331
Alabama	1,157	1,056	1,616	1,777	1,701	1,734	1,701	1,704	1,662	1,684	1,805	1,680
Alaska	6,775	6,772	9,670	9,936	9,427	9,518	9,136	9,152	9,482	9,609	10,055	11,422
Arizona	7,422	7,388	9,992	11,390	11,056	9,956	10,635	10,654	10,470	10,611	10,701	11,217
Arkansas	129	136	205	327	778	1,085	1,071	1,072	289	293	308	307
California	4,134	4,395	6,585	6,552	6,706	6,460	6,349	6,360	5,786	5,864	6,185	6,522
Colorado	407	483	668	678	668	650	669	670	756	766	767	764
Connecticut	24	16	18	0	0	0	0	0	0	0	0	0
Delaware	0	0	0	0	0	0	0	0	0	0	0	0
District of Columbia	0	0	0	0	0	0	0	0	0	0	0	0
Florida	63	51	57	54	54	50	60	61	42	43	57	67
Georgia	0	0	0	0	4	4	0	0	0	0	0	0
Hawaii	0	0	0	0	0	0	0	0	0	0	0	0
Idaho	268	256	400	451	420	365	444	445	390	395	429	419
Illinois	59	56	88	104	104	102	83	83	102	103	130	145
Indiana	7	8	4	0	0	0	0	0	0	0	0	0
Iowa	123	133	190	190	190	148	199	199	210	213	154	194
Kansas	234	401	698	817	863	972	968	970	1,080	1,095	1,171	1,232
Kentucky	0	0	0	0	0	0	0	0	0	0	0	0
Louisiana	507	532	794	842	787	771	774	776	758	768	813	897
Maine	86	72	131	128	125	128	125	125	129	130	114	153
Maryland	141	137	186	175	164	176	159	159	73	74	75	79
Massachusetts	105	99	67	71	46	48	41	41	76	77	72	80
Michigan	2,644	2,484	3,582	3,541	3,270	3,126	3,223	3,229	3,159	3,202	2,953	2,680
Minnesota	2,355	2,427	3,623	3,562	3,459	3,281	3,244	3,250	3,354	3,399	3,413	3,513
Mississippi	244	228	322	398	368	363	352	353	341	346	49	457
Missouri	48	20	81	68	80	79	105	105	94	95	73	88

Table A-1. (Continued)

State	FY1999	FY2000	FY2001	FY2002	FY2003	FY2004	FY2005	FY2006	FY2007	FY2008	FY2009	FY2010
Montana	2,069	2,137	3,067	3,194	3,034	2,948	2,964	2,969	2,890	2,929	3,192	3,174
Nebraska	434	465	668	738	659	662	693	695	776	786	816	822
Nevada	490	519	771	750	749	748	685	686	683	693	744	752
New Hampshire	0	0	0	0	0	0	0	0	0	0	0	0
New Jersey	104	55	103	52	66	63	54	54	58	59	59	60
New Mexico	5,275	4,976	7,683	7,799	8,354	7,962	7,905	7,918	7,958	8,065	8,580	8,398
New York	1,107	1,106	1,545	1,504	1,501	2,965	1,564	1,566	1,716	1,739	1,780	1,823
North Carolina	2,124	2,158	3,402	3,662	3,512	3,518	3,370	3,375	3,348	3,393	3,570	3,477
North Dakota	1,082	1,005	1,669	1,552	1,592	1,567	1,587	1,590	1,652	1,674	1,786	1,870
Ohio	7	0	0	0	0	0	0	0	0	0	0	0
Oklahoma	12,391	12,702	20,305	22,020	21,771	21,995	22,413	22,452	23,553	23,870	24,540	26,789
Oregon	1,298	1,524	2,306	2,458	2,632	2,435	2,393	2,397	2,161	2,190	2,200	2,166
Pennsylvania	0	0	0	0	0	0	0	0	0	0	0	0
Rhode Island	0	0	0	0	0	0	0	0	0	0	0	0
South Carolina	35	40	51	61	56	0	0	0	5	5	9	16
South Dakota	2,327	1,898	3,249	3,197	3,206	3,048	3,235	3,240	3,508	3,555	3,468	3,719
Tennessee	0	0	0	0	0	0	0	0	0	0	0	0
Texas	181	166	148	339	322	319	278	279	309	313	366	391
Utah	777	690	965	1,191	1,119	1,044	1,127	1,129	1,202	1,218	1,234	1,583
Vermont	91	90	128	139	132	134	134	134	169	172	199	235
Virginia	15	16	25	26	23	10	10	10	11	12	15	15
Washington	3,255	3,146	4,265	4,538	4,480	4,406	4,431	4,439	4,274	4,332	4,309	3,963
West Virginia	0	0	0	0	0	0	0	0	0	0	0	0
Wisconsin	1,657	1,852	2,615	2,345	2,493	2,538	2,463	2,467	2,246	2,277	2,428	2,432
Wyoming	351	287	499	509	501	553	522	522	558	566	713	728
Other	19	19	323	31	31	0	0	0	0	0	0	0

Source: U.S. Department of Education State Funding History Tables: FY1980-FY2008 available at http://www2.ed.gov/about/overview/ budget/history/index.html as of October 13, 2010; FY2011 U.S. Department of Education Budget Request; and the Estimated FY2010 Award Slate provided by ED.

Notes: The FY2010 amounts are estimates based on FY2010 preliminary data for the ESEA Title VII-A formula grant program as provided by the U.S. Department of Education (ED).

APPENDIX B. ESTIMATED FY2010 GRANT AWARDS PROFILE BY STATE

Table B-1. Number of Grants, Award Amounts, Number of Indian Students Served, State Average Per Pupil Expenditure, and Average Award per Indian Pupil for FY2010 ESEA Title VII-A Indian Education Formula Grant Program by State and by BIE-Funded Schools

State or BIE-Funded	Number of Grantees	Total of Awards ($)	Percentage of Total Award (%)	Number of Indian Students	Percentage of Indian Students (%)	State FY2008 APPE[a] ($)	Award per Indian Pupil ($)
All grantees	1,265	104,331,000	100.0	473,973	100.0	NA[b]	220
BIE-operated schools	51	2,844,210	2.7	14,204	3.0	NA	200
BIE grant and contract schools	67	4,188,165	4.0	20,522	4.3	NA	204
State Total[c]	1,147	97,298,625	93.3	439,247	92.7	10,431	222
Alabama	12	1,680,372	1.6	8,480	1.8	8,646	198
Alaska	49	11,421,849	10.9	32,590	6.9	15,451	350
Arizona	72	9,175,341	8.8	46,875	9.9	8,089	196
Arkansas	4	306,907	0.3	1,534	0.3	8,855	200
California	86	6,386,727	6.1	29,362	6.2	9,292	218
Colorado	10	763,540	0.7	3,627	0.8	9,326	211
Florida	3	672,249	0.1	329	0.1	8,995	204
Idaho	8	419,360	0.4	1,996	0.4	7,072	210
Illinois	1	145,106	0.1	578	0.1	11,055	251
Iowa	2	194,340	0.2	991	0.2	8,697	196
Kansas	17	1,232,196	1.2	5,179	1.1	10,526	238
Louisiana	8	897,090	0.9	3,886	0.8	10,176	231
Maine	3	90,642	0.1	317	0.1	12,603	286
Maryland	3	79,155	0.1	260	0.1	13,453	304
Massachusetts	2	80,123	0.1	254	0.1	13,921	315
Michigan	55	2,576,211	2.5	10,724	2.3	10,665	240
Minnesota	65	3,319,329	3.2	14,550	3.1	10,084	228
Mississippi	1	57,651	0.1	292	0.1	7,705	197
Missouri	4	87,811	0.1	416	0.1	9,375	211
Montana	38	3,174,384	3.0	14,363	3.0	9,777	221
Nebraska	15	822,116	0.8	3,472	0.7	10,476	237
Nevada	9	726,256	0.7	3,752	0.8	8,335	194
New Jersey	2	59,778	0.1	150	0.0	17,621	399
New Mexico	26	6,984,044	6.7	34,710	7.3	8,906	201
New York	14	1,822,680	1.7	4,521	1.0	17,824	403
North Carolina	18	3,282,092	3.1	17,410	3.7	7,987	189
North Dakota	23	1,557,360	1.5	7,743	1.6	8,897	201
Oklahoma	398	26,543,688	25.4	130,241	27.5	7,635	204
Oregon	27	2,054,475	2.0	9,178	1.9	9,904	224
South Carolina	1	16,416	0.0	77	0.0	9,155	213
South Dakota	31	2,610,895	2.5	13,692	2.9	8,422	191
Texas	8	391,481	0.4	2,031	0.4	8,501	193
Utah	19	1,541,371	1.5	6,637	1.4	6,337	232

Table B-1. (Continued)

State or BIE-Funded	Number of Grantees	Total of Awards ($)	Percentage of Total Award (%)	Number of Indian Students	Percentage of Indian Students (%)	FY2008 State APPE[a] ($)	Award per Indian Pupil ($)
Vermont	1	234,766	0.2	710	0.1	14,504	331
Virginia	1	15,473	0.0	62	0.0	10,960	250
Washington	60	3,585,499	3.4	17,058	3.6	9,292	210
Wisconsin	34	2,253,407	2.2	9,228	1.9	10,814	244
Wyoming	5	641,475	0.6	1,972	0.4	14,352	325

Source: This data was prepared by CRS using FY20 10 Preliminary Award Data for the ESEA Title VII-A formula grant program as provided by the U.S. Department of Education (ED).

a. APPE is the average per pupil expenditure.

b. NA is not applicable.

c. The BIE schools are not included in the statistics for each state.

End Notes

[1] U.S. Congress, Senate Committee on Labor and Public Welfare, Special Subcommittee on Indian Education, *Indian Education: A National Tragedy—A National Challenge*, Pursuant to S. Res. 80 A Resolution Authorizing an Investigation into the Problems of Education for American Indians, 91st Cong., 1st sess., November 3, 1969, S. Rept. 501 (Washington: GPO, 1969).

[2] P.L. 73-167, Act of April 16, 1934, 48 Stat. 596, as amended; 25 U.S.C. 452-457. For information on the Johnson O'Malley program, see CRS Report RL34205, *Federal Indian Elementary-Secondary Education Programs: Background and Issues*, by Cassandria Dortch, pp. 17-18.

[3] P.L. 81–815 and P.L. 81–874 (20 U.S.C. §7701 et seq.).

[4] The Impact Aid program (Title VIII of the Elementary and Secondary Education Act of 1965, as amended) compensates local educational agencies for "substantial and continuing financial burden" resulting from federal activities. For information on the Impact Aid program, see CRS Report R40720, *Federal Impact Aid: Title VIII of the Elementary and Secondary Education Act*, by Jeffrey J. Kuenzi.

[5] This report will use the term Secretary of Education regardless of the time period referenced.

[6] Decisions of the U.S. Supreme Court have characterized the role of the federal government with respect to Indian tribes as involving a trust relationship. Having identified the trust relationship, the Court has upheld congressional power to provide special treatment for Indians, declaring that "[a]s long as the special treatment can be tied rationally to the fulfillment of Congress' unique obligation toward the Indians, such legislative judgments will not be disturbed" (Morton v. Mancari, 417 U.S. 535, 555 (1974)). However, the Court has never interpreted the trust relationship to require any definite action on the part of Congress. When called upon to decide whether an administrative agency has breached its trust obligation or when called upon to enforce the trust obligation against an agency of the Executive Branch, moreover, the Court confines its review to whether the agency has a trust obligation imposed upon it by statute. See e.g., United States v. Mitchell, 463 U.S. 206 (1983).

[7] Section 7101 of the ESEA (20 U.S.C. § 7401).

[8] "Terminated" is defined in the act as an Indian tribe or band whose federal recognition was terminated after 1940 (20 U.S.C. §7491(3)(A)(i).

[9] ESEA Title VII, Part A, Subpart 5, Section 7151(3) (20 U.S.C. §7491(3)).

[10] The federal government's trust relationship to tribes has resulted in the enactment of many programs to serve and protect federally recognized Indian tribes through the provision of social services, natural resources management, economic development, and more.

[11] Federal recognition allows tribes to take advantage of numerous federal assistance programs that are exclusively for recognized tribes and establishes an intergovernmental relationship between the tribe and federal government. For more information on the process for federally recognizing Indian tribes, see CRS Report RS21 109, *The Bureau of Indian Affairs's Process for Recognizing Groups as Indian Tribes*, by M. Maureen Murphy.

[12] U.S. Congress, Senate Permanent Select Committee on Indian Affairs, *Indian Education Amendments*, To accompany S. 1645, 100th Cong., 1st sess., November 30, 1987, S.Rept. 100-233, p. 4.

[13] U.S. Congress, Senate Committee on Labor and Public Welfare and Committee on Interior and Insular Affairs, *Indian Education Act of 1971*, To accompany S. 2482, 92nd Cong., 1st sess., October 1, 1971, S. Rept. 92-384 (Washington: GPO, 1971), pp. 5-6.

[14] U.S. Congress, Senate Committee on Indian Affairs, *Reauthorization of the Elementary and Secondary Education Act of 1965*, The Administration's Proposal for the Reauthorization of the Elementary and Secondary Education Act, 103rd Cong., 2nd sess., May 4, 1994, S.Hrg. 103-801, pp. 22-23.

[15] Ibid.

[16] The Improving America's Schools Act of 1994 (P.L. 103-382).

[17] U.S. Congress, House Committee on Education and Labor, *Improving Americas Schools Act*, To accompany H.R. 6, 103rd Cong., 2nd sess., September 28, 1994, H.Rpt. 103-761, p. 6.

[18] LEAs include charter school LEAs and administrative and educational service districts (ESDs) that directly operate schools or enroll students.

[19] According to CCD in academic year 2008-09, 506 of the 16,154 LEAs with enrollment served fewer than 40 students. Of the LEAs serving fewer than 40 students, 116 were in Montana, 60 were in Maine, 50 were in California, three were in Alaska, and three were in Oklahoma.

[20] ESEA Title VII, Part A, Subpart 1, Section 7112(b) (20 U.S.C. §7422(b)).

[21] U.S. Congress, Senate Committee on Labor and Public Welfare and Committee on Interior and Insular Affairs, *Indian Education Act of 1971*, 92nd Cong., 1st sess., October 1, 1971, S. Rept. 92-384, pp. 1-5.

[22] ESEA Title VII, Part A, Subpart 1, Section 7112(c) (20 U.S.C. §7422(c)).

[23] U.S. Congress, House Committee on Education and Labor, Subcommittee on Elementary, Secondary, and Vocational Education, *Indian Education—Oversight, Part I Supplemental Programs*, 95th Cong., 1st sess., September 16, 20 and October 7, 1977, HRG-1977-EDL-0027, 78-H341-33 (Washington: GPO, 1978), p. 326 and U.S. Congress, Senate Committee on Indian Affairs, *Reauthorization of the Elementary and Secondary Education Act of 1965*, The Administration's Proposal for the Reauthorization of the Elementary and Secondary Education Act, 103rd Cong., 2nd sess., May 4, 1994, S.Hrg. 103-801, p. 22 and U.S. Congress, House Committee on Education and Labor, Subcommittee on Elementary, Secondary, and Vocational Education, *Hearings on Reauthorization of H.R. 6: The Elementary and Secondary Education Act of 1965*, Oversight Hearing on H.R. 6: ESEA Programs Serving Native Americans, Alaska Natives, and Native Hawaiians, 103rd Cong., 1st sess., April 27, 1993, Serial No. 103-30 (Washington: GPO, 1993), p. 573.

[24] Entities in Puerto Rico and the outlying areas are not eligible for federal recognition. Bureau of Indian Affairs, Interior, "Indian Entities Recognized and Eligible To Receive Services From the United States Bureau of Indian Affairs," 75 *Federal Register* 60810-60814, October 1, 2010.

[25] Under the original 1972 Act, BIE-funded schools were eligible for a 5% set-aside for schools located on or near reservations. The 1978 Education Amendments (Section 1146 of P.L. 95-561) allowed tribal schools and BIE-funded contract schools to apply as LEAs. Section 53 12(b)(3) of the Augustus F. Hawkins-Robert T. Stafford Elementary and Secondary School Improvement Amendments of 1988 (P.L. 100-297) allowed BIE-funded and operated schools to apply as LEAs.

[26] ESEA Title VII-A-1, Section 7114 (20 U.S.C. § 7424).

[27] In 2006, the Secretary of the Interior moved the Office of Indian Education Programs (OIEP) out of the BIA and made it equivalent to the BIA, renaming it the Bureau of Indian Education (BIE). Both bureaus are under the Assistant Secretary - Indian Affairs. This report uses "BIE" for current information and programs and "BIA" for historical periods.

[28] U.S. Congress, House Committee on Interior and Insular Affairs, *Recommendations for Indian Policy, Message from the President*, prepared by The White House, 91st Cong., July 8, 1970, H. Doc. 91-363 (Washington: GPO, 1970), p. 4.

[29] U.S. Congress, House Committee on Education and Labor, *Education Amendments of 1978*, to accompany H.R. 15, 95th Cong., 2nd sess., May 11, 1978, H.Rept. 95-1137, p. 126.

[30] This provision was enacted by the 1978 Education Amendments (Section 1144 of P.L. 95-561).

[31] ESEA Title VII, Part A, Subpart 1, Section 7117 (20 U.S.C. §7427).

[32] LEAs may maintain a student's ED Form 506 for the student's enrollment duration, and LEAs are required to maintain ED Form 506 for three years after the end of the project period and then destroy the form, according to the U.S. Department of Education, *Formula Grant Electronic Application System for Indian Education (Formula Grant EASIE) Frequently Asked Questions (FAQs)*, http://www2.ed.gov/ programs/ indianformula/ faq.html as of November 3, 2010.

[33] ESEA Title VII, Part A, Subpart 1, Section 7117(g) (20 U.S.C. §7427(g)). The provision requiring the use of a standard form was enacted by the 1978 Education Amendments (Section 1148 of P.L. 95-561).

[34] For more information on the BIE formula grant education program, known as the Indian School Equalization Program, see CRS Report RL34205, *Federal Indian Elementary-Secondary Education Programs: Background and Issues*, by Cassandria Dortch, p. 16.

[35] This provision was added by the No Child Left Behind Act of 2001 (Section 7117(h) of P.L. 107-110).

[36] U.S. Department of Education, Office of Indian Education, *Formula Grant Projects*, p. 28, http://www.indianeducation.org/files/Regional%20Formula.pdf accessed November 3, 2010.

[37] The audit requirement has been reduced since the 1978 Education Amendments (P.L. 95-56 1), which required a review of at least one third of all participating districts to ensure proper student counts and accurate applications. The 1988 reauthorization (P.L. 100-297) reduced the requirement to one-quarter of LEAs annually. The 1994 reauthorization (P.L. 103-3 82) required a sample.

[38] "Title VII Enrollment and Recruitment," Portland Public Schools Title VII / Indian Education Act Project, Talking Circle Newsletter, Fall 2009.

[39] The Pee Dee Indian Tribe of South Carolina, "Indian Education Title VII Program," available at http://www.peedeeindiantribeofsc.com/id8.html as of May 7, 2010.

[40] ESEA Title VII, Part A, Subpart 1, Section 7114(b) (20 U.S.C. §7424(b)).

[41] For more information on state academic standards, see CRS Report RL3 1407, *Educational Testing: Implementation of ESEA Title I-A Requirements Under the No Child Left Behind Act*, by Rebecca R. Skinner and Erin D. Lomax, pp. 4- 20.

[42] ESEA Title VII, Part A, Subpart 1, Section 7115 (20 U.S.C. §7425).

[43] School-wide programs, authorized under ESEA Title I, Part A (20 U.S.C. § 6314), became an option with the enactment of the Improving America's Schools Act of 1994 (P.L. 103-382).

[44] U.S. Congress, House Committee on Education and Labor, *Improving America's School Act of 1994*, To accompany H.R. 6, 103rd Cong., 2nd sess., February 16, 1994, H. Rept. 103-425, Part 1.

[45] U.S. Congress, Senate Committee on Labor and Human Resources, *Preparing American Indian Students for the 21st Century*, On S. 1150, 103rd Cong., 1st sess., August 21, 1993, S.Hrg. 103-447, p. 2.

[46] ESEA Title VII, Part A, Subpart 1, Section 7116 (20 U.S.C. §7426).

[47] U.S. Department of Education, *FY2011 Budget Request*, Indian Education, pp. E-10.

[48] The requirement that public hearings be conducted was added by the Augustus F. Hawkins-Robert T. Stafford Elementary and Secondary School Improvement Amendments of 1988 (Section 5314(b) of P.L. 100-297) to help develop the project plans.

[49] ESEA Title VII, Part A, Subpart 1, Section 7119 (20 U.S.C. §7429).

[50] U.S. Congress, Senate Committee on Indian Affairs, *Reauthorization of the Elementary and Secondary Education Act of 1965*, The Administration's Proposal for the Reauthorization of the Elementary and Secondary Education Act, 103rd Cong., 2nd sess., May 4, 1994, S.Hrg. 103-80 1, p. 15.

[51] U.S. Department of Education, *FY2011 Budget Request*, Indian Education, pp. E-9.

[52] ESEA Title VII, Part A, Subpart 1, Section 7113 (20 U.S.C. §7423).

[53] The lowest state APPE for use in the formula was set at 80% of the national APPE by the Improving America's Schools Act of 1994 (P.L. 103-3 82) to ensure states with low APPEs were not underfunded by using the greater of the state APPE or 80% on the national APPE.

[54] Section 7113(e) of the ESEA (20 U.S.C. § 7423(e)).

[55] A minimum grant award was established by the Improving America's Schools Act of 1994 (Section 9113(b) of P.L. 103-382).

[56] ESEA Title VII, Part A, Subpart 1, Section 71 14(c)(1) (20 U.S.C. §7424(c)(1)).

[57] ESEA Title VII, Part A, Subpart 1, Section 7118(c) (20 U.S.C. §7428(c)).

[58] ESEA Title VII, Part A, Subpart 1, Section 7118(b) (20 U.S.C. §7428(b)).

[59] This provision was added by the No Child Left Behind Act of 2001 (Section 7115(d) of P.L. 107-110).

[60] FY2010 estimates may not match actual awards as actual awards have been adjusted to account for allocation errors in prior years since the CRS used the Estimated FY2010 Award Slate provided by ED.

[61] U.S. Department of the Interior, Bureau of Indian Affairs, "Indian Entities Recognized and Eligible To Receive Services From the United States Bureau of Indian Affairs," 75 *Federal Register* 60810-60814, October 1, 2010.

[62] National Conference of State Legislatures, Federal and State Recognized Tribes, March 2009, http://www.ncsl.org/?tabid=13278#state.

[63] See definitions at 25 U.S.C. § 450b, 25 U.S.C. § 2021(20), and 25 U.S.C. § 2511(4).

[64] 20 U.S.C. § 1401(13). For more information on IDEA, see CRS Report RS22590, *The Individuals with Disabilities Education Act (IDEA): Overview and Selected Issues*, by Ann Lordeman and Nancy Lee Jones.

[65] For more information on the ESEA Title III English language acquisition program, see CRS Report RL33960, *The Elementary and Secondary Education Act, as Amended by the No Child Left Behind Act: A Primer*, by Rebecca R. Skinner, pp. 9-10.

[66] Under 25 U.S.C. §2021(20), for instance, the term "tribe" means any Indian tribe, band, nation, or other organized group or community, including an Alaska Native Regional Corporation or Village Corporation (as defined in or established pursuant to the Alaska Native Claims Settlement Act [43 USCS §§ 1601 et seq.]), which is recognized as eligible for the special programs and services provided by the United States to Indians because of their status as Indians.

[67] For more information on the process for federally recognizing Indian tribes, see CRS Report RS21 109, *The Bureau of Indian Affairs's Process for Recognizing Groups as Indian Tribes*, by M. Maureen Murphy.

[68] Federal recognition allows tribes to take advantage of numerous federal assistance programs that are exclusively for recognized tribes and establishes an intergovernmental relationship between the tribe and federal government.

[69] Office of Management and Budget, "Revisions to the Standards for the Classification of Federal Data on Race and Ethnicity," 62 *Federal Register* 58782, October 30, 1997.

[70] Ibid.

[71] U.S. Congress, Senate Committee on Labor and Public Welfare, Special Subcommittee on Indian Education, *Indian Education: A National Tragedy—A National Challenge*, Pursuant to S. Res. 80 A Resolution Authorizing an Investigation into the Problems of Education for American Indians, 91st Cong., 1st sess., November 3, 1969, S. Rept. 501 (Washington: GPO, 1969).

[72] DeVoe, J.F., and Darling-Churchill, K.E. (2008). *Status and Trends in the Education of American Indians and Alaska Natives: 2008* (NCES 2008-084). National Center for Education Statistics, Institute of Education Sciences, U.S. Department of Education. Washington, DC, p. 86.

[73] The status dropout rate is reported for 16- through 24-year-olds in the civilian, noninstitutionalized population in Aud, S., Hussar, W., Planty, M., Snyder, T., Bianco, K., Fox, M., Frohlich, L., Kemp, J., Drake, L. (2010). *The Condition of Education 2010* (NCES 20 10-028). National Center for Education Statistics, Institute of Education Sciences, U.S. Department of Education. Washington, DC, p. 204.

[74] The 1969 data were sourced from U.S. Congress, Senate Committee on Labor and Public Welfare, Special Subcommittee on Indian Education, *Indian Education: A National Tragedy—A National Challenge*, Pursuant to S. Res. 80 A Resolution Authorizing an Investigation into the Problems of Education for American Indians, 91st Cong., 1st sess., November 3, 1969, S. Rept. 501 (Washington: GPO, 1969). The 2007 data were sourced from U.S. Department of Education, Institute of Education Sciences, *National Indian Education Study 2007: Part II, The Educational Experiences of American Indian and Alaska Native Students in Grades 4 and 8 Statistical Analysis Report*, NCES 2010-462, Washington, DC, p. 17.

[75] The NAEP, directed by the U.S. Department of Education, is the largest nationally representative and continuing assessment of what America's students know and can do in various subject areas. Since NAEP assessments are administered uniformly across the nation, NAEP results serve as a common metric.

[76] Below basic scores signify that students do not have partial mastery of prerequisite knowledge and skills that are fundamental for proficient work at each grade assessed.

[77] Comparisons are statistically significant at the 0.05 level. U.S. Department of Education, Institute of Education Sciences, *National Indian Education Study 2009: Part I, Performance of American Indian and Alaska Native Students at Grades 4 and 8 on NAEP 2009 Reading and Mathematics Assessments*, NCES 2010-462, Washington, DC, pp. 15 and 54.

[78] Scoring at or above proficient means that for each grade assessed students demonstrated solid academic performance.

[79] Comparisons are statistically significant at the 0.05 level. U.S. Department of Education, Institute of Education Sciences, *National Indian Education Study 2009: Part I, Performance of American Indian and Alaska Native Students at Grades 4 and 8 on NAEP 2009 Reading and Mathematics Assessments*, NCES 2010-462, Washington, DC, pp. 15 and 54.

[80] Sections 1142 of the Education Amendments of 1978 (P.L. 95-561).

[81] U.S. Congress, House Committee on Education and Labor, Subcommittee on Elementary, Secondary, and Vocational Education, *Indian Education—Oversight, Part I Supplemental Programs*, 95th Cong., 1st sess., September 16, 20 and October 7, 1977, HRG-1977-EDL-0027, 78-H341-33 (Washington: GPO, 1978), pp. 321, 355.

[82] U.S. Congress, House Committee on Education and Labor, Subcommittee on Elementary, Secondary, and Vocational Education, *Indian Education—Oversight, Part I Supplemental Programs*, 95th Cong., 1st sess., September 16, 20 and October 7, 1977, HRG-1977-EDL-0027, 78-H341-33 (Washington: GPO, 1978), p. 321.

[83] U.S. Congress, House Committee on Education and Labor, *Education Amendments of 1978*, Report Together with Additional and Supplemental Views to Accompany H.R. 15, 95th Cong., 2nd sess., May 11, 1978, H. Rept. 95-1137, p. 125.

[84] Ibid.

[85] Section 9102 of the Improving America's Schools Act of 1994 (P.L. 103-382).

[86] Section 7115 of the No Child Left Behind Act of 2001 (P.L. 107-110).

[87] U.S. Department of Education, National Advisory Council on Indian Education, *Annual Report FY2005-2006*, June 2006, p. 3, http://www2.ed.gov/about/offices/list/oese/oie/nacie2006ar. pdf.

[88] Section 411 of P.L. 92-3 18.

In: American Indians. Volume 1
Editors: Albert O. Hughes and Eric A. Sanders
ISBN: 978-1-61122-351-4
© 2012 Nova Science Publishers, Inc.

Chapter 3

THE INDIAN CHILD WELFARE ACT (ICWA): A LEGAL OVERVIEW[*]

Jane M. Smith

SUMMARY

From the 19th century to the passage of the Indian Child Welfare Act (ICWA) in 1978, the federal government, states, and private adoption agencies sought to remove Indian children from their tribes and families in order to "civilize" the children or provide them with better lives. Congress passed the ICWA to end this practice and the high rate at which Indian children were being removed from their homes and placed with non-Indians.

One survey reported that 25%-35% of all Indian children were being separated from their families and placed in foster homes, adoptive homes, or institutions. The House Committee on Interior and Insular Affairs termed the disparity between placement rates for Indians and non-Indians "shocking." The committee concluded that many non-Indian social workers who recommended removal of Indian children from their families and communities were ignorant of Indian cultural values and social norms, and biased against typical Indian family life. This bias too often resulted in finding neglect or abandonment when there was none. The committee noted also that the decision to take Indian children from their natural homes was frequently carried out without due process of law and that most cases did not go through adjudication because parents voluntarily waived their parental rights in the face of coercion from the state.

Accordingly, Congress passed the ICWA to establish standards for removing Indian children from their homes, prioritizing placement of Indian children with extended family members and other Indians, and giving tribes a recognized role in the placement of Indian children by, among other things, recognizing tribal court jurisdiction over Indian child placements and adoptions. In addition, the ICWA includes important procedural protections for Indian parents, custodians, and tribes to provide due process of law.

---

[*] This is an edited, reformatted and augmented version of the Congressional Research Service Publication, CRS Report for Congress R42047, dated October 6, 2011.

BACKGROUND

From the 19th century to the passage of the Indian Child Welfare Act (ICWA)[1] in 1978, the federal government, states, and private agencies sought to separate Indian children from their tribes and families in order to "civilize" the children or provide them with better lives.[2] Congress undertook to reverse this practice when it passed the ICWA in response to the high rate at which states were separating Indian children from their parents, families, and tribes through involuntary removal of Indian children from Indian homes and involuntary termination of parental rights.[3] One survey reported that "approximately 25–35 percent of all Indian children are separated from their families and placed in foster homes, adoptive homes, or institutions."[4] The House Committee on Interior and Insular Affairs—the predecessor of the present-day House Committee on Natural Resources—termed the disparity between placement rates for Indians and non-Indians "shocking."[5] The committee expressed concern about the welfare of Indian children who are traumatized by removal from their families and then "adjusting to a social and cultural environment much different from their own."[6] The committee concluded, "[i]n judging the fitness of a particular family, many social workers, ignorant of Indian cultural values and social norms, make decisions that are wholly inappropriate in the context of Indian family life and so they frequently discover neglect or abandonment where none exists."[7] The committee noted also that "[t]he decision to take Indian children from their natural homes is, in most cases, carried out without due process of law" and that most cases did not go through adjudication because parents voluntarily waived their parental rights in the face of coercion from the state.[8]

Congress declared two policy aims of the ICWA: (1) "to protect the best interests of Indian children," and (2) "to promote the stability and security of Indian tribes and families."[9] The ICWA is premised on the belief that "protection of the child's relationship with the tribe is in the child's best interest."[10] It identifies Indian children as a "resource" that is "vital to the continued existence and integrity of Indian tribes."[11] Thus, the ICWA recognizes that Indian tribes have a unique interest in their minor members or potential members. The Bureau of Indian Affairs (BIA) described the ICWA's policy as follows: "Congress through the [ICWA] has expressed its clear preference for keeping Indian children with their families, deferring to tribal judgment on matters concerning the custody of tribal children, and placing Indian children who must be removed from their homes within their own families or Indian tribes."[12]

To achieve these policy aims, the ICWA establishes "minimum Federal standards for the removal of Indian children from their families and the placement of such children in foster or adoptive homes which will reflect the unique values of Indian culture, and by providing for assistance to Indian tribes in the operation of child and family services programs."[13] In addition, the ICWA provides procedural protections for parents and tribes in state court proceedings.

WHEN THE ICWA APPLIES

The ICWA applies to child custody proceedings involving Indian children. "Child custody proceedings" include "foster care placement," "termination of parental rights," "preadoptive placement," and "adoptive placement."[14] It does not apply to placements resulting from juvenile proceedings concerning an act which if committed by an adult would be a crime, or custody determinations made in conjunction divorce proceedings.[15] Although the ICWA is associated primarily with involuntary child custody proceedings, it applies to voluntary proceedings as well.[16] The ICWA defines "Indian child" as "any unmarried person who is under age eighteen and is either (a) a member of an Indian tribe or (b) is eligible for membership in an Indian tribe and is the biological child of a member of an Indian tribe."[17]

The *BIA Guidelines*[18] provide "[w]hen a state court has reason to believe a child involved in a custody proceeding is an Indian, the state court shall seek verification of the child's status from either the [BIA] or the child's tribe."[19] Under the *BIA Guidelines*, the tribe's determination of the child's or parent's status as a member or the child's status as eligible for membership is conclusive.[20] In the absence of a tribal determination, the BIA's determination is conclusive.[21]

The courts of six states have adopted the "existing Indian family" doctrine to determine whether the ICWA applies.[22] Under this doctrine, the ICWA does not apply when "neither the child nor the child's parents have maintained a significant social, cultural, or political relationship with his or her tribe."[23] Courts usually apply the doctrine in cases involving children of mixed heritage who have been living in a non-Indian environment for an extended period.[24] The Kansas Supreme Court first formulated the doctrine based on the belief that, "[a] careful study of the legislative history behind the [ICWA] and the [ICWA] itself discloses that the overriding concern of Congress and the proponents of the [ICWA] was the maintenance of the family and tribal relationships existing in Indian homes and to set minimum standards for the removal of Indian children from their existing Indian environment."[25]

The doctrine is applied differently depending on the state. Alabama courts have limited the existing Indian family doctrine to circumstances where the parents are unmarried and the non- Indian mother voluntarily places the child for adoption.[26] In *Ex Parte C.L.J.*,[27] the Alabama Court of Civil Appeals explicitly limited the doctrine to those circumstances and declined to apply the doctrine to a child whose mother did not obtain membership in her tribe until after the child had been removed from her custody and it was clear the state was going to move to terminate her parental rights. Even though the child had not been raised in an Indian family, the court held the ICWA applied. In contrast, the Kentucky Supreme Court applied the doctrine to a proceeding involving a child who was a ward of the tribal court but who had lived with a non-Indian family for years.[28] The court gave no reason as to why the tribal court would not continue to have exclusive jurisdiction over the child. Indiana, Louisiana, Missouri, and Tennessee courts apply it even when the mother is Indian.[29] In *In re: James Ronald Hampton*,[30] the Louisiana supreme court applied the existing Indian family doctrine to deprive an Indian mother of her rights under the ICWA to revoke her consent to a voluntary adoption by a non-Indian family. Nevada courts have determined to apply the existing Indian family doctrine on a "case-by-case basis to avoid results that are counter to the ICWA's policy goal of protecting the best interest of a Native American child."[31]

The existing Indian family doctrine appears to be on the decline. The Kansas, Oklahoma, and South Dakota supreme courts, initially leading courts in adopting the doctrine, have since rejected it.[32] Washington and Iowa have rejected it through legislation.[33]

ADOPTIONS UNDER THE ICWA

To counter the high rate at which states were removing Indian children from their families and Indian communities, the ICWA provides uniform and heightened standards for involuntarily terminating parental rights, preferences for placing Indian children in Indian adoptive homes, and procedural protections for parents and Indian tribes in state court proceedings.

Termination of Parental Rights

The termination of parental rights occurs when the parent-child relationship is legally severed. Termination can be voluntary, such as when parents consent to adoption, or involuntary, upon a finding of abandonment, neglect, or abuse of the child. Upon termination of parental rights, a child is available to enter a parent-child relationship with adoptive parents.

The ICWA does not restrict a parent's ability to voluntarily terminate his or her parental rights. It limits the circumstances under which state courts may terminate parental rights involuntarily.

Because Congress found that frequently states were terminating the parental rights of Indian parents based on biased evidence of neglect and abandonment, Section 1912(f) of the ICWA establishes the evidence that state courts must consider, the standard of proof, and the substantive standard that the evidence must establish in order for a state court to involuntarily terminate parental rights. A court must find "beyond a reasonable doubt," based on evidence which must include expert testimony, that "the continued custody of the child by the parent or Indian custodian is likely to result in serious emotional or physical damage to the child."[34] The "beyond a reasonable" doubt standard is higher than the "clear and convincing evidence" standard required for due process and employed by the states in parental termination proceedings,[35] and is "designed to fulfill [the] ICWA's goal of ending practices by state social welfare personnel that result in removal of Indian children from their homes based on nonconformity with non-Indians' stereotypes of what a proper family should be."[36]

The *BIA Guidelines* explain that removal of an Indian child from his or her family "must be based on competent testimony from one or more experts qualified to speak specifically to the issue of whether continued custody by the parents or Indian custodians is likely to result in serious physical or emotional damage to the child."[37] In requiring expert witness testimony by a witness with relevant experience or education, Section 1912 seeks to counter the bias of non-Indians against Indian communities, families, and circumstances cited in the ICWA.[38] The House Report from the Committee on Interior and Insular Affairs explained the need for these standards with statistical evidence that physical abuse existed in just one percent of the cases in which an Indian child was removed from the family.[39] In the remaining 99 percent of the cases, the state gave vague reasons such as "neglect" or "social deprivation" or presented evidence that somehow living with the parents damaged the child emotionally.[40] By imposing strict standards and requiring expert testimony, the ICWA seeks to limit the circumstances in which Indian children are removed from their homes to those that present a real danger to the child.

Most state courts do not require expert testimony when the evidence justifying removal of the child is "culturally neutral."[41] Therefore, a state court will not get expert testimony if the basis for removal is physical abuse such as shaken baby syndrome or newborn drug addiction.[42]

The ICWA's Placement Preferences

In the interest of maintaining Indian children within the Indian community and tribe, section 1915 establishes the order of preference for placement of Indian children that state courts must follow. Indian tribes may alter the order of preference by resolution.[43]

Section 1915(a) provides that in "any adoption proceeding" in a state court, "a preference shall be given, in the absence of good cause to the contrary, to a placement with (1) a member of the child's extended family; (2) other members of the Indian child's tribe; or (3) other Indian families."[44] By its terms, Section 1915 applies to all adoptions, voluntary and involuntary. Some view these preferences as a departure from the general federal policy of disfavoring race matching in adoptions and foster placements.[45]

The *BIA Guidelines* identify the following considerations for determining good cause: the request of the parents or the child, if the child is of sufficient age; "the extraordinary physical or emotional needs of the child as established by testimony of a qualified expert witness," and the unavailability of suitable families for placement after "diligent" search.[46] The party seeking to avoid the statutory preferences bears the burden of establishing good cause.[47] The states are divided on whether the best interests of the child constitute good cause to depart from the placement preferences.[48] Those state courts that find good cause based on the child's best interests generally place greater importance on the child's permanent placement,[49] while those state courts that reject the child's best interests as a basis for a good cause finding generally place greater importance on the child's identity as an Indian and the tribe's interest in that identity.[50]

Procedural Protections

The House Report from the Committee on Interior and Insular Affairs stated point blank: "[t]he decision to take Indian children from their natural homes is, in most cases, carried out without due process of law."[51] One commentator has stated that the ICWA provides greater procedural protections for parents, tribes, and Indian custodians than are provided to non-Indian parents.[52] These protections are designed to ensure that parents, tribes, and Indian custodians are fully informed and may participate in state court proceedings, and that federal courts may review state court judgments.

Consent

In response to the conclusion by Congress that states were coercing waivers of parental rights and obtaining consent from uninformed parents, Section 1913(a) of the ICWA requires that in cases of voluntary placement in foster care or voluntary termination of parental rights, consent will not be valid unless it is in writing, recorded before a judge, and accompanied by a certificate from the judge that the "the terms and consequences of the consent were fully explained in detail and were fully understood" by the consenting person.[53] Section 1913(a) requires also that the court must certify that the parent understood the explanation, either in English or as translated in a language he or she did understand.[54] Consent given within ten days after birth of a child is not valid.[55]

The ICWA also gives Indian parents opportunity to withdraw their consent. Parents of an Indian child may withdraw their consent for termination of parental rights at any time before the final decree of termination or adoption.[56] Upon withdrawal of consent, the child must be returned to the parent.[57] Even after the final decree of termination or adoption has been entered, the parents have two years to withdraw consent and petition the court to vacate the decree on the ground that his or her consent was obtained through fraud or duress.[58] Upon a finding of fraud or duress, the court shall vacate the decree and return the child to the parent.[59] By providing that parents may withdraw their consent and petition the court to vacate the adoption upon an allegation of fraud or duress, the ICWA creates incentives to ensure that parents give their consent knowingly and freely. However, these provisions also generate uncertainty about the security and finality of adoptions of Indian children.

Based on all these procedural protections, one commentator has stated that Indian birth parents are afforded more procedural protections than non-Indian birth parents in voluntary termination proceedings.[60]

Notice

An important element of due process is notice of the action that the state is proposing to take.[61] The House Report from the Committee on Interior and Insular Affairs pointed to the importance of notice in the context of Indian children.

The conflict between Indian and non-Indian social systems sometimes operates to defeat due process. The extended family provides an example. By sharing the responsibility of child rearing, the extended family tends to strengthen the community's commitment to the child. At the same time, however, it diminishes the possibility that the nuclear family will be able to mobilize itself quickly enough when an outside agency acts to assume custody. Because it is not unusual for Indian children to spend considerable time away with other relatives, there is no immediate realization of what is happening—possibly not until the opportunity for due process has slipped away.[62]

Section 1912(a) provides that in an involuntary proceeding in state court, the party seeking termination of parental rights must notify the parent and the child's tribe by return receipt registered mail.[63] If the identity or location of the Indian child's parent is not known, the party seeking foster care placement or termination of parental rights must notify the Secretary of the Interior (Secretary).[64] The Secretary has 15 days in which to notify the parents.[65] The court cannot hold a proceeding for ten days after the parent or Indian custodian and tribe or the Secretary received notice.[66] State courts must grant up to 20 additional days upon request from the parent, Indian custodian, or tribe before proceeding.[67] Section 1912(a) is intended to provide meaningful notice to both the parents and the tribe so that they may participate in the proceedings and, if they wish, challenge the involuntary termination of parental rights or the removal of the child from the family.

Right to Intervene

Section 1911(c) establishes the right of the Indian child's Indian custodian or tribe to intervene in any state court proceeding for termination of parental rights at any point in the proceeding.[68] This right of intervention applies in both involuntary and voluntary terminations. However, because the ICWA requires that tribes get notice of involuntary proceedings only, tribes are more likely to know about, and therefore intervene in, involuntary proceedings than in voluntary proceedings.

The House Report from the Committee on Interior and Insular Affairs noted that frequently Indian parents leave their children with members of their extended families.[69] Under 1911(c) such a family member has a right to intervene, even though he or she has no recognized legal relationship with the child. Section 1911(c) recognizes the importance of that relationship and ensures that such a family member, as well as the child's tribe, has the opportunity to be a party to the termination proceedings. Granting Indian custodians and tribes the right to intervene as parties provides another mechanism that increases the likelihood that Indian children will remain in Indian communities and maintain ties to their tribes.

Right to Counsel

For indigent parents or Indian custodians challenging the removal of a child or the termination of parental rights, the ICWA provides the right to counsel. Section 1912(b) provides that when a court determines indigence, the parent or Indian custodian has a right to a court-appointed counsel in any placement or termination proceeding.[70] A state court has discretion to appoint counsel for the child if it determines it to be in the best interest of the child.[71] If state law does not provide for appointment of counsel, the state court must notify the Secretary of the Interior who will pay reasonable fees and expenses upon certification from the presiding judge.[72]

Reports and Other Documents

One of the complaints voiced in the legislative history was that state court judges were making decisions about Indian children based on evidence that the Indian parties could not see.[73] Section 1912(c) seeks to remedy this by providing any party to a foster care placement or termination of parental rights proceeding with the right to examine "all reports or other documents filed with the courts upon which any decision with respect to such action may be based."[74] This provision seeks to ensure that the court bases its decision on evidence in the record filed with the court that all parties have had an opportunity to examine.

Remedial Services and Rehabilitation Programs

The ICWA requires that before a state court terminates parental rights, the state must take steps to try to maintain the Indian family. Section 1912(d) requires the state to demonstrate that "active efforts have been made to provide remedial services and rehabilitative programs designed to prevent the breakup of the Indian family and that these efforts have proved unsuccessful" before terminating parental rights.[75] Such active efforts should extend to the extended family and the tribe and may include "providing transportation, arranging appointments with providers, assisting with childcare, and taking other rehabilitative measures, optimally in collaboration with the child's tribe."[76] This provision is intended to protect the integrity of Indian families and increases the likelihood that a child will remain in the Indian community by requiring that states involve the extended family and the tribe.

Federal Court Review

The ICWA provides for federal court review of state court decisions. Section 1914 states that a child who is the subject of a state court proceeding, the parent or Indian custodian, or the child's tribe "may petition any court of competent jurisdiction" to invalidate an action based on a violation of the ICWA's jurisdictional provisions, procedural provisions, or consent provisions.[77] A "court of competent jurisdiction" includes a federal court.[78] Thus, federal courts may review and invalidate state court decrees, upon a showing that the state court improperly exercised jurisdiction, failed to allow the Indian custodian or tribe to intervene, failed to give full faith and credit to a tribal court decree, failed to respect the procedural rights of the Indian custodian or tribe, or failed to obtain informed and knowing consent from the parents. However, when tribes or Indian parties have tried to use federal courts to invalidate state court decisions rendered in violation of the ICWA, they have met with mixed results.[79]

Federal courts may review tribal court decrees, but only after the party seeking review has exhausted his or her remedies in the tribal court.[80] Thus, a party seeking review of a tribal court decree must appeal the challenged decision through the tribal court system and obtain a decision from the highest tribal court before challenging the decree in federal court.

FOSTER CARE PLACEMENT UNDER THE ICWA

Foster care is the term applied to the temporary placement of a child with a licensed caregiver when a child is removed, voluntarily or involuntarily, from his or her home and made a ward of the state or tribe. The foster care giver has day-to-day responsibility for the child and the state or tribe makes the legal decisions for the child.

Section 1912(e) establishes the standard of proof, the type of evidence, and the substantive standard that state courts must apply in removing an Indian child from his or her home and placing the child in foster care. Section 1912(e) provides that for involuntary proceedings, state courts must find, based on "clear and convincing evidence," including the testimony of qualified expert witnesses, that "continued custody of the child by the parent or Indian custodian is likely to result in serious emotional or physical damage to the child" before placing the child in foster care.[81] The "clear and convincing evidence" standard is higher than the "preponderance of the evidence" standard necessary for due process and employed by most states in foster care placement proceeding for non-Indian children.[82] The *BIA Guidelines* provide that "[e]vidence that only shows the existence of community or family poverty, crowded or inadequate housing, alcohol abuse, or non-conforming social behavior does not constitute clear and convincing evidence that continued custody is likely to result in serious emotional or physical harm to the child."[83] Rather, in order to meet the standard, "the evidence must show the existence of particular conditions in the home that are likely to result in serious emotional or physical damage to the particular child."[84]

Section 1915(b) provides that for foster care or preadoptive placement, a state court must place the child "in reasonable proximity to his or her home," "in the least restrictive setting which most closely approximates a family, and in which his special needs, if any, may be met."[85] These standards are similar to the standards applied under state law for foster placement of non-Indian children. The ICWA, however, provides a hierarchy of preferences. Placement should be: with a member of the child's extended family; a foster home licensed, approved, or specified by the child's tribe; an Indian foster home licensed or approved by an authorized non-Indian licensing authority; or, an institution for children approved by an Indian tribe or operated by an Indian organization which has a program suitable to meet the child's needs.[86] Like the preferences for adoption, these preferences make it more likely that Indian children will not be removed from an Indian environment.

Parents and tribes enjoy the same procedural rights in foster care placement proceedings as they have in parental rights termination proceedings.

THE ICWA'S JURISDICTIONAL SCHEME

By recognizing both exclusive and concurrent tribal court jurisdiction over custody proceedings involving Indian children, the ICWA provides an important mechanism by which tribes may participate in the placement of Indian children. The ICWA recognizes that tribal courts have exclusive jurisdiction over child custody proceedings involving Indian children who are residing on the reservation or who are wards of the tribal court, regardless of residency. It recognizes that tribal courts have concurrent jurisdiction over child custody proceedings involving children who reside off the reservation. To ensure that other jurisdictions respect tribal court orders, the ICWA provides that "[t]he United States, every State, every territory or possession of the United States, and every Indian tribe shall give full faith and credit to the public acts, records and judicial proceedings of any Indian tribe applicable to Indian child custody proceedings to the same extent that such entities give full faith and credit to the public acts, records and judicial proceedings of any other entity."[87]

Exclusive Jurisdiction

Before Congress passed the ICWA, the U.S. Supreme Court recognized that tribal courts have exclusive jurisdiction over adoptions involving tribal members residing on the reservation. In *Fisher v. District Court of the Sixteenth Judicial District of Montana*,[88] members of the Northern Cheyenne Tribe (Tribe) had gained custody of a member child through a tribal court proceeding.[89] The members sought to adopt the child through a state court proceeding. The biological mother of the child, who was also a member of the Tribe, moved to dismiss the state court proceeding on the ground that the tribal court had exclusive jurisdiction over the proceeding.[90] The Supreme Court stated the test for whether the state court could exercise jurisdiction was at the least, "whether the state action infringed on the right of the reservation Indians to make their own laws and be ruled by them."[91] The Court concluded that the tribal court had exclusive jurisdiction owing to the Tribe's right to govern itself independent of state law.[92] In response to the argument that the Tribe could not divest the state of jurisdiction it exercised over tribal adoptions prior to organization of the Tribe in 1935, the Court noted the tribal courts were established pursuant to the Indian Reorganization

Act. If the state courts in fact exercised jurisdiction over tribal adoptions, that jurisdiction has been preempted by federal statute.[93] Finally, the Court rejected the members' assertion that depriving them of access to state courts constituted impermissible racial discrimination, noting that the tribal court's exclusivity derives from the "quasi-sovereign status" of the Tribe under federal law.[94] "Moreover, even if a jurisdictional holding occasionally results in denying an Indian plaintiff a forum to which a non-Indian has access, such disparate treatment of the Indian is justified because it is intended to benefit the class of which he is a member by furthering the congressional policy of Indian self-government."[95]

The ICWA recognizes this exclusive jurisdiction over child custody proceedings involving Indian children residing or domiciled on the reservation.[96] It explicitly provides in section 1911(a) that "[a]n Indian tribe shall have jurisdiction exclusive as to any State over any child custody proceeding involving an Indian child who resides or is domiciled within the reservation of such tribe."[97] Thus, a parent of a child residing or domiciled on the reservation cannot circumvent tribal jurisdiction by going to state court.[98] Section 1911(a) provides for exclusive tribal court jurisdiction over Indian children who are wards of the tribal court, regardless of the child's residence or domicile.[99]

Section 1911(a) provides an exception for states in which a federal law, such as P.L. 280,[100] vests civil jurisdiction over the reservation in the state. Under Section 1918(a), tribes in P.L. 280 states may reassume exclusive jurisdiction over child custody proceedings upon approval by the Secretary of the Interior (Secretary) of a petition for reassumption.[101] Reassumption, however, is not necessary in order for tribes in P.L. 280 states to exercise concurrent inherent jurisdiction over child custody proceedings[102]

For the ICWA, the child's domicile or residence is determined, under federal law, by the domicile or residence of the parents. In *Mississippi Band of Choctaw v. Holyfield*,[103] the only Supreme Court case to consider the ICWA, the Court considered whether the tribal court had exclusive jurisdiction over the voluntary termination of parental rights and subsequent adoption of twin Indian children whose biological parents resided on the reservation but who purposefully left the reservation so that the children would not be born on the reservation, thereby avoiding the ICWA's reach. The Court held that the tribal court had exclusive jurisdiction over the proceedings. The state supreme court had held that domicile or residence was a matter of state law and that under state law, the children were never domiciled or residing on the reservation. The Supreme Court reversed, holding that Congress intended that domicile or residence would be determined by a uniform federal standard, and the standard looked to the residence of the parents to determine the residence of the children. "Tribal jurisdiction under § 1911(a) was not meant to be defeated by the actions of individual members of the tribe, for Congress was concerned not solely about the interests of Indian children and families, but also about the impact on the tribes themselves of the large number of Indian children adopted by non-Indians."[104] The Court noted, "[t]he protection of this tribal interest [in Indian children] is at the core of ICWA, which recognizes that the tribe has an interest in the child which is distinct from but on parity with the interest of the parents."[105]

Concurrent Jurisdiction

The ICWA ensures concurrent tribal-state jurisdiction by providing that in state child custody proceedings involving Indian children residing off the reservation, state courts must transfer the proceeding to tribal court upon petition of the Indian child's parent, Indian custodian, or tribe, unless either parent objects, the tribal court declines jurisdiction, or good cause is shown.[106] The Supreme Court said in *Holyfield* that when there is concurrent jurisdiction, tribal court jurisdiction is presumed.[107] The fact that either parent may object to transfer to tribal court means that state courts frequently hear cases involving children of mixed heritage.[108]

The ICWA does not define good cause and the legislative history indicates that Congress left it undefined intentionally so that state courts would have flexibility in making good cause determinations.[109] The *BIA Guidelines* identify the following circumstances as constituting good cause: the child's tribe lacks a tribal court; the petition is filed when the proceeding is at an advanced stage and the petitioner did not file the petition promptly; an Indian child older than twelve objects; presenting evidence in tribal courts would present an undue hardship on parties or witnesses; or a child older than five, whose parents are unavailable, has had little or no contact with the tribe or its members.[110] Courts are divided on whether to consider the child's best interest in determining good cause.[111]

PROPOSED AMENDMENTS TO THE ICWA

Over the years, there have been many bills introduced in Congress to amend the ICWA.[112] In general, the amendments have been aimed at ensuring tribal notice and the opportunity for limited tribal intervention in voluntary adoptions,[113] restricting the time in which parents may revoke their consent to voluntary termination of their rights,[114] and providing criminal penalties for misrepresentation regarding an Indian child.[115] In addition, many of the proposed amendments have clarified when tribal courts have exclusive jurisdiction; extended exclusive jurisdiction to tribes with reservations located in P.L. 280 states and to tribes without reservations, including tribes in Oklahoma; and, made clear that tribes in Alaska have jurisdiction concurrent with state courts.[116] Only one bill has been introduced to limit the applicability of the ICWA.[117]

There have been no bills introduced in the 111th or 112th Congresses to amend the ICWA.

CONCLUSION

The ICWA has achieved success in reducing the rate at which Indian children are removed from their homes and the rate at which Indian children are placed in non-Indian homes.[118] Nonetheless, Indian children are still removed from their homes and placed in foster care at a rate higher than that for non-Indian children.[119] In 2008, Congress passed the Fostering Connections to Success and Increasing Adoptions Act,[120] which made tribes eligible for direct funding for foster care and adoption assistance under Title IV-E of the Social Security Act,[121] the act under which states receive federal funding for foster placement and adoption assistance. It is too early to know the results of this access to increased funding, but it may improve the tribes' ability to protect their children in a way that also protects the tribes.

End Notes

[1] 25 U.S.C. §§1901 *et seq.*

[2] Barbara Ann Atwood, Children, Tribes, and States: Adoption and Custody Conflicts over American Indian Children 155-15 8 (2010); *see also* Lorie M. Graham, "The Past Never Vanishes": A Contextual Critique of the Existing Indian Family Doctrine, 23 Am. Ind. L. Rev. 1 (1998-1999).

[3] H.Rept. 95-1386, at 8-11.

[4] *Id.* at 9.

[5] *Id.*

[6] *Id.*

[7] *Id.* at 10.

[8] *Id.* at 11.

[9] 25 U.S.C. § 1902.

[10] Chester County Dep't of Social Services. v. Coleman, 372 S.E.2d 912, 914 (S.C.Ct. App. 1988).

[11] 25 U.S.C. § 1901(3).

[12] Bureau of Indian Affairs Guidelines for State Courts; Indian Child Custody Proceedings, 44 Fed. Reg. 67,584, 67,585 (1979) (BIA Guidelines).

[13] *Id.*

[14] 25 U.S.C. § 1903(1).

[15] *Id.*

[16] Mississippi Band of Choctaw Indians v. Holyfield, 490 U.S. 30 (1989).

[17] 25 U.S.C. § 1903(4).

[18] The *BIA Guidelines* are not binding on the states. Rather, they are intended to provide guidance to state courts in administering the ICWA. Courts frequently follow the *BIA Guidelines* as an administrative interpretation of the ICWA. *See, e.g., In re C. W.*, 479 N.W. 2d 105, 113 (Neb. 1992) (relying on *BIA Guidelines*); Felix Cohen's Handbook of Federal Indian Law (2005) (Cohen) 11.02[1] citing *In re Junious M.*, 193 Cal. Rptr 40, 43 n7 (Ct. App. 1983).

[19] *BIA Guidelines, supra* note 12 at 67,586.

[20] *Id.* In *Nielson v. Ketchum*, 640 F.3d 1117 (10th Cir. 2011), however, the Court of Appeals for the Tenth Circuit rejected the tribe's determination that the child was a member. The Cherokee Nation adopted a "Citizenship Act," which made every newborn who was direct descendant of an original enrollee a temporary citizen of the Cherokee Nation for a period of 240 days following birth. The purpose of the act was to "protect[] the rights of the Cherokee Nation under the ICWA." *Id.* at 2. The child at issue was a direct descendant of an original enrollee but his mother was not enrolled. Thus, the ICWA applied only if the Citizenship Act effectively conferred citizenship on him for purposes of the ICWA. Noting that Congress rejected a definition of Indian child which would have included all children eligible for membership such as the child at issue, the court rejected the tribe's position that the child was a member. The court concluded that involuntary temporary membership, such as that conferred by the Citizenship Act, did not qualify as membership for the purposes of the ICWA.

[21] *Id.* The *BIA Guidelines* identify the following common circumstances as providing reason to believe that a child may be an Indian child: a party, an Indian tribe, or a public or private agency informs the court the child is Indian; any public or state licensed agency involved in child protection or family support obtains information indicating the child is Indian; the child gives reason to believe he or she is Indian; the residence or domicile of the child or the parents is a predominantly Indian community; and an officer of the court involved in the proceeding has knowledge that the child may be Indian.

[22] The following states have judicially adopted the existing Indian family doctrine: Alabama (*S.A. v. E.J.P.*, 571 So.2d 1187 (Ala. App. 1990)); Indiana (*In re Adoption of T.R.M.*, 525 N.E.2d 298 (Ind. 1988), *cert. denied sub nom, In re Adoption of T.R.M.*, 490 U.S. 1069 (1989)); Louisiana (*In re: James Ronald Hampton and Jan Harris Milz Hampton.*, 658 So.2d 331 (La. Ct. App. 1995), *cert. denied*, 517 U.S. 1158 (1996)); Missouri (*In re S.A.M.*, 703 S.W.2d 603 (Mo. Ct. App. 1986)); Nevada (*In the Matter of the Parental Rights as to N.J.*, 221 P.3d 1255, 1264 (Nev. 2009)); and Tennessee (*In re Morgan*, 1997 Tenn. App. LEXIS 818 (Tenn. Ct. App. 1997)). The following states have rejected the doctrine: Alaska (*In re Adoption of Crews*, 781 P.2d 973 (Alaska 1989), *cert. denied sub nom, Jasso v. Finney*, 494 U.S. 1030 (1990)); Arizona (*Michael J. Jr. v. Michael J. Sr.*, 7 P.3d 960 (Ariz. Ct. App. 2000)); Idaho (*In re Baby Boy Doe*, 849 P.2d 925 (Idaho 1993), *cert. denied sub nom, Swenson v. Oglala Sioux Tribe*, 510 U.S. 960 (1993)); Illinois (*In re Adoption of S.S.*, 662 N.E.2d 832 (Ill. 1993)); Iowa (Iowa Code §232B.5 (2011)); Kansas (*Matter of A.J.S.*, 204 P.3d 543 (Kan. 2009)); Michigan (*In re Elliott*, 554 N.W.2d 32 (Mich. Ct. App. 2000)); Minnesota (*In re Welfare of S.N.R.*, 617 N.W.2d 77 (Minn. Ct. App. 2000)); Montana (*In re Adoption of Riffle*, 922 P.2d 510 (Mont. 1996)); New Jersey (*In re Adoption of a Child of Indian Heritage*, 543 A.2d 925 (N.J. 1988)); New York (*In the matter of Baby Boy C. Jeffrey A.*, 805 N.Y.S.2d 313 (N.Y. App. 2005)); North Dakota (*Hoots v. K.B.(In re A.B.)*, 663 N.W.2d 625 (N.D. 2003) *cert. denied*, 541 U.S. 972 (2004)); Oklahoma (*Matter of Baby Boy L.*, 103 P.3d

1099 (Okla. 2004)); South Dakota (*Matter of Adoption of Baade*, 462 S.W.2d 485 (S.D. 1990)); Utah (*In re D.A. C.*, 933 P.2d 993 (Utah Ct. App. 1997)); Washington (Rev. Code Wash. §13.34.040(3)); and Wyoming (*S.N.K. v State*, 78 P.3d 1032 (Wyo. 2005)). In California the state supreme court has not ruled on the issue and the lower courts are divided. *In re Alicia S. 76* Cal. Rptr 2d 507 (Ct. App. 1998) (rejecting doctrine); *In re Bridget R.*, 49 Cal. Rptr 2d 507 (Ct. App. 1996) (accepting doctrine and finding it necessary for constitutionality of the ICWA).

[23] Atwood, *supra* note 2 at 204; *see In re: James Ronald Hampton and Jan Harris Milz Hampton*, 658 So.2d 331, 336- 337 (Ct. App. La. 1995), *cert. denied*, 517 U.S. 1158 (1996) (court determined that even if it applied the ICWA and did not terminate Indian mother's rights, the child would not be raised in an Indian family because the Indian mother had few ties with her Indian heritage).

[24] *Id.* at 206-207, 209; *see, e.g., In the Matter of the Parental Rights as to N.J.*, 221 P.3d 1255 (Nev. 2009) (court applied the existing Indian family doctrine in termination proceeding in which non-Indian mother objected and Indian father and tribe did not object); *In re: James Ronald Hampton and Jan Harris Milz Hampton*, 658 So.2d 331, 336-337 (Ct. App. La. 1995), *cert. denied*, 517 U.S. 1158 (1996) (court applied the existing Indian family doctrine because it found the child's father was unknown and her mother was a member of the Cheyenne River Sioux Tribe who had not lived on the reservation since she was a child and did not maintain ties with her Indian heritage; the child was placed with a non-Indian family and the court determined application of the ICWA would not result in the child being raised in an Indian family); *S.A. v. E.J.P.*, 571 So.2d 1187 (Ala. App. 1990) (court applied the existing Indian family doctrine when child was illegitimate, non-Indian mother placed child for adoption, and Indian father had little contact with the child).

[25] *Matter of the Adoption of Baby Boy L.*, 643 P.2d 168, 175 (Kan. 1982).

[26] *Ex Parte C.L.J.*, 946 So.2d 880 (Ala. Civ. App. 2006).

[27] *Id.*

[28] *Rye v. Weasel*, 934 S.W.2d 257 (Ky. 1996).

[29] *Matter of Adoption of T.R.M.*, 525 N.E.2d 298 (Ind. 1988); *In re: James Ronald Hampton and Jan Harris Milz Hampton*, 658 So.2d 331 (La. 1995); *C.E.H. v. R.H.*, 8837 S.W.2d 947 (Mo. Ct. App. 1992); *In re: Morgan*, 1997 Tenn. App. LEXIS 818 (Tenn. App. 1997).

[30] *In re: James Ronald Hampton*, 658 So.2d 331 (La. 1995).

[31] *In the Matter of the Parental Rights as to N.J.*, 221 P.3d 1255, 1264 (Nev. 2009).

[32] *Matter of A.J.S.*, 204 P.3d 543 (Kan. 2009); *Matter of Baby Boy L.*, 103 P.3d 1099 (Okla. 2004); *Matter of Adoption of Baade*, 462 S.W.2d 485 (S.D. 1990).

[33] R.C.W. §26.33.040(1)(a); Iowa Code §232B.5(2).

[34] 25 U.S.C. §1912(f).

[35] Atwood, *supra* note 2 at 176-177; *see also, In the Matter of the Parental Rights as to N.J.*, 221 P.3d 1255, 1260 (Nev. 2009) (discussing differences between the state standard and the ICWA standard).

[36] *See* H.Rept. 95-1386, *supra* note 3 at 10; Cohen, *supra* note 18 at §1 1.04[4].

[37] *BIA Guidelines*, *supra* note 12, at 65,953.

[38] Cohen, § 1 1.04[4]; Cynthia R. Mabry and Lisa Kelly, Adoption Law: Theory, Policy, and Practice (2006) 399 (Adoption Law), quoting *Matter of Welfare of B. W.*, 454 N.W.2d 437 (Minn. App. 1990).

[39] H.Rept. 95-13 86, *supra* note 3 at 10.

[40] *Id.*

[41] Atwood, *supra* note 2 at 178.

[42] *Id.*

[43] 25 U.S.C. §1915(c).

[44] 25 U.S.C. §1915(a).

[45] Atwood, *supra* note 2 at 185-193; Adoption Law, *supra* note 38 at 411-413 (explaining that the federal Interethnic Adoption Provisions, Section 1808 of P.L. 104-188, prohibit placement agencies from denying any individual the opportunity to be an adoptive or foster parent on the basis of race.)

[46] *BIA Guidelines*, *supra* note 12 at 67,594.

[47] *Id.*

[48] Atwood, *supra* note 2 at 228.

[49] *Id.* at 228-229. See also Christine Metteer, Hard Cases Making Bad Law: The Need for Revision of the Indian Child Welfare Act, 38 Santa Clara L. Rev. 419, 445 (1998) (Metteer) (citing *In re Adoption of F.H.*, 851 P.2d 1361, 1365 (Alaska 1993) as an example of a court finding good cause for deviation from the ICWA's placement preferences partly based on avoiding uncertainty in favor of adoption).

[50] Metteer, *id.* at 447 (citing *In re Custody of S.E. G.*, 521 N.W.2d 357, 365 (Minnesota 1994) as rejecting the good cause exception based simply on the child's best interests and considering cultural needs in the placement).

[51] H.Rept. 95-1386, *supra* note 3 at 11.

[52] Atwood, *supra* note 2 at 174.

[53] 25 U.S.C. §1913(a).

[54] *Id.*

[55] *Id.*

[56] 25 U.S.C. §1913(b).

[57] *Id.*

[58] 25 U.S.C. §1913(c).

[59] *Id.*

[60] Atwood, *supra* note 2 at 174.

[61] *Goldberg v. Kelly*, 397 U.S. 254, 268 (1970).

[62] H.Rept. 95-1386, *supra* note 3 at 11.

[63] 25 U.S.C. §1912(a).

[64] *Id.*

[65] *Id.*

[66] *Id.*

[67] *Id.*

[68] 25 U.S.C. §1911 (c).

[69] H.Rept. 95-1386, *supra* note 3 at 10, 11.

[70] 25 U.S.C. §1912(b).

[71] *Id.*

[72] *Id.*

[73] H.Rept. 95-1386 22 (1978).

[74] 25 U.S.C. §1912(c).

[75] 25 U.S.C. §1912(d).

[76] Atwood, *supra* note 2 at 176.

[77] 25 U.S.C. §1914 provides for invalidation based on violations of §§1911, 1912, or 1913. Section 1911 governs jurisdiction of tribal and state courts and provides a right of intervention for Indian custodians and tribes and for full faith and credit of tribal court decrees. Section 1912 provides procedural protections: notice; counsel; examination of reports; remedial service and rehabilitation programs; and standards of proof. Section 1913 governs consent by parents to voluntary termination of parental rights and foster care placement.

[78] *Doe v. Mann*, 415 F.3d 1038, 1046-1047 (9th Cir. 2005).

[79] *See, e.g., Kiowa Tribe v. Lewis*, 777 F.2d 587 (10th Cir. 1985) (declining review of state court judgment because ICWA did not affect full faith and credit due state court decisions); *Doe v. Mann*, 415 F.3d 1038 (9th Cir. 2005), *cert. denied*, 126 S.Ct. 1909 (2006) (finding section 1914 authorized federal court review of state court decision).

[80] *Boozer v. Wilder*, 381 F.3d 931 (9th Cir. 2004).

[81] 25 U.S.C. §1912(e).

[82] Atwood, *supra* note 2 at 177.

[83] *BIA Guidelines*, *supra* note 12 at 67,593.

[84] *Id.*

[85] 25 U.S.C. §1915(b).

[86] *Id.*

[87] 25 U.S.C. §1911(d).

[88] *Fisher v. District Court of the Sixteenth Judicial District of Montana*, 424 U.S. 382 (1976).

[89] *Id.* at 383.

[90] *Id.* at 383-384.

[91] *Id.* at 386 (internal quotations and citations omitted).

[92] *Id.* at 387.

[93] *Id.* at 390.

[94] *Id.*

[95] *Id.* at 390-391.

[96] 25 U.S.C. §1911(a).

[97] 25 U.S.C. §1911(a).

[98] Atwood, *supra* note 2 at 170.

[99] 25 U.S.C. §1911(a).

[100] 28 U.S.C. § 1360. P.L. 280 "mandated the transfer of civil and criminal jurisdiction over 'Indian country' from the federal government to the governments of five states [(California, Minnesota, Nebraska, Oregon, and Wisconsin)], and permitted other states to assume such jurisdiction voluntarily. In 1958, Alaska was added to the list of mandatory Public Law 280 jurisdictions." *Native Village of Venetie v. Alaska*, 944 F.2d 548, 559-560 (9th Cir. 1989). P.L. 280, therefore, vests jurisdiction over custody proceedings involving Indian children residing on a reservation in state court.

[101] 25 U.S.C. § 1918(a).

[102] Atwood, *supra* note 2 at 171. The Alaska state supreme court and the federal Court of Appeals for the Ninth Circuit have held that Alaska Native village tribal courts have inherent original jurisdiction, concurrent with the state's jurisdiction, to initiate child custody proceedings for Alaska Native children residing off a

reservation. *State of Alaska v. Native Village of Tanana*, 249 P.3d 734 (Alaska 2011); *John v. Baker*, 982 P.2d 738 (Alaska 1999); *Native Village of Venetie*, 944 F.2d at 561-562.

[103] 490 U.S. 30 (1989).

[104] *Id.* at 49.

[105] *Id.* at 52 (internal quotations and citation omitted).

[106] 25 U.S.C. §1911(b).

[107] *Holyfield*, 490 U.S. at 36.

[108] Atwood, *supra* note 2 at 173; *see* cases cited *supra* note 24.

[109] *BIA Guidelines*, *supra* note 12 at 67,584, citing S.Rept. 95-597, 95th Cong., 1st Sess. 17 (1977).

[110] *Id.*

[111] Atwood, *supra* note 2 at 173-174, citing *In re Appeal in Maricopa County Juvenile Action No. JS-8287*, 828 P.2d 1245 (Ariz. Ct. App. 1991)(court considered best interests of the child); *In re Robert T.*, 246 Cal. Rptr 168 (Ct. App. 1988) (same); *In re Alexandria Y.*, 53 Cal. Rptr2d 679 (Cal. App. 1996)(same); *In re Adoption of F.H.*, 851 P.2d 1361 (Alaska 1993) (same). *See, e.g., Shageluk IRA Council v. State of Alaska*, (S.Ct. Alaska March 18, 2009) (affirming lower court decision not to transfer case to tribal court because lower court did not consider best interests of the child); *In re M.A.*, 40 Cal. Rptr. 3d 439 (Ct. App. 2006) (court did not consider best interests of the child).

[112] *See, e.g.,* H.R. 4733, 107th Cong. (2002); S. 1213, 106th Cong. (1999); H.R. 1082, 105th Cong. (1997); S. 569, 105th Cong. (1997); H.R. 3275, 104th Cong. (1996); H.R. 3828, 104th Cong. (1996); H.R. 1448, 104th Cong. (1995); S. 1962, 104th Cong. (1995); S. 764, 104th Cong. (1995).

[113] H.R. 4733, 107th Cong. (2002), sec. 9, 10, 11; S. 1213, 106th Cong. (1999), sec. 6-8; H.R. 1082, 105th Cong. (1997), sec.6-8; S. 569, 105th Cong. (1997), sec. 6, 7, 8; H.R. 3828, 104th Cong. (1996), sec. 6, 7, 8; S. 1962, 104th Cong. (1995), sec. 6, 7, 8.

[114] H.R. 4733, 107th Cong. (2002), sec. 8; S. 1213, 106th Cong. (1999), sec. 5; H.R. 1082, 105th Cong. (1997), sec. 5; S. 569, 105th Cong. (1997), sec. 5; H.R. 3828, 104th Cong. (1996), sec 5; S. 1962, 104th Cong. (1995), sec. 5.

[115] H.R. 4733, 107th Cong. (2002), sec. 18; S. 1213, 106th Cong. (1999), sec. 10; H.R. 1082, 105th Cong. (1997), sec. 9; S. 569, 105th Cong. (1997), sec. 10; H.R. 3828, 104th Cong. (1996), sec. 9; S. 1962, 104th Cong. (1995), sec. 9.

[116] H.R. 4733, 107th Cong. (2002), sec. 2(5),(6),(7); H.R. 1082, 105th Cong. (1997), sec. 2; H.R. 3828, 104th Cong. (1996), sec. 1; S. 1962, 104th Cong. (1995), sec. 2.

[117] H.R. 3275, 104th Cong. (1996).

[118] Atwood, *supra* note 2 at 193; Ann E. MacEachron, Nora S. Gustavsson, Suzanne Cross, Allison Lewis, The Effectiveness of the Indian Child Welfare Act of 1978, 70 Social Service Review 451 (1996). MacEachron et al. report that between 1975 and 1986, there was a 93 percent drop in adoption rates of Indian children and a 31 percent decrease in the placement of Indian children in foster care. *Id.* at 457. They also report that the discrepancy between foster care placement rates for Indians and non-Indians was smaller in 1986 than it was in 1975. *Id.* at 458.

[119] Atwood, *supra* note 2 at 194.

[120] P.L. 110-351, 110th Cong., 2d Sess. (2008).

[121] 42 U.S.C. §§601, 670-679a.

In: American Indians. Volume 1
Editors: Albert O. Hughes and Eric A. Sanders

ISBN: 978-1-61122-351-4
© 2012 Nova Science Publishers, Inc.

Chapter 4

ADDRESSING CHILD HUNGER AND OBESITY IN INDIAN COUNTRY[*]

Anne Gordon and Vanessa Oddo

EXECUTIVE SUMMARY

American Indian (AI) and Alaska Native (AN) children have approximately twice the levels of food insecurity, obesity, and Type II diabetes, relative to the averages for all U.S. children of similar ages. Those living on or near reservations or other tribal lands (often referred to as Indian Country) have historically been particularly disadvantaged. Section 141 of the Healthy, Hunger-Free Kids Act of 2010 (HHFKA) requires that the Department of Agriculture (USDA) provide a report to Congress on USDA programs that serve AI children living in Indian Country and may reduce these risks. This report describes how USDA nutrition programs serve children in Indian Country and how provisions of HHFKA and other recent initiatives might improve those services.

The major USDA programs that serve children and families in Indian Country include the National School Lunch Program (NSLP); the Supplemental Nutrition Assistance Program (SNAP); the Special Supplemental Nutrition Program for Women, Infants, and Children (WIC); the Food Distribution Program on Indian Reservations (FDPIR); the Child and Adult Care Food Program (CACFP); and the Summer Food Service Program (SFSP). NSLP offers lunches free or at a reduced price to school children from low-income families. SNAP offers food assistance to low-income households in the form of debit cards that can be used to purchase food items at authorized retailers. WIC provides food packages to pregnant and postpartum women, infants, and children up to age 5 to meet their special nutritional needs as well as nutrition education, breastfeeding promotion and support, and referrals to health care and social service providers. The FDPIR provides USDA food packages to low-income AIs/ANs living in Indian Country who do not participate in SNAP. CACFP provides reimbursement for meals served to low- income children in child care settings. SFSP offers

---

[*] This is an edited, reformatted and augmented version of the USDA Food and Nutrition Service, dated January 12, 2012.

meals to children when schools are out. WIC and FDPIR are frequently administered by tribes themselves, whereas NSLP, SNAP, CACFP, and SFSP are administered by the States in which the reservations are located.

Based on data from the March 2009 Current Population Survey, the NSLP has the widest reach; about 550,000 children identified as AI/AN alone received free or reduced-price school lunches in an average month in 2008, and 328,000 children who identified as AI/AN and white. SNAP also serves a large number of AI/AN individuals; for example, it served 540,000 people who identified as AI/AN alone and 260,000 who identified as AI/AN and white in an average month in 2008. During an average month in 2008, WIC served approximately 126,000 individuals identified as AI/AN alone, and 85,000 who identified as AI/AN and white. FDPIR, which is available only to households living in Indian Country, served about 80,000 individuals per month in fiscal year 2011, based on administrative data. Specific data on the number of AI/AN children served in CACFP and SFSP are unavailable.

Several provisions of HHFKA would help USDA improve the nutritional quality of meals served to children in Indian Country or increase access to program benefits. The law required updating nutrition standards for USDA-subsidized meals in schools and child care settings. The USDA proposed rule for nutrition standards and menu planning in the NSLP and School Breakfast Program would be an important step in reducing risk of obesity and type II diabetes; for example, the new standards include restrictions on the fat content of milk and requirements to increase offerings of fruits, vegetables, and whole grains. The new law will also improve access to school meals by allowing schools in low-income areas more options for serving free meals to all students without requiring parent applications, which could improve food security among children on reservations. USDA is one of the agencies sponsoring *Let's Move! In Indian Country*, a public/private initiative to provide technical assistance and social marketing materials to parents, schools, and communities in Indian Country to encourage healthy eating and physical activity.

I. INTRODUCTION

American Indians living on reservations or in other tribal areas (Indian Country) are among the most disadvantaged populations in the United States. The Healthy, Hunger-Free Kids Act of 2010 (HHFKA), section 141, requires the Department of Agriculture (USDA) to report to Congress on the ways that Federal nutrition programs can help overcome child hunger and nutrition problems on Indian reservations. To meet this requirement, this report addresses three questions:

1. What is the level of food insecurity, obesity, and Type II diabetes[1] among American Indian children living in Indian Country?[2]
2. What is the scope and reach of Federal nutrition programs in Indian Country?
3. How can the HHFKA improve food security and reduce obesity and diabetes risk among American Indian children living in Indian Country?

Before addressing these issues, we briefly describe the population of American Indians (AIs) as a whole and those living in Indian Country. We define AIs, in general, as those who report American Indian as their race in the U.S. Census or other national surveys and are not Alaska Natives (ANs).[3] In some instances, however, we report data on AIs and ANs together, as that is all that is available, and ANs are less than 10 percent of the combined group. Whenever not stated otherwise, we use those reporting AI or AN as their only race.

AI/ANs make up about 1 percent[4] of the total U.S. population (U.S. Census Bureau 2011d). Compared with the U.S. population as a whole, AI/ANs are a relatively young population, with approximately one-third younger than 20 years old (see Table I.1). Among those older than 25, 23 percent have less than a high school diploma, 31 percent have as their highest level of education a high school diploma or the equivalent, and 46 percent have some postsecondary education, compared with 14 percent, 29 percent, and 57 percent, respectively, in the U.S. population as a whole. AI/AN households are larger than those of the general U.S. population (3.01 versus 2.58 people per household) and have higher poverty rates. More than 24 percent of AI/AN households were below the Federal poverty line in 2010, compared with 15 percent of the U.S. population (the highest since 1993). Additionally, 24 percent of AI/AN households received Supplemental Nutrition Assistance Program (SNAP; formerly Food Stamp) benefits in 2010, whereas 13 percent of the U.S. population received SNAP benefits (Table I.1).

Most AI/ANs do not live in Indian Country. Of the population that identified as AI/AN alone in the 2010 census, 31 percent lived in Indian Country (U.S. Census Bureau 2010b). This is slightly less than in 2000 (see Figure I.1) (Ogunwole 2006). In 2010, for those who identified as American Indian and Alaska Native in combination with one or more other races, 7 percent lived in Indian Country.

As of the 2000 Census, there were differences in household composition and income between AI/ANs living in and outside of Indian Country (Ogunwole 2006; Table I.2). Cole (2002) reported large differences among Special Supplemental Nutrition Program for Women, Infants, and Children (WIC) enrollees with respect to family size, receipt of public assistance, and income.[5] For example, among AIs living in Indian Country, 24 percent had a family size of six or more, compared with 10 percent of AIs living off reservations. In addition, Cole (2002) notes higher rates of poverty among WIC participants on reservations than among those living off reservations, using 1998 data. Ogunwole (2006) corroborates these patterns for AI/ANs as a whole, noting larger family sizes and higher poverty levels in Indian Country (Table I.2).

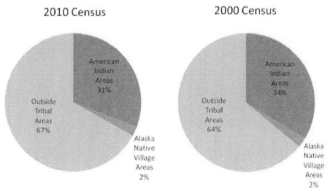

Sources: U.S. Census Bureau (2011 b) for 201 0 data; Ogunwole (2006) for 2000 data.

Figure I.1. Residence of AI/AN Population.

Table I.1. Characteristics of the American Indian and Alaska Native Population in the United States, 2010

	AI/AN Alone		Black or African American Alone		White Alone		Hispanic or Latino (All Races)		U.S. Total Population	
	N	%	N	%	N	%	N	%	N	%
Total Population[a]	2,932,248	100	38,929,319	100	223,553,265	100	50,477,594	100	308,745,538	100
Percentage of U.S. Population[a]		0.9		12.6		72.4		16.3		100
Population by Age[a]										
<5 years	244,615	8.3	2,902,590	7.5	12,795,675	5.7	5,114,488	10.1	20,201,362	6.5
5–9 years	243,259	8.3	2,882,597	7.4	13,293,799	5.9	4,790,771	9.5	20,348,657	6.6
10–14 years	245,049	8.4	3,034,266	7.8	13,737,332	6.1	4,525,242	9.0	20,677,194	6.7
15–19 years	263,805	9.0	3,448,051	8.9	14,620,638	6.5	4,532,155	9.0	22,040,343	7.1
≥ 20 years	1,935,520	66.0	28,088,003	72.2	169,105,821	75.6	31,514,938	62.4	225,477,982	73.1
Educational Attainment[b]										
Less than 9th grade	134,144	8.9	1,243,847	5.3	7,804,932	5.0	6,148,937	22.5	12,461,624	6.1
9th to 12th grade, no diploma	207,091	13.8	3,010,139	12.8	11,492,936	7.3	4,172,326	15.3	16,955,981	8.3
High school diploma or equivalent	461,653	30.7	7,458,620	31.7	45,587,413	29.0	7,224,578	26.5	58,222,345	28.5
Some college, no degree	384,512	25.5	5,852,043	24.9	33,715,436	21.4	4,708,625	17.2	43,513,542	21.3
Associate's degree	114,905	7.6	1,752,795	7.4	12,348,730	7.8	1,497,794	5.5	15,525,958	7.6
Bachelor's degree	133,579	8.9	2,747,713	11.7	29,268,752	18.6	2,431,354	8.9	36,159,141	17.7
Graduate degree	67,644	4.5	1,465,489	6.2	17,219,003	10.9	1,130,382	4.1	21,246,049	10.4
Number of Households[a]	939,707	32.0	14,129,983	36.3	89,754,352	40.1	13,461,366	26.7	116,716,292	37.8
Average Household Size[a]	3.01	NA	2.63	NA	2.46	NA	3.52	NA	2.58	NA
Population Below Poverty Level in Past 12 months[b]	701,213	28.4	10,099,631	27.1	27,951,752	12.5	12,306,535	24.8	46,215,956	15.3
Households with Income Below Poverty Level in Past 12 months[b]	132,017	23.7	2,030,834	23.3	5,112,925	8.7	2,300,703	22.2	8,598,062	11.3
Households Received Food Stamps/SNAP in the Past 12 Months[b]	197,932	24.3	3,587,600	26.1	8,295,458	9.3	2,741,108	20.7	14,535,659	12.7

Notes: Data presented are for American Indians and Alaska Natives (AI/ANs) alone (0.9 percent of U.S. population); the total population for AI/ANs in combination with one or more races is 5,220,579 (1.7 percent) (U.S. Census Bureau 201 1d). Among those in combination, a small percentage (7.3 percent) live in Indian Country (U.S. Census Bureau 201 1b). Among AI/ANs alone, 34 percent live in Indian Country. Similarly, data presented for Blacks or African Americans and whites are for those who identified as a single race. Educational attainment is for those 25 years and older. Household participation in SNAP as reported by FNS administrative data was considerably higher in FY 2010 (18,618,436); SNAP participation is underreported in surveys.

[a] U.S. Census Bureau 201 1d; data from U.S. Census 2010.

[b] U.S. Census Bureau 201 1a; data from American Community Survey 1-Year Estimates 2010.　　　　　NA = not applicable.

Table I.2. Characteristics of American Indians and Alaska Natives in 2000, Overall and in Indian Country

	American Indians and Alaska Natives Overall	American Indians in Indian Country[a]
	Percentage	Percentage
Percentage of U.S. Total Population	0.87	NR
Distribution of AI/ANs by Area of Residence	64.1[b]	33.5
Median Age	28.5	25.2
Educational Attainment		
Less than high school graduate	29.1	33.1
High school graduate	29.2	32.2
Some college or associate's degree	30.2	26.5
Bachelor's degree or more	11.5	8.1
Family Households	73.2[c]	78.5[c]
Average Household Size	3.06	3.35
Poverty Rate	25.7[d]	NR

Sources: Ogunwole 2006; data from U.S. Census 2000.

Notes: Data presented are for those reporting American Indian or Alaska Native race (AI/ANs) alone. The total population for AI/ANs alone was 2,447,989 (0.9 percent of the total U.S. population); the number of AI/ANs in combination with one or more races is 4,315, 865 (1.5 percent of the total U.S. population) (Ogunwole 2006). Educational attainment as reported is for those aged 25 years and older.

[a] *Indian Country* refers to American Indian areas that include American Indian reservations and/or off-reservation trust lands (Federal), Oklahoma tribal statistical areas, tribal designated statistical areas, American Indian reservations (State), and State-designated American Indian statistical areas.

[b] Percentage of AI/ANs residing outside tribal areas.

[c] Percentage of family households.

[d] Percentage of specified group in poverty determined for individuals under 15 years.

NR = not reported.

American Indians also have higher levels of health problems than other Americans. This report details the extent of hunger, obesity, and Type II diabetes among children in Indian Country and discusses the Federal nutrition assistance programs that serve them. We use the most recent available statistics and, when possible, include comparable statistics on other groups to frame the scope of the problem for this population. In addition, we briefly report on current Federal initiatives and potential positive impacts of implementation of HHFKA in Indian Country.

II. Hunger and Nutrition-Related Health Problems among American Indians

This chapter reviews the problems of food insecurity, overweight and obesity, and Type II diabetes among children in Indian Country.

Table II.1. Food Insecurity among American Indians and Alaska Natives

Data Source	Year(s)	Scale Used	Households	Low Food Security		Very Low Food Security		Total Food Insecure	
				AI/AN	Non-AI/AN	AI/AN	Non-AI/AN	AI/AN	Non-AI/AN
Current Population Survey[a]	2006–2008	House hold	All Households	NR		NR		23%	1 5%
Current Population Survey[b]	2001–2004	House hold	Households with Children	20.9%	11.9%	7.1%	3.8%	28.0%	15.7%
Current Population Survey[b]	2001–2004	Household	Households w/ Children: Income < 185% Poverty	30.0%	2 5.8%	11.7%	9.0%	41.7%	34.8%
Current Population Survey[b]	2001–2004	Child	Households with Children					29.7%	16.6%
Current Population Survey[b]	2001–2004	Child	Households w/Children: Income < 185% Poverty					43.1%	36.1%

Sources: Data from the Current Population Survey, 2006–2008, are from U.S. Census Bureau and Bureau of Labor Statistics 2008. Data from the Current Population Survey, 200 1–2004, are from Gundersen 2008.

Notes: Differences between populations were statistically significant. Sample sizes were not reported.

[a] Comparison group is all U.S. households. Data on AI/ANs is for AI/ANs *only*.

[b] In 2001–2002, the Current Population Survey measured race using a one-choice question; in 2003–2004 it measured race using a question that allowed multiple answers. In 2003–2004, all households reporting AI/AN as a race, including those who also selected other races, were included in Gundersen's analysis.

NR = not reported.

A. Food Insecurity

High levels of poverty and unemployment, low education levels, and the relative isolation of many reservations make American Indians particularly vulnerable to food insecurity, which is defined as uncertain or limited access to enough food for an active healthy life because of a lack of money or resources (Coleman-Jensen et al. 2011). Approximately 24 percent of American Indians in the United States live below the poverty line (U.S. Census Bureau 2011a) and in some reservations, such as the Pine Ridge Reservation in South Dakota, more than half of the people live in poverty (Institute of Medicine [IOM] 2011).

AI/AN-only households are much more likely than other households to be food insecure—the most recent available data (Current Population Survey [CPS] 2006–2008) indicated that 23 percent of AI/AN households (nearly one in four) were food insecure versus 15 percent of all U.S. households in 2008 (Table II.1).[6] An earlier study by Gundersen (2008), which pooled data from the 2001 to 2004 CPS, found that, among households with children, nearly twice as many AI/AN households were food insecure than among non-AI/AN households with children (28 versus 16 percent). However, when comparing households with incomes less than 185 percent of poverty, the disparity was less pronounced (42 versus 35 percent). Gundersen found there were similar disparities between AI/AN households with children and other households with children when assessing very low food security (the lowest level, involving some household members cutting the size of meals or skipping meals) or food insecurity among children (worry about food or lack of food for children in the household) (Table II.1).

Source: Food desert by Census tract: US Department of Agriculture, Economic Research Service http://www.usda.gov/wps/portal/usda/usdahome. Map was created at http://ims2.missouri.edu/tool/maps/default.aspx.

Note: Orange shading indicates food deserts; green shading indicates reservation borders; brown indicates overlap.

Figure II.1. Locations of Food Deserts and American Indian Reservations in the Contiguous United States.

In Indian Country, access to food can be a challenge. Many reservations have significant food deserts, which are defined as low-income communities without ready access to healthy and affordable food (Ver Ploeg et al. 2009). Isolated settlements create logistical and cost challenges, limiting people's ability to access affordable nutritious food because they live far from a large grocery store and do not have easy access to transportation (see Figure II. 1). However, data on food insecurity specific to American Indians living in Indian Country are not currently available. Gundersen (2008), in his multivariate analysis of factors affecting food insecurity using the 2001–2004 CPS supplements, found that American Indian households with children in rural areas (as a proxy for locations in Indian Country) were no more likely to be food insecure than those in metropolitan areas. However, rural residence was positively associated with food insecurity for American Indian households without children. In addition, American Indians had significantly higher levels of food insecurity than the rest of the population, even after controlling for a wide range of demographic and socioeconomic characteristics.

Table II.2. Prevalence of Obesity among American Indians and Alaska Natives in the United States

Data Source	Year	Living in Indian Country	Age Range	Total AI/ANs in sample	BMI ≥ 85th Percentile	BMI 85th to < 95th Percentile	BMI ≥ 95th Percentile
					%	%	%
WIC Participant Characteristics[a]	1998	X	2 years	9,742			21.4
WIC Participant Characteristics[a]	1998	X	3 years	9,114			15.9
WIC Participant Characteristics[a]	1998	X	4 years	7,236			14.1
WIC Participant Characteristics[b]	2008		2–5 years	419,919	35.4		17.6
Indian Health Service Clinical Reporting System[c]	2008	X	2–5 years	NR	45.0		25.0
Pediatric Nutrition Surveillance System[d]	2010		2–5 years	35,604		20.1	21.1
Early Childhood Longitudinal Program, Birth Cohort[e]	2005		4 years	650			31.2
Indian Health Service Clinical Reporting System[c]	2008	X	6–11 years	NR	49.0		31.0
Indian Health Service Clinical Reporting System[c]	2008	X	12–19 years	NR	51.0		31.0
National Health Interview Survey[f]	2009		≥ 18 years	1,856		34.0	32.5

Notes: Percentages from the National Health Interview Survey are BMI for overweight (34.0%) and obese (32.5%) adults, which are defined by specific cutoffs, not percentiles.

[a] Cole 2002; data from WIC Participant Characteristics Data 1998.

[b] Conner et al. 2002; data from WIC Participant Characteristics Data 2008.

[c] Strauss 2010; data from Indian Health Service Clinical Reporting System 2008.

[d] CDC 2010b; data from Pediatric Nutrition Surveillance System 2010.

[e] Anderson and Whitaker 2009; data from Early Childhood Longitudinal Program, Birth Cohort 2005.

[f] Pleis, Disraeli, and McGregor 2010; data from National Health Interview Survey 2009.

BMI = body mass index; NR = not reported; WIC = Special Supplemental Nutrition Program for Women, Infants, and Children.

B. Overweight and Obesity

1. Overweight and Obesity among AI/ANs Nationally

The increasing prevalence of overweight and obesity among children in the United States is well documented (Anderson and Whitaker 2009; Centers for Disease Control and Prevention 2009; Wang and Beydoun 2007). Overweight and obesity have also increased dramatically among AI/AN children. Strauss (2010) reports an 11.5 percent increase in prevalence of overweight from 1999 to 2008 (from 36.4 percent in 1999 to 40.6 percent in 2008) among AI/AN 0- to 5-year-olds surveyed in the Pediatric Nutrition Surveillance System (PedNSS). Strauss also reports a 17.4 percent increase in obesity among this sample. Current estimates suggest that overweight and obesity affects one-third to one-half of AI/AN children (Table II.2).

Nationally representative data on AI/AN children in Indian Country are limited. Existing infrastructure that collects and aggregates body mass index (BMI) data primarily includes the Indian Health Services' (IHS) Clinical Reporting System, the PedNSS, and the WIC program. However, age-specific obesity prevalence rates are not available from the IHS, which is the only source specific to those living on or near reservations. PedNSS and WIC data include only or mostly low-income families. Anderson and Whitaker (2009) present nationally representative data on AI/AN children from the Early Childhood Longitudinal Study, Birth Cohort, but their data are only for 4-year-olds.

Although the precise developmental period for overweight and obesity is not clear, obesity in AI/AN children typically begins in early childhood (Thomas and Cook 2005), with disparities between AI/ANs and other races/ethnicities established by adolescence (Gordon-Larsen et al. 2003). This is consistent with obesity prevalence as reported in the 2010 PedNSS, a surveillance system that monitors low-income infants, children, and women. Approximately 20 percent of AI/AN children sampled were overweight, and an additional 21 percent were obese. In comparison, 16 percent of the total PedNSS population were overweight and another 14 percent were obese. Similar prevalence rates were reported among another low-income AI/AN population, WIC participants, in a study by Cole (2002) that compared the characteristics of American Indian WIC participants in and out of Indian Country. In this sample, American Indians living in Indian Country were considerably more obese than those not living in Indian Country. Among WIC children living in Indian Country, 21.4 percent of 2-year-olds; 15.9 percent of 3-year-olds; and 14.1 percent of 4-year-olds were obese. Comparatively, obesity was less prevalent for AI/AN children not living in Indian Country; 16.2 percent of 2-year-olds; 11.6 percent of 3-year-olds; and 10.0 percent of 4-year-olds were obese.

More recent data (2008) estimate that 20 percent of AI/AN children 2 to 4 years old participating in WIC are obese (Harper 2011). For those AI/AN children (aged 2 to 4 years) living in areas served by Indian Tribal Organizations (ITOs), obesity prevalence increases to 22 percent (Harper 2011). Prevalence of obesity among AI/AN children aged 12 to 19 years was at least 30 percent in 2008 (Strauss 2010).

Although AI/ANs are not a homogeneous group, obesity rates among specific tribes are similar, regardless of ancestry. Among children of all ages, obesity prevalence was at least 20 percent for the various tribal areas covered in special studies (Table II.3).

Table II.3. Prevalence of Obesity among American Indians in Specific Tribal Areas

Data Source	Year(s)	Tribal Area	Age Range	Total AI/ANS in Sample	BMI ≥ 85th Percentile %	BMI 85 to < 95th Percentile %	BMI ≥ 95th Percentile %
Pediatric Nutrition Surveillance System[a]	2009	Cheyenne River Sioux (SD)	2–4 years	NR			15–20
Pediatric Nutrition Surveillance System[a]	2009	Intertribal Council of Arizona	2–4 years	NR			> 20
Pediatric Nutrition Surveillance System[a]	2009	Navajo Nation (AZ, NM, UT)	2–4 years	NR			15–20
Pediatric Nutrition Surveillance System[a]	2009	Rosebud Sioux (SD)	2–4 years	NR			> 20
Pediatric Nutrition Surveillance System[a]	2009	Standing Rock Sioux (ND)	2–4 years	NR			> 20
Pediatric Nutrition Surveillance System[a]	2009	Three Affiliated Tribes (ND)	2–4 years	NR			> 20
Pathways Study[b]	1997–2000	White Mountain Apache, San Carlos Apache, Navajo, Sicangu Lakota, Oglala Lakota, Tohono O'od ham, Gila River Indian Community	7.6 years	1,704	48.9		28.6
Gila River Indian Survey[c]	2003	Gila River Indian Community (AZ): Pima and Tohono O'odham Indians	11.3 years	4,857			28.7

Notes: The Gila River Indian survey was a longitudinal study.

[a] CDC 2009; data from Pediatric Nutrition Surveillance System 2009.

[b] Caballero et al. 2003; data from Pathways Study 1997–2000.

[c] Franks et al. 2010; data from Gila River Indian Survey 2003.

BMI = body mass index; NR = not reported.

Table II.4. Prevalence of Diabetes among American Indians and Alaska Natives in the United States

Data Source	Year(s)	Living in Indian Country	Age Range	Type of Diabetes	Total AI/ANs in Sample	Prevalence per 1,000
SEARCH for Diabetes Youth Study[a]	2001		0–9 years	Type II	66,6 1 7	0.03
SEARCH for Diabetes Youth Study[a]	2001		10–19 years	Type II	72,387	1.74
Indian Health Service Clinical Reporting System[b]	1998	X	< 15 years	NS	7,736	1 .23
Indian Health Service Clinical Reporting System[c]	2004	X	< 15 years	NS	NR	2.2
Indian Health Service Clinical Reporting System[b]	1998	X	15–19 years	NS	7,736	5.42
Indian Health Service Clinical Reporting System[c]	2004	X	15–19 years	NS	NR	7.4
Behavioral Risk Factor Surveillance Survey[d]	2007		18–34 years	NS	1 ,320	28.0
National Health Interview Survey[e]	2008		≥ 18 years	NS	1,856	93.8

Notes: Prevalence reported for the SEARCH study was American Indians only. Type of diabetes refers to Type I and Type II diabetes; Type I diabetes is insulin-dependent diabetes and typically begins in childhood, and Type II diabetes is noninsulin-dependent diabetes (American Diabetes Association 2000).

a SEARCH for Diabetes in Youth Study Group 2006; data from SEARCH Survey 2001.

b Acton et al. 2002; data from Indian Health Service Clinical Reporting System (outpatient) data 1998.

c Acton et al. 2006; data from Indian Health Service Clinical Reporting System (ambulatory patient-care) data, 1994–2004.

d Roberts et al. 2009; data from Behavioral Risk Factor Surveillance Survey 2007.

e Pleis, Ward, and Lucas 2010; data from National Health Interview Survey 2008.

NR = not reported; NS = not specified.

2. Factors Associated with Overweight and Obesity

The determinants of overweight and obesity in the United States are complex, but the trend of increasing overweight and obesity among American Indians and Alaska Natives, as well as the Nation at large, is associated with environments that promote increased food intake and decreased activity (Strauss 2010; Halpern 2007). Historically, the AI/AN diet was higher in complex carbohydrates and lower in fat than current diets and primarily made up of homegrown foods (Halpern 2007). However, there has been a shift in Indian Country, whereby American Indians are eating less traditional food and more food that is commercially prepared and processed, a trend also reported among the U.S. population as a whole. This dietary shift was summarized in a review of reservation-based studies by Story and colleagues

(2003) who reported that in the 1 990s, dietary fat intake among American Indians was at the high end of or above the currently recommended 25 to 35 percent of total calories, ranging from 31 to 47 percent. AI/ANs have also shifted from a subsistence lifestyle to a lifestyle that involves less physical activity (Mendlein et al. 1997). Research has found low physical activity levels among those AI/ANs living on or near reservations (Mendlein et al. 1997; Yurgalevitch et al. 1998).

Socioeconomic factors may also play a role in the development of childhood obesity among AI/ANs. While the circumstances of each tribe are unique, most AI/ANs have experienced severe economic and housing problems (Hillabrant et al. 2001). Unemployment and poverty have been at high levels in the majority of American Indian communities. Kumanyika and Grier (2006) suggest that higher rates of obesity among AI/ANs may result from socioeconomic influences such as reduced access to space for physical activity and targeted advertising and marketing of energy-dense foods. In addition, lack of access to stores with a variety of healthy food options may contribute to obesity as well as food insecurity (IOM 2011; Zenk et al. 2005). Likewise, the higher cost of nutrient-dense foods may be associated with higher rates of obesity among AI/ANs (Richards and Patterson 2006).

C. Type II Diabetes

1. Type II Diabetes among American Indians and Alaska Natives Nationally

As with overweight and obesity, AI/ANs are disproportionately affected by diabetes, with some estimates suggesting that AI/ANs are 2.3 times more likely to have diabetes than are individuals in the U.S. general population (Acton et al. 2003; Indian Health Service 2009). Furthermore, approximately 16.5 percent of the total AI/AN adult population served by the IHS have been diagnosed with diabetes, which is twice the diagnosed rate among non-Hispanic whites in the United States (Harper et al. 2008). Although Type II diabetes has traditionally been a health concern among adults, its prevalence among children has increased in the American Indian community, a finding consistent with increases in obesity (Ríos Burrows 1998). The SEARCH study sought to assess the diabetes burden among U.S. children less than 20 years of age; this population-based observational study of physician diagnosed diabetes collected data from six centers (in CA, CO, HI, OH, SC, and WA) and estimated the prevalence of Type II diabetes to be 0.03 per 1,000 among AI children aged 0–9 years. Comparatively, prevalence of Type II diabetes among all groups surveyed (aged 0–9 years) was 0.01 per 1,000. Among AI children aged 10–19 years, prevalence of Type II diabetes was 1.74 per 1,000, whereas the prevalence among all groups surveyed was notably lower (see Figure II.2). For Type I and Type II diabetes, prevalence was 0.23 per 1,000 among AI children aged 0–9 years and 2.28 per 1,000 among AI children aged 10–19 years. Analogous to obesity, diabetes prevalence among children may be higher among adolescents and those living on or near reservations, as described in Table II.4.

2. Type II Diabetes among AI/ANs from Specific Tribal Areas

There is convincing evidence that prevalence of Type II diabetes among Pima Indians is higher than among other AI tribes (Knowler et al. 1990; Savage et al. 1979)—it is the highest recorded prevalence of diabetes worldwide (Knowler et al. 1978). In one study, prevalence among Pima Indians was 22.3 per 1,000 for 10- to 14-year-olds and 50.9 per 1,000 for 15- to 19-year-olds (Dabelea et al. 1998). Dabelea and colleagues (1998) reported that this was a large increase from when this population was first surveyed from 1967 to 1976. Because of these historical data, this study is a more reliable indicator of increasing prevalence than can be obtained in cross-sectional data.

Although reported prevalence is lower among other tribes, Moore and colleagues (2003) reported results (consistent with the national trend) that Type II diabetes is more prevalent than Type I diabetes among AI/AN youth. More specifically, Moore and colleagues (2003) found that the prevalence of Type II diabetes was nearly two times higher than Type I diabetes among American Indian youth in Montana and Wyoming. As detailed in Table II.5, diabetes prevalence varies widely across tribal areas.

3. Factors Associated with Diabetes

Diabetes imposes increased health risks among AI/AN youth, such as accelerated development of cardiovascular diseases, renal disease, and loss of visual acuity, all of which contribute to excess morbidity and mortality (Story et al. 2003). Akin to obesity, the increasing prevalence has been attributed to lifestyle changes in diet and physical activity (Weir and Lipscombe 2004). Among youth with Type II diabetes, an estimated 50 to 90 percent have a BMI ≥ 85th percentile for age (American Diabetes Association 2000). Among the SEARCH study sample, the prevalence of obesity among AI youth with Type II diabetes was 79.4 percent. Obesity prevalence was only 12.5 percent among youth with Type I diabetes (Liu et al. 2010). Other risk factors for Type II diabetes include family history, hypertension, and dyslipidemia[7] (Rao, Disraeli, and McGregor 2004).

Exposure to diabetes in utero and low birthweight increase risk in AI/AN children (Dabelea et al. 1998). As in the population overall, AI/AN children with Type II diabetes are more likely to be adolescents (i.e., 10–19 years) and female (Fagot-Campagna and Ríos Burrows 1999; Harwell et al. 2001; Moore et al. 2003).

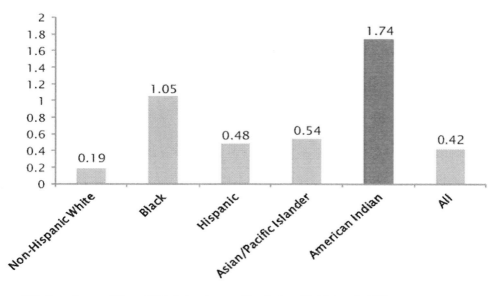

Figure II.2. Prevalence of Type II Diabetes Among Youth Age 10-19 (per 1,000).

Table II.5. Prevalence of Diabetes among American Indians in Specific Tribal Areas

Data Source	Year(s)	Tribal Area	Age Range	Type of Diabetes	Total AI/ANs in Sample	Prevalence per 1,000
SEARCH Navajo Youth[a]	2001	Included these IHS units: Chinle, Crownpoint, Fort Defiance, Gallup, Kayenta, Shiprock, Tuba City, Winslow	0–9 years	Both	47,553	0.11
Indian Health Service and MDPHHS[b]	1999–2001	Billings Area: Montana & Wyoming	5–9 years	Type 2	6,283	4.0
SEARCH Navajo Youth[a]	2001	Included these IHS units: Chinle, Crownpoint, Fort Defiance, Gallup, Kayenta, Shiprock, Tuba City, Winslow	10–14 years	Both	27,107	0.81
Gila River Indian Study[c]	1987–1996	Gila River Indian Community (AZ): Pima and Tohono O'odham Indians	10–14 years	Type 2	672	22.3
Indian Health Service[b]	1999–2001	Billings Area: Montana & Wyoming	10–14 years	Type 2	6,002	21.0
SEARCH Navajo Youth[a]	2001	Included these IHS units: Chinle, Crownpoint, Fort Defiance, Gallup, Kayenta, Shiprock, Tuba City, Winslow	15–19 years	Both	23,354	2.78
Gila River Indian Community Study[c]	1987–1996	Gila River Indian Community (AZ): Pima and Tohono O'odham Indians	15–19 years	Type 2	530	50.9
Indian Health Service and MDPPHS[b]	1999–2001	Billings Area: Montana & Wyoming	15–19 years	Type 2	5,135	4.3
Behavioral Risk Factor Surveillance Survey[d]	2004	North Dakota Tribal Communities	≥18 years	NS	404	13.8
Indian Health Service Clinical Reporting System[e]	1998	Northern Plains: IO, MT, NE, ND, SD, WY	<35 years	NS	NR	13.72
Indian Health Service Clinical Reporting System[e]	1998	Southeast: MS, NC	<35 years	NS	NR	34.93
Indian Health Service Clinical Reporting System[e]	1998	Southwest: AZ, CO, NV, NM, UT	<35 years	NS	NR	11.84
Indian Health Service Patient Management System[f]	2005	Phoenix Service Unit	18–64 years	Both	30,121	92.7

Notes: Type of Diabetes refers to Type I and Type II diabetes; Type I diabetes is insulin–dependent diabetes and typically begins in childhood, and Type II diabetes is non–insulin–dependent diabetes (American Diabetes Association 2000).

[a] Dabelea et al. 2009; data from SEARCH Survey 2001.

[b] Moore et al. 2003; data from Indian Health Service and Montana Department of Public Health and Human Services Surveillance 1999–2001.

[c] Dabelea et al. 1998; data from Gila River Indian Community Study 1987–1996.

[d] Holm et al. 2010; data from Behavioral Risk Factor Surveillance Survey 2004.

[e] Acton et al. 2002; data from Indian Health Service Clinical Reporting System (outpatient) data 1998.

[f] O'Connell et al. 2010; data from Indian Health Service Resource Patient Management System 2005.

IHS = Indian Health Service; MDPHHS = Montana Department of Public Health and Human Services; NR = not reported; NS = not specified.

III. FEDERAL FOOD ASSISTANCE PROGRAMS SERVING AMERICAN INDIAN CHILDREN IN INDIAN COUNTRY

A. Overview

FNS has a long history of providing low-income children and families better access to food through its food assistance programs and related nutrition education efforts. In the last decade, FNS food assistance programs have focused on both increasing participation among eligible families and updating program benefits and services to reflect advances in nutritional science as well as the increasing epidemic of childhood obesity.

Given their high levels of poverty, many American Indians/Alaskan Natives (AI/ANs) living in Indian Country are eligible to participate in FNS programs. To reach this population, FNS works in partnership with Indian Tribal Organizations (ITOs) and State agencies to provide funding to cover the food benefits and administrative costs for AI/ANs that reside in Indian Country. This chapter reviews the major FNS programs that serve AI/AN families with children in Indian Country.[8] Four major programs are the core of the food safety net—the Food Distribution Program on Indian Reservations (FDPIR), SNAP, WIC, and the National School Lunch Program (NSLP). They comprise an important part of the Federal government's efforts to alleviate food insecurity, obesity, and risk for Type II diabetes and its complications among children in Indian County. This chapter describes participation by AI/ANs and benefits and services offered by these four key programs and briefly summarizes information on other child nutrition programs.

B. Food Distribution Program on Indian Reservations

FDPIR provides USDA foods to low-income AI/AN households living on or near Indian reservations as an alternative to SNAP, because SNAP offices or authorized food stores are sometimes not easily accessible to such households. In 2011, members of 276 tribes receive benefits under the FDPIR through 100 ITOs and five State agencies. The USDA purchases and ships FDPIR foods to the ITOs and State agencies. These agencies then arrange their distribution to eligible households. Households are certified based on income and resource standards set by the Federal government, and must be recertified at least every 12 months, with the exception of elderly and disabled households, which may be certified for up to 24 months. Although households may not participate in FDPIR and SNAP in the same month, FDPIR households are often eligible to participate in other food assistance programs such as WIC or the NSLP (Harper et al. 2008). The size of FDPIR programs varies; approximately half of local FDPIR programs serve fewer than 250 households per month, with nearly all of the remaining programs serving between 250 and 1,200 households per month. Five programs serve more than 1,200 households per month.

In 2011, FDPIR had an estimated 77,641 participants (Table III.1). Participation was lower than in the previous two years, perhaps reflecting changes in SNAP program benefits implemented in 2009 (and discussed below). Usher et al. (1990) reported that over half of the FDPIR participating households contained children. Most households were headed by two parents. Nearly 10 percent of participating households did not have any income, with 33 percent of households reporting a gross income of no more than 50 percent of the poverty level. This population also heavily relied on home food production and other FNS programs to meet their dietary needs. In the 1990 study, 70 percent of households participated in the NSLP, 44 percent in the School Breakfast Program (SBP), and 17 percent in the WIC program. Although this information is quite dated, it indicates the program has historically served a very disadvantaged population.[9]

USDA has improved the nutritional quality of foods delivered through FDPIR in the last decade (Harper et al. 2008). Consistent with the Dietary Guidelines for Americans, 2010, the program focuses on reducing added sugars, sodium, and fat. The FDPIR food package now offers leaner meat, more fresh fruits and vegetables, whole grain foods, and low-fat milk. It no longer offers items such as butter that are high in saturated fat. On average, the FDPIR food package meets many of the nutritional needs of participating household members. As delivered, the food package provides protein, total fat, essential fatty acids, and carbohydrates at levels that fall within acceptable ranges under the Dietary Reference Intakes. Individuals consuming only the FDPIR foods in the quantities provided would achieve a Healthy Eating Index 2005 score of 81 out of 100. In comparison, the general U.S. population has an estimated score of 58 (Harper et al. 2008).[10]

Table III.1. Characteristics of Federal Food Assistance Programs

	FDPIR[a,]	SNAP	WIC	NSLP
Average Participation by Individuals				
FY 2011[b]	77,641	44,570,892	8,951,459	31,806,334
FY 2010	84,577	40,301,878	9,175,020	31,746,677
FY 2009	95,369	33,489,975	9,121,779	31,311,514
FY 2008	90,153	28,222,630	8,704,510	31,015,756
Average Participation for Individual American Indians or Alaska Natives Only (2008)	35,356	541,246	126,184	549,577
Average Participation for Individuals Reporting Two Races: White and American Indian or Alaska Native (2008)[c]	623	262,069	84,730	328,263
Average Cost of Benefit Per Person (2008)	$55.38[d]	$102.19	$43.41	NA

Sources: USDA, FNS 2011b; data from FNS Program Administrative data 2008–2011; for average participation by individuals and average cost of benefit per person. Trippe and Schechter 2010; data from Current Population Survey 2009; for average participation for individual American Indians or Alaska Natives only (2008) and average participation for individuals reporting two races: white and American Indian or Alaska Native (2008).

Notes: All participation rates are "per month" averages, except for the NSLP which are "per day." FDPIR specifically targets households living on Indian reservations and American Indian households residing in approved areas near reservations or in Oklahoma.

[a] FDPIR average participation based on National Databank data.

[b] Fiscal Year 2011 data exclude September 2011 data, thus average is for 11 months (October 2010 through August 2011).

[c] Participation for American Indians and Alaska Natives in 2008 is from the March 2009 Current Population Survey.

[d] FDPIR Average Cost of Benefit Per Month (2008) based on FY 2010 Budget Explanatory Notes. The total monthly food package cost does not reflect retail value of the average monthly food package. For FY 2009, the food package had retail value estimated at $78.44 per month (USDA FNS 2011b).

NA = not applicable; NR = not reported.

C. Supplemental Nutrition Assistance Program

SNAP is a cornerstone of the Nation's safety net. Eligible participants have a gross income of 130 percent of poverty or less. After various deductions for items such as shelter and countable resources, net income must be no more than 100 percent of poverty. Typically, able-bodied adults without dependents between 18 and 50 years of age can get SNAP benefits only for 3 months in a 36-month period if they do not work, search for work, or participate in a workfare or employment and training program.

As the largest food assistance program in the United States, SNAP has played a critical role in feeding the U.S. population during the recession. In FY 2011, SNAP served approximately 44.5 million participants per month. AI/ANs in 2008 accounted for nearly 2 percent of all participants in the program and received an estimated $55 million in benefits, making SNAP the largest nutrition program for AI/ANs (Table III.1). Based on data from the March 2009 CPS, about 541,000 SNAP participants reported being AI/AN only and an additional 262,000 SNAP participants reported being AI/AN and another race (Trippe and Schechter 2010; Table III.1).

D. Special Supplemental Nutrition Program for Women, Infants, and Children

The Special Supplemental Nutrition Program for Women, Infants, and Children (WIC) provides a variety of services to promote the health and nutrition of low-income pregnant, breastfeeding, and nonbreastfeeding postpartum women; infants from birth to age 1; and children from 1 to 5 who are at risk for nutritional deficiencies. WIC provides supplemental food packages that are targeted to meet their special nutritional needs and nutrition services, which include nutrition education, breastfeeding promotion and support, and referrals to health care providers. WIC participants receive supplemental food in the form of vouchers (paper food instruments or electronic benefit transfer cards) that allow them to obtain specific types of food at authorized stores. WIC participants receive a "prescription" for foods that meet the unique nutritional requirements for women (pregnant, breastfeeding, and postpartum), infants, and children.

Since 2008, WIC has had approximately 9 million participants nationally (Table III.1), among whom were 126,000 reporting their race as AI/AN alone and 85,000 AI/ANs who also said they were white (Table III.1). WIC PC 2008 indicates that as of April 2008, approximatly 44,000 AI/AN participants received services from WIC programs operated by ITOs as State agencies. Furthermore, 24,461 American Indians enrolled in WIC were children served by ITO WIC agencies.[11] FNS administrative data for FY 2011 indicate that on average, 1,813 AI/AN participants participated per month in each ITO WIC agency, with enrollment at the 34 ITO State agencies ranging from 90 to 11,998 (Table III.2).

In order to address concerns about childhood obesity and advances in nutritional science, WIC food packages were updated in 2009 to offer more nutrient-dense foods on the basis of recommendations from an Institute of Medicine panel (IOM 2005). The new food packages are aligned more closely with current nutrition science and infant feeding guidelines of the American Academy of Pediatrics. These new food packages provide participants with a variety of foods and notably include fruits and vegetables and whole grains. WIC State agencies and ITOs also have more flexibility to prescribe food packages to accommodate the cultural food preferences of participants. For example, soft corn or whole wheat tortillas are now an allowable option in place of whole wheat bread. In addition, the new packages provide improved incentives for the establishment of successful, long-term breastfeeding by varying the packages among women who are fully formula feeding their infants as compared to those who are partially or fully breastfeeding.

Since 2004, State and ITO WIC programs have received Federal grants for peer-counseling programs to promote breastfeeding; in 2010, funding for peer-counseling programs increased from $15 million to $50 million per year. Peer counselors are experienced mothers who have breastfed and who are trained, supervised, and compensated according to FNS guidelines. Peer counselors talk by telephone or meet with WIC mothers who are breastfeeding and seek support or help with breastfeeding questions or concerns (Collins et al. 2010). All of the State and ITO WIC agencies have received peer counseling funding.

E. Child Nutrition Programs

Most schools on reservations participate in the NSLP, including Bureau of Indian Education schools and local schools; the SBP may be less available. Finegold et al. (2005) reported that an issue with SBP is that long bus rides do not always leave time for schools to serve breakfast to students before classes start. Participation in the Child and Adult Care Food Program (CACFP) appears to be largely among Head Start Centers, which are required to offer the program, but some Boys & Girls Clubs or recreation programs also offer it, based on sponsor lists from selected States in the West, Southwest, and Mountain/Plains regions with large reservations. The Summer Food Service Program, which provides free meals to children in low-income areas in the summer, also is available on reservations in several of these States, most frequently at school sites.

One way in which access to meals is facilitated for Indian children is that children whose families receive FDPIR, SNAP, or TANF benefits are categorically eligible for free meals at schools and at day care centers and homes participating in NSLP and CACFP, respectively, without the need to provide income information. Both the NSLP and CACFP also provide reimbursement for after-school snacks and CACFP now provides reimbursement in all States for a full afterschool meal, most often supper. However, there are little data to indicate how frequently these benefits or the Fresh Fruit and Vegetable Program are offered in Indian Country.

IV. OPPORTUNITIES FOR IMPROVED SERVICES UNDER THE HEALTHY, HUNGER-FREE KIDS ACT AND RELATED INITIATIVES

Recent policy changes and initiatives in the Federal nutrition assistance programs have focused on healthier meal options, easier access for those in need, and support for broader lifestyle interventions at the family, school, or community level to reduce or prevent food insecurity, obesity, Type II diabetes, and associated long-term health problems. USDA is in the process of implementing the changes included in HHFKA. These changes have the potential for enhancing the ability of USDA nutrition programs to serve children and their families in Indian Country. USDA also participates in comprehensive, cross-agency collaborations to prevent or reduce child obesity, most notably First Lady Michelle Obama's *Let's Move! in Indian Country*, which was introduced in May 2011 as part of the larger national *Let's Move!* initiative.[12] This chapter reviews the potential for positive changes from provisions of HHFKA and from the *Let's Move!* program.

A. Healthier Meal Options

HHFKA requires implementation of revised meal patterns for NSLP and SBP meals and requires regular updating of CACFP meal patterns as well. FNS policy is to make meals served in both programs consistent with the most recent Dietary Guidelines for Americans. A proposed rule has been published with new standards and meal patterns for NSLP and SBP meals (Federal Register January 13, 2011); the law also calls for proposed rules for CACFP meal patterns to be issued within 18 months of passage. These meal patterns will make school meals and CACFP meals healthier and thus may help mitigate obesity and diabetes risk among AI children living on reservations. School districts that comply with the new school meal regulations are eligible for higher reimbursement rates from USDA (six cents per meal) beginning in fall 2012. HHFKA also requires schools and day care providers to serve only fat-free (skim) and low-fat (1 percent) milk and requires that children have access to potable water.

Table III.2. American Indians and Alaska Natives Participating in WIC Programs Sponsored by Indian Tribal Organizations

	FY 2010			FY 2011		
	Average	Range	Median	Average	Range	Median
Average Monthly Participation	1,847	90–11,998	647	1,813	75–11,939	643
Average Participation of Women	384	13–2,496	135	400	15–2,580	133
Average Participation of Children (Age 1–4)	1,037	46–6,951	372	1,102	47–6,909	379
Average Participation of Infants	426	1 6–2,658	141	418	14–2,478	137
Average Monthly Food Cost Per Person (All Categories)	$46.34	$32.96–$74.91	$42.50	$47.90	$34.69–S71.45	$44.03

Source: USDA, Food and Nutrition Service 2011b; Monthly Participation Data, FY 2010–2011.

Note: Ranges indicate the range in the caseloads across ITOs. Averages are across all months in FY 2010, 11 months in FY 2011. Averages are unweighted and are based on the 34 ITOs that administer WIC as State agencies. Per-person cost estimates are total dollars divided by number of participants.

B. Increased Access to Food Assistance

Several provisions of the HHFKA have the potential to increase access to school meals and other food assistance programs for American Indian children in Indian Country. Schools in high-poverty areas will have new ways to qualify for universal free school meals, including community eligibility (in which schools with over 40 percent of students directly certified can offer all meals free, and claim free meals based on the number of directly certified students times 1.6). In addition, the law says USDA may pilot or implement use of the American Community Survey poverty data rather than school meal applications as a way to establish eligibility for universal free school meals. USDA has also been expanding direct certification for school meals (based on matching student lists with records of other assistance programs, including SNAP and FDPIR) without parents needing to complete an application. The HHFKA includes bonuses as incentives for States with high direct certification rates, and a phaseout of the letter method of direct certification, which required parents to sign and return a letter indicating their child was eligible for free meals. Parents who do still need to apply for free or reduced-price meals can no longer be required to provide their Social Security number, just the last four digits. All of these provisions make access to the school meal programs easier.

Previously, after-school programs in 14 States could be reimbursed through CACFP for serving after-school meals to at-risk children. HHFKA extended this option to programs in all States. To be eligible, these programs must be located in low-income areas, offer after-school enrichment or educational activities (other than team sports), and provide snacks and/or meals free to all participants.

C. Let's Move! in Indian Country

Although not specifically part of HHFKA, *Let's Move!* is a public/private initiative led by First Lady Michelle Obama, with the goal of ending the epidemic of child obesity in a generation. USDA is one of the Federal agencies sponsoring *Let's Move!* The program is intended to improve coordination at the levels of the family, the school (or child care center), and the community in making changes in eating and physical fitness behaviors, particularly among children. *Let's Move! in Indian Country* (started in May 2011) is targeting American Indians in Indian Country. The Web site (noted above) has social marketing and technical assistance materials. Some materials have been tailored for American Indians, while others are for a general audience. One emphasis in the materials is on expanding access to Federal food programs on reservations; for example, the site urges parents to work with schools to establish the SBP if it is not already offered and to participate in the HealthierUS School Challenge, a USDA program that supports and recognizes schools that achieve standards for healthy school meals and a healthy school environment (Department of the Interior 2011).

APPENDIX A. DEFINING THE TARGET POPULATION

Because American Indians are a small proportion (less than 2 percent) of the Nation's population, detailed data on the characteristics of American Indians are largely derived from the decennial Census or from combining several years of the American Community Survey (a continuing survey that replaced the Census long form). In 2000, the Census began allowing respondents to report multiple races, which led to a large jump in the numbers reporting themselves as American Indians or Alaska Natives. In Census 2010, 44 percent of those who checked they were AI/AN also checked another race, most often white (U.S Census Bureau 2011b). The Current Population Survey, a national survey of the demographic and labor force characteristics of U.S. households, began to allow multiple race responses in 2003 (Gundersen 2008); again, race data from before and after this change are not comparable.

Administrative data sources on American Indians use other approaches. The IHS eligible population includes all persons living on reservations and those living nearby who can document they are members of a recognized tribe. The IHS, a Federal agency, maintains a database of all those who use its services and publishes selected aggregate statistics from these data; it provides the data as well to academic programs focused on American Indians for research purposes, but, for privacy reasons, does not make public-use versions available.

The Special Supplemental Nutrition Program for Women, Infants, and Children Participant Characteristics Study (WIC PC), sponsored by USDA's Food and Nutrition Service, collects administrative data on a census of all WIC participants every two years. WIC's target population includes low-income pregnant women, postpartum mothers (breastfeeding mothers for up to a year after birth; nonbreastfeeding mothers for up to six months), and children younger than 5 years old. Nonetheless, it provides a large body of information on disadvantaged Indian families both on and off reservations (Cole 2002).

The WIC PC system switched from a combined race/ethnicity variable to one that asked separate race and ethnicity questions for WIC PC 2006. To implement this change, Hispanic participants had to indicate a race for the first time; large numbers were coded as AI/AN, particularly in California, leading to a major jump in the number of AI/AN WIC participants in WIC PC data (Conner et al. 2010).

Although section 141 of the HHFKA, in calling for this report, referred to American Indians "on reservations," we use a slightly broader group in this report—those in "Indian Country." As specified in law (U.S. Code, Title 18, Part 1, Chapter 53, Section 1151, for example), the term *Indian Country* refers to reservations and other tribal lands; this is what the Census Bureau refers to as "American Indian areas." American Indian areas include American Indian reservations and/or off-reservation trust lands (Federal), Oklahoma tribal statistical areas, tribal designated statistical areas, American Indian reservations (State), and State-designated American Indian statistical areas. We use the term *Indian Country* for American Indian areas in this report.

There are two data sources where the populations considered are "on or near reservations," which are slightly different than the definition of Indian Country just described. The first is the IHS's data on enrolled participants, described above. The second is the Cole (2002) study of American Indian WIC Participants "on or near reservations." Cole (2002), in her study of WIC participants on and off reservations, mapped the distance between the local WIC agency serving each participant and the nearest reservation, and defined "on or near reservations" as WIC participants served by WIC local agencies that included all or part of a reservation in their service area or were located within 20 miles of a reservation. In the main text of this report, these two definitions are also referred to as Indian Country.

APPENDIX B. FOOD SECURITY MEASURES

Food security is assessed using an 18-item survey developed by USDA (Bickel et al. 2000; Economic Research Service 2011). Data are collected annually from a nationally representative sample of about 50,000 households in the December supplement to the CPS.[13] Estimates for AI/AN households combine samples from at least three successive years of the CPS to obtain an adequate sample size. Households with children in which the household head responds affirmatively to 3 or more questions are considered food insecure; these households in turn are divided into two groups: households who respond affirmatively to 3 to 5 questions are said to have low food security, while households where the head responds affirmatively to 6 or more of the 18 questions are said to have very low food security. More specifically, households are said to have very low food security if one or more members cut the size of meals or skipped meals because they could not afford to buy food.

Eight of the 18 questions only apply in households with children less than 18 years old. A scale based on just these eight questions is known as the children's food security scale, although it is also a household-level measure. Households who respond affirmatively to two or more of the eight child-related questions are said to have food insecurity among children, while those who respond affirmatively to five or more are said to have very low food security among children.[14]

APPENDIX C. OVERWEIGHT AND OBESITY MEASURES
FOR CHILDREN

Overweight and obesity are both labels for ranges of weight that are greater than what is considered healthy for a given height, as these ranges have been shown to increase the likelihood of health problems such as diabetes and cardiovascular disease. Body mass index (BMI) was the indicator used to assess overweight and obesity in the data presented in this report.

BMI-for-age and gender are used to assess weight among children 2 to 19 years of age (Ogden and Flegal 2010). BMI is a weight-for-height index defined as weight in kilograms divided by the square of height in meters. BMI is plotted on the CDC BMI-for-age growth charts to obtain a percentile ranking, which indicates a child's BMI relative to other children throughout the U.S. (the reference population). BMI-for-age weight-status categories and the corresponding percentiles are shown in Table C.1. For children ages 2–19, overweight is defined as 85th to less than the 95th percentile among the same age and gender. For this age group, obese is defined as greater than or equal to the 95th percentile among the same age and gender (Ogden and Flegal 2010). Notably, excess weight in infants (0–11 months) and toddlers (1 to < 2 years) is assessed using recumbent length instead of height. For this youngest age group, overweight is defined as weight at or above the 95th percentile of the sex-specific 2000 CDC weight-for-recumbent-length growth charts, which are independent of age (CDC 2010a).

It is critical to note that the definitions of the terms *overweight* and *obese* have changed in the last decade (Table C.2). Prior to 2007, *overweight* was defined as a BMI at or above the 95th percentile of a specified reference population and the designation of "at risk for overweight" was used for BMI values that were between the 85th and the 95th percentiles of BMI for age (Ogden and Flegal 2010). The American Medical Association expert committee proposed changes to the terminology to more effectively convey the seriousness and medical nature of excess weight for children above the 95th percentile.

Table C.1. Definitions of Overweight and Obese Terminology

Age	BMI Measure Used	Current Definition of Overweight	Current Definition of Obese
0–11 months	weight-for-recumbent length	≥ 95th percentile	NA
1 to < 2 years	weight-for-recumbent length	≥ 95th percentile	NA
2–19 years	weight-for-height	85th to < 95th percentile	≥ 95th percentile

Table C.2. Changes in Terminology

BMI Index for 2- to 19-Year-Olds	1994 Terminology	2007 Terminology
5th to < 85th percentile	Healthy Weight	Healthy Weight
85th to < 95th percentile	At Risk for Overweight	Overweight
95th percentile	Overweight	Obese

REFERENCES

Acton, K., Ríos Burrows, N., Geiss., L. & Thompson, T. (2003). "Diabetes Prevalence Among American Indians and Alaska Natives and the Overall Population—United States, 1994–2002." *MMWR*, vol. *52*, no. 30, p. 702.

Acton, K., Ríos Burrows, N., Moore, K., Querec, L., Geiss, L. & Engelgau, M. (2002). "Trends in Diabetes Prevalence Among American Indian and Alaska Native Children, Adolescents, and Young Adults." *American Journal of Public Health,* vol. *92*, no. 9, p. 1485.

Acton, K., Ríos Burrows, N., Wang, J. & Geiss, L. (2006). "Diabetes Prevalence Among American Indians and Alaska Natives and the Overall Population—United States, 1994–2002." *MMWR*, vol. *55*, no. 44, p. 1201.

American Diabetes Association (2000). "Type 2 Diabetes in Children and Adolescents." *Diabetes Care*, vol. *23*, p. 381.

Anderson, S., & Whitaker, R. (2009). "Prevalence of Obesity Among US Preschool Children in Different Racial and Ethnic Groups." *Archives of Pediatrics and Adolescent Medicine*, vol. *163*, no. 4, p. 344.

Bickel, G., Nord, M., Price, C., Hamilton, W. & Cook, J. (2000). "*Guide to Measuring Household Food Security, Revised 2000.*" U.S. Department of Agriculture, Economic Research Service. Washington DC: USDA.

Brown, B., Noonan, C. Bentley, B. Conway, K. Corcoran, M. FourStar, K., Gress, S. & Wagner S. (2010). "Acanthosis Nigricans Among Northern Plains American Indian Children." *The Journal of School Nursing*, vol. *26*, no. 6, p. 450.

Caballero, B., Himes, J. Lohman, T. Davis, S. M., Stevens, J., Evans, M., Going, S. & J. Pablo (2003). "Body Composition and Overweight Prevalence in 1704 Schoolchildren from 7 American Indian Communities." *The American Journal of Clinical Nutrition*, vol. *78*, no. 2, p. 308.

Centers for Disease Control and Prevention (2009). "*State Prevalence Among Low-Income Children Aged 2 to 4 Years.*" Pediatric Nutrition Surveillance System. Available at http://www.cdc.gov/obesity/ childhood/data.html. Accessed November 10, 2011.

———. "*Prevalence of Overweight, Infants and Children Less Than 2 years of Age, Growth Charts.*" 2010a. Available at http://www.cdc.gov/ growthcharts/.

———. (2010b). "*Summary of Trends in Growth and Anemia Indicators by Race/Ethnicity, Table 18 D.*" Pediatric Nutrition Surveillance System. Accessed at http://www.cdc.gov/pednss/how_to/ interpret_data/ index. htm.

Cole, N. (2002). "*Characteristics of Native American WIC Participants, On and Off Reservations.*" U.S. Department of Agriculture, Food and Nutrition Service, Office of Analysis, Nutrition and Evaluation. Nutrition Assistance Program Report Series, WIC-02-NAM. Alexandria, VA: USDA Food and Nutrition Service.

Coleman-Jensen, Alisha, Mark Nord, Margaret Andrews, & Steven Carlson. (2011). "*Household Food Security in the United States: 2010.*" Economic Research Report No. ERR-125. Washington, DC: USDA Economic Research Service, September.

Collins, A., Dun Rappaport, C., Burstein., N. (2010). "*WIC Breastfeeding Peer Counseling Study, Final Implementation Report*" U.S. Department of Agriculture, Food and Nutrition Service, Office of Research and Analysis, WIC-10-BPC, Alexandria, VA: USDA, June.

Conner, P., Bartlet, S., Mendelson, M., Condon, K. & Sutcliffe, J. (2010). "*WIC Participant and Program Characteristics 2008.*" U.S. Department of Agriculture, Food and Nutrition Service, Office of Research and Analysis, WIC-08-PC. Alexandria, VA: USDA Food and Nutrition Service.

Dabelea, D., DeGroat, J., Sorrelman, C., Glass, M., Percy, C., Avery, C., Hu, D., D'Agostino, R. Beyer, J. & Imperatore, G. (2009). "Diabetes in Navajo Youth." *Diabetes Care*, vol. *32*, supplement no. 2, p. S141.

Dabelea, D., Hanson, R., Bennett, P., Roumain, J., Knowler, W. & Pettitt, D. (1998). "Increasing Prevalence of Type II Diabetes in American Indian Children." *Diabetologia*, vol. *41*, no. 8, , pp. 904–910.

Economic Research Service (2011). "*Food Security in the United States.*" Accessed at http://www.ers.usda.gov/briefing/Foodsecurity/, November 19.

Fagot-Campagna, A. & Ríos Burrows, N. (1999). "The Public Health Epidemiology of Type 2 Diabetes in Children and Adolescents: A Case Study of American Indian Adolescents in the Southwestern United States." *Clinica Chimica Acta*, vol. *286*, no. 1–2, pp. 81–95.

Finegold, K., Pindus, N., Wherry, L., Nelson, S., Triplett, T. & Capps, R. (2005). *"Background Report on the Use and Impact of Food Assistance Programs on Indian Reservations."* Economic Research Service, Food and Nutrition Assistance Research Program, no. CCR-4. Washington, DC: USDA Economic Research Service, January.

Franks, P., Hanson, R., Knowler, W., Sievers, M., Bennett, P. & Looker, H. (2010). "Childhood Obesity, Other Cardiovascular Risk Factors, and Premature Death." *New England Journal of Medicine*, vol. *362*, no. 6, pp. 485–493.

Gordon-Larsen, P., Adair, L. & Popkin, B. (2003). "The Relationship of Ethnicity, Socioeconomic Factors, and Overweight in US Adolescents." *Obesity*, vol. *11*, no. 1, pp. 121–129.

Gundersen, C. (2008). "Measuring the Extent, Depth, and Severity of Food Insecurity: An Application to American Indians in the USA." *Journal of Population Economics*, vol. *21*, no. 1, pp. 191–215.

Halpern P. (2007). "Obesity and American Indians/Alaska Natives." Report submitted to the U.S. Department of Health and Human Services, Office of the Assistant Secretary for Planning and Evaluation. Washington, DC: DHHS OASPE, April.

Harper, E. (2011). *"WIC Participant Characteristics, 2008."* Personal Communication, December 5.

Harper, E., Orbeta, R., Southworth, L., Meade, K., Cleveland, R., Gordon, S., Buckley, M. & Hirschman, J. (2008). *"FDPIR Food Package Nutritional Quality: Report to Congress."* U.S. Department of Agriculture, Food and Nutrition Service, Office of Research and Analysis, Special Nutrition Programs Report FD-08-FDPIR. Alexandria, VA: USDA November.

Harwell, T., McDowall, J., Moore, K., Fagot-Campagna, A., Helgerson, S. & Gohdes, D. (2001). "Establishing Surveillance for Diabetes in American Indian Youth." *Diabetes Care*, vol. *24*, no. 6, p. 1029.

Hillabrant, W., Rhoades Jr., M., Pindus, N. & Trutko, J. (2001). *"The Evaluation of the Tribal Welfareto-Work Grants Program: Initial Implementation Findings."* Princeton, NJ: Mathematica Policy Research, Inc.

Holm, J., Vogeltanz-Holm, N., Poltavski, D. & McDonald, L. (2010). "Assessing Health Status, Behavioral Risks, and Health Disparities in American Indians Living on the Northern Plains of the U.S." *Public Health Reports*, vol. *125*, no. 1, pp. 68–78.

Indian Health Service (2009). *"Special Diabetes Program for Indians: 2007 Report to Congress."*

Institute of Medicine (2005). *"WIC Food Packages: Time for a Change"* Washington, DC: The National Academies Press.

———. (2011). *"Hunger and Obesity: Understanding a Food Insecurity Paradigm: Workshop Summary."* Washington, DC: The National Academies Press.

Knowler, W., Bennett, P. Hamman, R. & Miller. M. (1978). "Diabetes Incidence and Prevalence in Pima Indians: A 19-Fold Greater Incidence than in Rochester, Minnesota." *American Journal of Epidemiology*, vol. *108*, no. 6, p. 497.

Knowler, W., Pettitt, D. Saad, M. & Bennett, P. (1990). "Diabetes Mellitus in the Pima Indians: Incidence, Risk Factors and Pathogenesis." *Diabetes/Metabolism Reviews*, vol. *6*, no. 1, pp. 1–27.

Kumanyika, S., & Grier, S. (2006). "*Targeting Interventions for Ethnic Minority and Low-Income Populations.*" The Future of Children, pp. 187–207.

Liu, L., Lawrence, J., Davis, C., Liese, A., Pettitt, D., Pihoker, C., Dabelea, D. Hamman, R., Waitzfelder, B. & Kahn, H. (2010). "Prevalence of Overweight and Obesity in Youth with Diabetes in USA: The SEARCH for Diabetes in Youth Study." *Pediatric Diabetes*, vol. *11*, no. 1, pp. 4–11.

Mendlein, J., Freedman, D., Peter, D., Allen, B., Percy, C., Ballew, C., Mokdad, A. & White, L. (1997). "Risk Factors for Coronary Heart Disease Among Navajo Indians: Findings from the Navajo Health and Nutrition Survey." *The Journal of Nutrition*, vol. *127*, no. 10, p. 2099S.

Moore, K., Harwell, T., McDowall, J., Helgerson, S. & Gohdes, D. (2003). "Three-Year Prevalence and Incidence of Diabetes Among American Indian Youth in Montana and Wyoming, 1999 to 2001." *The Journal of Pediatrics*, vol. *143*, no. 3, pp. 368–371.

Nord, M., & Prell, M. (2011). "*Food Security Improved Following the 2009 ARRA Increase in SNAP Benefits*". Economic Research Report, no. ERR-116.

O'Connell, J., Yi, R., Wilson, C., Manson, S. & Acton, K. (2010). "Racial Disparities in Health Status: A Comparison of the Morbidity Among American Indian and U.S. Adults with Diabetes." *Diabetes Care*, vol. *33*, no. 7, pp. 1463–1470.

Ogden, C., & Flegal, K. (2010). "*Changes in Terminology for Childhood Overweight and Obesity: National Health Statistics.*" National Health Statistics Reports; No 25. Hyattsville, MD: National Center for Health Statistics.

Ogden, C., Carroll, M., Curtin, L., Lamb, M. & Flegal, K. (2010). "Prevalence of High Body Mass Index in US Children and Adolescents, 2007-2008." *JAMA*, vol. *303*, no. 3, pp. 242-249.

Ogunwole, S. "*We the People: American Indians and Alaska Natives in the United States.*" Census 2000 Special Reports, 2006.

Pleis J., Ward, B. & Lucas, J. (2010). "Summary Health Statistics for U.S. Adults: National Health Interview Survey 2009." National Center for Health Statistics, *Vital and Health Statistics,* vol. *10*, no. 249.

Rao, S., Disraeli, P. & McGregor, T. (2004). "Impaired Glucose Tolerance and Impaired Fasting Glucose." *American Family Physician*, vol. *69*, no. 8, pp. 1961–1968.

Richards, T. & Patterson, P. (2006). "Native American Obesity: An Economic Model of the 'Thrifty Gene' Theory." *American Journal of Agricultural Economics*, vol. *88*, no. 3, p. 542.

Ríos Burrows, N., Acton, K., Geiss, L. & Venkat Narayan, K. (1998). "Trends in Diabetes Prevalence in American Indians and Alaska Natives: An Increasing Burden among Younger People." *Diabetes*, vol. *47*, no. suppl 1, pp. A187.

Ríos Burrows, N., Geiss, L., Engelgau, M. & Acton, K. (2000). "Prevalence of Diabetes Among Native Americans and Alaska Natives, 1990–1997: An Increasing Burden." *Diabetes Care*, vol. *23*, no. 12, p. 1786.

Roberts, H., Jiles, R., Mokdad, A., Beckles, G. & Ríos-Burrows, N. (2009). "Trend Analysis of Diagnosed Diabetes Prevalence Among American Indian/Alaska Native Young Adults—United States, 1994–2007." *Ethnicity & Disease*, vol. *19*, no. 3, pp. 276–279.

Savage, P., Bennett, P., Senter, R. & Miller, M. (1979). "High Prevalence of Diabetes in Young Pima Indians: Evidence of Phenotypic Variation in a Genetically Isolated Population." *Diabetes*, vol. *28*, no. 10, p. 937.

SEARCH for Diabetes in Youth Study Group (A. Liese, D'Agostino Jr., R., Hamman, R., Kilgo, P., Lawrence, J., Liu, L., Loots, B., Linder, B., Marcovina, S., Rodriguez, B., Standiford, D. & Williams, D.) (2006). "The Burden of Diabetes Mellitus Among US Youth: Prevalence Estimates from the SEARCH for Diabetes in Youth Study." *Pediatrics*, vol. *118*, no. 4, pp. 1510–1518.

Story, M., Stevens, J., Himes, J., Stone, E., Holy Rock, B., Ethelbah, B. & Davis, S. (2003). "Obesity in American-Indian Children: Prevalence, Consequences, and Prevention." *Preventive Medicine*, vol. *37*, pp. S3–S12.

Strauss, K. (2010). "Evidence-Based Public Health Responses to the Overweight Crisis in American Indian and Alaska Native Communities." *The IHS Primary Care Provider*, vol. *35*, no. 6, pp. 116–122.

Thomas, S. & Cook, D. (2005). "Breastfeeding Duration and Prevalence of Overweight Among 4- to 5-Year Olds." *The IHS Primary Care Provider*, vol. *30*, no. 4.

Trippe, C. & Schechter, B. (2010). "*Individuals by Race and Receipt of Food Assistance, 2008.*" Memorandum submitted to Bob Dalrymple and Jenny Genser, Office of Research and Evaluation, USDA Food and Nutrition Service. Washington, DC: Mathematica Policy Research, September 1.

U.S. Census Bureau (2011a). "*American Community Survey 1-year Estimates.*" American FactFinder. Available at http://factfinder2.census. gov/faces/nav/jsf/pages/ index.xhtml, 2011a. Accessed November 10, 2011.

U.S. Census Bureau (2011b). "American Indian and Alaska Native Map." *Census Redistricting Data (Public Law 94-171) Summary File*, Table P1 and 2010 Census Summary File. Available at http://www. census.gov/geo/www/maps/ aian2010_ wall_map/aian_wall_ map.html. Accessed November 19, 2011.

———. (2011c). "U.S. Census 2000." *American FactFinder*. Available at http://factfinder2.census.gov/faces/nav/jsf/pages/index.xhtml. Accessed November 10, 2011.

———. (2011d). "U.S. Census 2010." *American FactFinder*. Available at http://factfinder2.census.gov/ faces/nav/jsf/pages/index.xhtml. Accessed November 10, 2011.

U.S. Census Bureau and Bureau of Labor Statistics (2011). "Current Population Survey: Food Security Supplement, Three Year Averages." *Healthy People 2010 Database*, Objective: 19–18. — October 2011. Available at http://wonder.cdc.gov. Accessed November 7.

U.S. Department of Agriculture (2011). "Food and Nutrition Service Program Data." *Alexandria, VA: USDA Food and Nutrition Service*, November 2011a. Available at http://www.fns.usda.gov/fns/data.htm. Accessed November 10.

———. (2011b). "Food and Nutrition Service: Monthly Data, Agency Level, Participation and Food Cost by Category per Person." *Alexandria, VA: USDA Food and Nutrition Service*, November. Available at http://www.fns.usda.gov/pd/ wicmain.htm. Accessed November 10, 2011.

U.S. Department of the Interior (2011). "*Healthy Schools.*" Available at http://www.doi.gov/letsmove/indiancountry/eathealthy/Healthy-Schools.cfm. Accessed November 14, 2011.

Usher, C., Shanklin, D. & Wildfire, J. (1990). "Evaluation of the Food Distribution Program on Indian Reservations." *Alexandria, VA: U.S. Department of Agriculture, Food and Nutrition Service.*

Ver Ploeg M., Breneman, V., Farrigan, T., Hamrick, K., Hopkins, D., Kaufman, P., Lin, B., Nord, M., Smith, T., Williams, R., Kinnison, K., Olander, C., Singh, A. & Tuckermanty, E. (2009). "*Access to Affordable and Nutritious Food: Measuring and Understanding Food Deserts and Their Consequences.*" Economic Research Service, no. AP-036. Washington, DC: USDA Economic Research Service.

Wang, Y., & Beydoun, M. (2007). "The Obesity Epidemic in the United States—Gender, Age, Socioeconomic, Racial/Ethnic, and Geographic Characteristics: A Systematic Review and Meta-Regression Analysis." *Epidemiologic Reviews*, vol. *29*, no. 1.

Weir, E., & Lipscombe, L. (2004). "Metabolic Syndrome: Waist Not Want Not." *Canadian Medical Association Journal*, vol. *170*, no. 9, p. 1390.

Yurgalevitch, S., Kriska, A., Welty, T., Go, O., Robbins, D. & Howard, B. (1998). "Physical Activity and Lipids and Lipoproteins in American Indians Ages 45–74." *Medicine & Science in Sports & Exercise,* vol. *30*, no. 4.

Zenk, S. N., Schulz, A. J., Israel, B. A., James, S. A., Bao, S. & Wilson, M. L. (2005). "Neighborhood racial composition, neighborhood poverty, and the spatial accessibility of supermarkets in metropolitan Detroit." *American Journal of Public Health.* vol *95*, no.4, pp. 660-667.

End Notes

[1] Type II diabetes is non–insulin-dependent diabetes and the most common form of diabetes. Type I diabetes is insulin-dependent diabetes and typically begins in childhood (American Diabetes Association 2000).

[2] See Appendix A for specific definitions used for Indian Country; most data are based on the Census definition of American Indian areas.

[3] Appendix A describes variations in racial categories across data sets and issues in comparing them.

[4] Total population for those reporting their race as AI/AN alone is 2,932,248 (0.9 percent of the U.S. population) and the total population for AI/AN in combination with one or more other races is 5,220,579 (1.7 percent of the U.S. population).

[5] Because data on the characteristics of AI/ANs in Indian Country from the 2010 Census are not yet available, we rely on older data for these comparisons.

[6] Appendix B describes the food security scale and subscales and their interpretation.

[7] Dyslipidemia is defined as an abnormal amount of lipids (e.g., cholesterol and/or fat) in the blood.

[8] FNS permits ITOs to serve as State agencies for FDPIR and WIC. Other programs are operated through the States, but an ITO may be a local site or sponsor sites.

[9] FNS recently awarded a three-year contract for *The Study of the Food Distribution Program on Indian Reservations (FDPIR): 2013.* The study will determine the demographic profile of households and individuals that currently participate and provide descriptive information on key aspects of FDPIR operations through case record analyses and interviews with participating households and staff.

[10] The Healthy Eating Index is a measure of how well population groups adhere to the Dietary Guidelines for Americans. A score of 100 indicates full adherence to recommended intakes of foods and nutrients.

[11] WIC PC 2008 tabulation provided by Ed Harper at FNS, personal communication, December 5, 2011.

[12] More information on *Let's Move! in Indian Country* can be found at http://www.letsmove.gov/ indiancountry.

[13] Data are collected both for an annual reference period and a 30-day reference period. All figures discussed here are for the annual reference period.

[14] A scale based on the 10 questions that are asked of all households is sometimes used—these questions are known as the "adult" scale, or a measure of food insecurity among adults in the household. Gundersen (2008) also presents some results for this scale.

In: American Indians. Volume 1   ISBN: 978-1-61122-351-4
Editors: Albert O. Hughes and Eric A. Sanders   © 2012 Nova Science Publishers, Inc.

Chapter 5

INDIAN ISSUES: OBSERVATIONS ON SOME UNIQUE FACTORS THAT MAY AFFECT ECONOMIC ACTIVITY ON TRIBAL LANDS. TESTIMONY OF ANU K. MITTAL, GOVERNMENT ACCOUNTABILITY OFFICE DELIVERED AT THE HEARING ON "REGULATORY BARRIERS TO AMERICAN INDIAN JOB CREATION"[*]

United States Government Accountability Office

WHY GAO DID THIS STUDY

Indian tribes are among the most economically distressed groups in the United States. In 2008, the U.S. Census Bureau reported that the poverty rate among American Indian and Alaska Natives was almost twice as high as the population as a whole—27 percent compared with 15 percent. Residents of tribal lands often lack basic infrastructure, such as water and sewer systems, and sufficient technology infrastructure. Without such infrastructure, tribal communities often find it difficult to compete successfully in the economic mainstream.

This testimony statement summarizes GAO's observations on (1) five broad categories of unique issues that may create uncertainty and therefore affect economic activity in Indian country and (2) tribes' use of special gaming and small business contracting provisions. It is based on prior GAO reports.

This testimony statement contains no new recommendations.

---

[*] This is an edited, reformatted and augmented version of the Highlights of GAO-11-543T, Presented April 7, 2011 before the House Committee on Oversight and Government Reform.

WHAT GAO FOUND

GAO's previous work has identified five broad categories of unique issues that may create uncertainty for tribes or, in some cases, private companies wishing to pursue economic activities on Indian reservations.

Accruing land in trust. Having a land base is essential for tribal economic development activities such as agriculture, energy development, and gaming. However, a February 2009 Supreme Court decision has raised uncertainty about the process for taking land in trust for tribes and their members.

Tribal environmental standards. The Clean Water Act, Safe Drinking Water Act, and Clean Air Act authorize the Environmental Protection Agency to treat Indian tribes in the same manner as states. In some cases, however, states are concerned that tribes with this authority may impose standards that are more stringent than the state standards, which could result in a patchwork of standards within the state and potentially hinder economic activity.

Indian tax provisions. Tribes face uncertainties regarding the types of activities that they can finance with tax-exempt bonds. Also, in 2008, GAO reported that there were insufficient data to (1) identify the users of a tax provision that allows for accelerated depreciation of certain property used by businesses on Indian reservations and (2) assess whether the provision had increased economic development on Indian reservations.

Obtaining rights-of-way. Securing rights-of-way across Indian land is important in providing Indian lands with the infrastructure needed to support economic activity. In 2006, GAO reported that obtaining rights-of-way through Indian lands was a time-consuming and expensive process.

Legal status of tribes. The unique legal status of tribes has resulted in a complex set of rules that may affect economic activities. For example, Indian tribes have sovereign immunity, which can influence a business's decision to contract with a tribe. Also, the limitations imposed by federal law on Indian tribes' civil jurisdiction over non-Indians on Indian reservations can create uncertainties over where lawsuits arising out of contracts with tribes can be brought.

In contrast to these unique issues that may pose challenges to economic activity in Indian country, some Indian tribes have taken advantage of special provisions for gaming and small business contracting. The National Indian Gaming Commission reports that tribal gaming operations generated $26.5 billion in revenue for 2009. However, not all tribes have gaming operations and the majority of the revenue is generated by a fraction of the operations. Similarly, Alaska Native Corporations (ANC) have been granted special procurement advantages. In 2006, GAO reported that obligations to firms owned by ANCs that participated in the Small Business Administration's 8(a) program increased from $265 million in fiscal year 2000 to $1.1 billion in 2004. We have ongoing work looking at the use of these special procurement advantages.

Chairman Lankford, Ranking Member Connolly, and Members of the Subcommittee:

I am pleased to be here today to participate in your hearing on the challenges of trying to increase economic activity in Indian Country. Indian tribes are among the most economically distressed groups in the United States. For example, in 2008, the U.S. Census Bureau reported that American Indians and Alaska Natives were almost twice as likely to live in poverty as the rest of the population—27 percent compared with 15 percent. Residents of tribal lands also often lack basic infrastructure, such as water and sewer systems, and sufficient technology infrastructure, such as telecommunications lines that are commonly found in other American communities. Without such infrastructure, tribal communities often find it difficult to compete successfully in the economic mainstream.

Our testimony today will cover (1) five broad categories of unique issues that may create uncertainty and therefore affect economic activity in Indian Country—land issues, tribal environmental standards, Indian tax provisions, rights-of-way, and certain issues related to the legal status of tribes—and (2) tribes' use of special gaming and small business contracting provisions. This statement is based on previously published work issued from December 2001 through March 2011. See the list of related GAO products at the end of this statement and other products cited for detailed descriptions of the scope and methodology used to conduct our work. We conducted our work in accordance with generally accepted government auditing standards or GAO's Quality Assurance Framework, as appropriate to each engagement.

BACKGROUND

Tribal lands vary dramatically in size, demographics, and location. They range in size from the Navajo Nation, which consists of about 24,000 square miles, to some tribal land areas in California comprising less than 1 square mile. Over 176,000 American Indians live on the Navajo reservation, while other tribal lands have fewer than 50 Indian residents. Some Indian reservations have a mixture of Indian and non-Indian residents. In addition, most tribal lands are rural or remote, although some are near metropolitan areas.

The federal government has consistently recognized Indian tribes as distinct, independent political communities with inherent powers of a limited sovereignty which has never been extinguished. To help manage tribal affairs, tribes have formed governments or subsidiaries of tribal governments including schools, housing, health, and other types of corporations. The United States has a trust responsibility to recognized Indian tribes and maintains a government-to-government relationship with those tribes. As of October 2010, there were 565 federally recognized tribes—340 in the continental United States and 225 in Alaska.[1]

According to tribal officials and government agencies, conditions on and around tribal lands—including the lack of technology infrastructure such as telecommunications lines—generally make successful economic development more difficult. In addition, a 1999 Economic Development Administration (EDA) study that assessed the state of infrastructure in American Indian communities found that these communities also had other disadvantages that made successful business development more difficult.[2] This study found that the high cost and small markets associated with investment in Indian communities continued to deter widespread private sector involvement.

To help address the needs of Indian tribes, various federal agencies provide assistance, including economic development assistance. The Bureau of Indian Affairs (BIA) in the Department of the Interior is charged with the responsibility of implementing federal Indian policy and administering the federal trust responsibility for about 2 million American Indians and Alaska Natives. BIA assists tribes in various ways, including providing for social services, developing and maintaining infrastructure, and providing education services. BIA also attempts to help tribes develop economically by, for example, providing resources to administer tribal revolving loan programs and guaranteed loan programs to improve access to capital in tribal communities. In addition to the support provided by BIA, other agencies with significant programs for tribes include the Department of Health and Human Services, which provides funding for the Head Start Program and the Indian Health Service; the Department of Housing and Urban Development, which provides support for community development and housing-related projects; and the Department of Agriculture, which provides support for services pertaining to food distribution, nutrition programs, and rural economic development.

SOME UNIQUE ISSUES THAT MAY AFFECT ECONOMIC ACTIVITY IN INDIAN COUNTRY

Our prior work has highlighted five broad categories of unique issues that have the potential to create uncertainty for tribes or, in some cases, private companies wishing to pursue economic activities on Indian reservations. Some of the issues that we have identified during our past work include (1) accruing land in trust for tribes and individual tribal members, (2) tribal environmental standards, (3) Indian tax provisions, (4) obtaining rights-of-way, and (5) certain legal issues that arise from the unique legal status of tribes. In addition to these five issues there may be others, such as access to financing, which may also hinder economic activity on Indian reservations. The five broad categories should only be considered as illustrative of some of the unique circumstances that exist in Indian country, which tribes or other business entities will need to take into account when they consider undertaking economic activities on tribal lands.

Land in Trust Issues May Create Uncertainty

Having a land base is essential for many tribal economic development activities such as agriculture, grazing, timber, energy development, and gaming. Since the early days of colonization, Indian lands have diminished significantly, in large part because of federal policy. By 1886, Indian lands had been reduced to about 140 million acres, largely on reservations west of the Mississippi River. Federal policy encouraging assimilation in the late 1800s and early 1900s further reduced Indian lands by two-thirds, to about 49 million acres by 1934. In 1934, however, the enactment of the Indian Reorganization Act changed the government's Indian policy to encourage tribal self-governance.[3] Section 5 of the act provided the Secretary of the Interior with discretionary authority to take land in trust on behalf of Indian tribes or their members. Trust status means that the federal government holds title to the land in trust for tribes or individual Indians. Once land is taken in trust it is no longer subject to state and local property taxes and zoning ordinances.[4] In 1980, Interior established a regulatory process intended to provide a uniform approach for taking land in trust.[5] Under the regulations, tribes or individual Indians who purchase or own property on which they pay property taxes can submit a written request to the Secretary of the Interior to have the land taken in trust; if approved, the ownership status of the property would be converted from taxable status to nontaxable Indian trust status. Some state and local governments support the federal government's taking additional land in trust for tribes or individual Indians, while others strongly oppose it because of concerns about the impacts on their tax base and jurisdictional control. Since 1934, the total acreage held in trust by the federal government for the benefit of tribes and their members has increased from about 49 million to about 54 million acres.[6]

We reported in July 2006 that BIA generally followed its regulations for processing land in trust applications from tribes and individual Indians to take land into trust, but had no deadlines for making decisions on these applications.[7] BIA generally responded to our recommendations to improve the processing of such applications, but this issue continues to create uncertainty in Indian country, in part, because of a February 24, 2009, Supreme Court decision and ongoing litigation. The Supreme Court held that the Indian Reorganization Act only authorizes the Secretary of the Interior to take land into trust for a tribe or its members if that tribe was under federal jurisdiction when the law was enacted in 1934.[8] The court did not define what constituted being under federal jurisdiction but did find that a particular tribe, which was not federally recognized until 1983, was not under federal jurisdiction in 1934. It is not clear how many tribes or pending land in trust applications will be affected by this decision, but the decision raises a question about the Secretary's authority to take land in trust for the 50 tribes that have been newly recognized since 1960 and their members.[9] The Secretary's decisions to take land in trust for two of these tribes—the Match-e-be-nash-she-wish Band of Potawatomi Indians of Michigan and the Cowlitz Indian tribe of Washington—have been challenged in court.[10]

Having or securing the land does not lead to economic development if that land sits idle. In the past we have reported on concerns about idle Indian lands and BIA's process for leasing Indian lands,[11] but we have not done any recent work on these issues.

Tribal Environmental Standards May Create Uncertainty

The Clean Water Act, Safe Drinking Water Act, and Clean Air Act authorize the Environmental Protection Agency (EPA) to treat Indian tribes in the same manner as it does states,[12] referred to as TAS (treated as states),[13] for the purposes of implementing these laws on tribal lands. On the one hand, tribes want to be treated as states and assume program responsibilities to protect their environmental resources because they are sovereign governments and have specific knowledge of their environmental needs. Tribes also generally believe that TAS status and program authority are important steps in addressing the potential impacts of economic development affecting their land. On the other hand, in some cases, states are concerned that tribes with program authority may impose standards that are more stringent than the state's, resulting in a patchwork of standards within the state and potentially hindering the state's economic development plans.

In October 2005, we reported that since 1986, when Congress amended the first of the three environmental laws to allow TAS status for tribes, a number of disagreements between tribes, states, and municipalities had arisen, over land boundaries, environmental standards, and other issues.[14] The disagreements had been addressed in various ways, including litigation, collaborative efforts, and changes to federal laws. For example, in *City of Albuquerque v. Browner*,[15] the city challenged EPA's approval of the nearby Pueblo of Isleta tribe's water quality standards, which are more stringent than those of New Mexico. EPA's approval was upheld. In other disagreements, some tribes and states have addressed the issues more collaboratively. For example, the Navajo Nation and the Arizona Department of Environmental Quality entered into a cooperative agreement that, among other things, recognizes the jurisdiction of the Navajo Nation within its reservation and establishes a plan to share the cost of pilot projects. Regarding the use of federal legislation to address disagreements, a federal statute enacted in August 2005, requires Indian tribes in Oklahoma to enter into a cooperative agreement with the state before EPA can approve a tribe's TAS request.[16] At the time of our October 2005 report, the Pawnee Nation was the only Oklahoma tribe that had been awarded TAS status to set its own water quality standards, and we have not conducted any more recent work on this issue.

Uncertainties Regarding the Use of Selected Indian Tax Provisions

The tax code has also been used to promote economic activity in Indian country. We have reported on tax provisions regarding (1) the uncertainties that tribes faced regarding the types of activities that they could finance with tax-exempt bonds and (2) the impact of accelerated depreciation provisions.

In September 2006, we reported on Indian tribal governments' use of tax- exempt bonds under section 787 1(c) of the Internal Revenue Code.[17] Section 7871(c), which was originally enacted in 1983, generally limits the use of tax-exempt bonds by Indian tribal governments to the financing of certain activities that constitute "essential government functions."[18] In 1987, section 7871(e) was added to the code to limit the essential governmental functions standard further to provide that an essential governmental function does not include any function which is not customarily performed by state and local governments with general taxing powers. To date the Internal Revenue Service has not issued regulations defining essential government function.[19] The lack of a definition has created uncertainty among tribes regarding the types of activities that they can finance using tax-exempt bonds. In addition, this custom-based essential governmental function standard has proven to be a difficult administrative standard and has led to audit disputes, based on difficulties in determining customs, the evolving nature of the functions customarily performed by state and local governments, and increasing involvement of state and local governments in quasi-commercial activities. In trying to determine what the customary practices were of state and local governments that tribes should be held accountable to, we reported that state and local governments had provided financial support for a variety of facilities, including rental housing, road transportation, parking facilities, park and recreation facilities, golf facilities, convention centers, hotels, and gaming support facilities.

Section 1402 of the American Recovery and Reinvestment Act of 2009 added a $2 billion bond authorization for a new temporary category of tax-exempt bonds with lower borrowing costs for Indian tribal governments known as "Tribal Economic Development Bonds" under section 7871(f) of the Internal Revenue Code to promote economic development on Indian lands.[20] In general, this new authority provides tribal governments with greater flexibility to use tax-exempt bonds to finance economic development projects than is allowable under the existing essential governmental function standard of section 787 1(c). The Internal Revenue Service allocated the $2 billion of bond issuance authority provided by section 1402 to 134 tribal governments in two rounds. Furthermore, the act required the Secretary of the Treasury to study the effect of section 1402 and report to Congress on the results of the study, including the Secretary's recommendation regarding the provision. According to the Treasury Department, the House Ways and Means Committee and the Senate Finance Committee indicated that, in particular, Treasury should study whether to repeal on a permanent basis the existing more restrictive essential governmental function standard for tax-exempt governmental bond financing by Indian tribal governments under section 7871(c).[21] The act required that the study be completed no later than 1 year after enactment, which would have made the deadline February 17, 2010. The Treasury Department published a notice in the Federal Register in July 2010 seeking comments from tribal governments regarding the tribal economic development bond to assist the department in developing recommendations for the required study, but, to our knowledge, the department has not yet issued the report to Congress. There is continuing uncertainty in this area because it is unknown what the Treasury Department may recommend regarding changes to section 7871(c) and ultimately what changes, if any, Congress may adopt.

A second tax measure intended to promote economic activity in Indian country is the Indian reservation depreciation provision, enacted in 1993. The provision acts as an incentive for investment on Indian reservations because it permits taxpayers to accelerate their depreciation for certain property used by businesses on Indian reservations.[22] The provision's special depreciation deduction schedule permits eligible taxpayers to take a larger and earlier deduction for depreciation from their business incomes than they otherwise would be allowed, thereby reducing any tax liability. Reducing tax liability earlier is an incentive for economic development because having a lower tax payment today is worth more to the taxpayer than having a lower tax payment in the future. However, in June 2008, we reported that there were insufficient data to identify users of the provision and assess whether the provision had increased economic development on Indian reservations.[23]

Obtaining Rights-of-Way Across Indian Land Can Involve Uncertainty

Securing rights-of-way across Indian lands is an important component of providing Indian lands with the critical infrastructure needed to support economic activity. We have reported on the uncertainties that telecommunication service providers and a nonprofit rural electric cooperative have faced in trying to negotiate rights-of-way involving Indian lands.

In January 2006, we reported that according to several telecommunications service providers and tribal officials, obtaining a right-of-way through Indian lands is a time-consuming and expensive process that can impede service providers' deployment of telecommunications infrastructure.[24] The right-of-way process on Indian lands is more complex than the right-of-way process for non-Indian lands because BIA must approve the application for a right-of-way across Indian lands. BIA grants or approves actions affecting title on Indian lands, so all service providers installing telecommunications infrastructure on Indian lands must work with BIA or its contractor (a realty service provider) to obtain a right-of-way through Indian lands.[25] To fulfill the requirements of federal regulations for rights-of-way over Indian lands and obtain BIA approval, service providers are required to take multiple steps and coordinate with several entities during the application process. These steps must be taken to obtain a right-of-way over individual Indian allotments as well as tribal lands. Several of the steps involve the landowner, which could be an individual landowner, multiple landowners, or the tribe, depending on the status of the land. Specifically, the right-of- way process requires (1) written consent by the landowner to survey the land; (2) an appraisal of the land needed for the right-of-way; negotiations with the landowner to discuss settlement terms; written approval by the landowner for the right-of-way; and (5) BIA approval of the right-of-way application.[26] One telecommunication service provider told us that an individual Indian allotment of land can have over 200 owners, and federal regulations require the service provider to gain approval from a majority of them. The service provider stated that the time and cost of this process is compounded by the fact that a telecommunications service line often crosses multiple allotments. In addition, if the service provider cannot obtain consent for the right-of-way from the majority of landowners, the provider is forced to install lines that go around the allotment, which is also expensive.

Rights-of-way can also be necessary to deliver energy to consumers. In September 2004, we reported that the Copper Valley Electric Association, a nonprofit rural electric cooperative, had been unable to reach agreements with several individual Alaska Natives for rights-of-way across their land.[27] In 1906, the Alaska Native Allotment Act authorized the Secretary of the Interior to allot individual Alaska Natives a homestead of up to 160 acres.[28] We found 14 cases where conflict exists regarding Copper Valley's rights-of-way within Native allotments. Resolution to a number of these conflicts had been intermittently pursued since the mid- 1990s, but at the time of our report, only a few cases had been resolved using existing remedies. Copper Valley had three remedies to resolve these conflicts: (1) negotiating rights-of-way with Native allottees in conjunction with BIA; (2) relocating its electric lines outside of the allotment; or (3) exercising the power of eminent domain, also known as condemnation, to acquire the land.[29] We reported that Copper Valley had ceased trying to resolve these conflicts because it maintains that the existing remedies are too costly, impractical, and/or potentially damaging to relationships with the community. More importantly, Copper Valley officials told us that on principle they should not have to bear the cost of resolving conflicts that they believe the federal government had caused.

Section 1813 of the Energy Policy Act of 2005 required the Secretaries of Energy and of the Interior to conduct a study of issues regarding energy rights-of-ways on tribal land and issue a report to Congress on the findings, including recommending appropriate standards and procedures for determining fair and appropriate compensation to Indian tribes for granting, expanding and renewing rights-of-way.[30] Issued in May 2007, the study focused on rights-of-way for electric transmission lines and natural gas and oil pipelines associated with interstate transit and local distribution. The study recommended that valuation of rights-of-way continue to be based on terms negotiated between the parties and that if negotiations failed to produce an agreement that has a significant regional or national effect on the supply, price, or reliability of energy resources, Congress should consider resolving such a situation through specific legislation rather than making broader changes that would affect tribal sovereignty or self-determination generally.

Certain Issues Related to the Legal Status of Tribes May Complicate the Resolution of Disputes

The unique legal status of tribes has resulted in a complex set of rules that may affect economic development efforts. As we reported earlier this year, as a general principle, the federal government recognizes Indian tribes as "distinct, independent political communities" with inherent powers of selfgovernment.[31] Therefore, Indian tribes have sovereign immunity as well as plenary and exclusive power over their members and territory subject only to the limitations imposed by federal law. However, sovereign immunity may influence a private company's decision to contract with an Indian tribe and the limitations imposed by federal law on Indian tribes' civil jurisdiction over non-Indians on Indian reservations may create uncertainties regarding where lawsuits arising out of those contracts can be brought.

Like the federal and state governments, Indian tribes are immune from lawsuits unless they have waived their sovereign immunity in a clear and unequivocal manner or a federal treaty or law has expressly abrogated or limited tribal sovereign immunity. For example, the Indian Tribal Economic Development and Contracts Encouragement Act of 2000 requires the Secretary of the Interior to approve any agreement or contract with an Indian tribe that encumbers Indian lands for 7 or more years; however, it prohibits the Secretary from approving the agreement or contract unless it provides remedies for breaching the agreement or contract, references a tribal law or court ruling disclosing the tribe's right to assert sovereign immunity, or includes an express waiver of sovereign immunity. If the tribe does not waive its sovereign immunity in the agreement or contract, private companies might be hesitant to undertake the work because they will not be able to sue the tribe if any disputes arise. In addition to waiving sovereign immunity in agreements or contracts on a case-by-case basis, some tribes have formed separate entities to conduct business that are not immune from lawsuits.

The Supreme Court has ruled that, as a general proposition, the inherent sovereign powers of an Indian tribe do not extend to the activities of non- tribal members.[32] However, the Court has also recognized two exceptions to this general proposition: (1) tribes may regulate the activities of nonmembers who enter into consensual relationships with the tribe or its members through commercial dealing, contracts, leases, or other arrangements and (2) tribes may exercise civil authority over the conduct of non-Indians on fee lands within the reservation when that conduct threatens or has some direct effect on the political integrity, economic security, or the health or welfare of the tribe. In 2008, the Supreme Court ruled that a tribal court did not have jurisdiction to adjudicate a discrimination claim against a non-Indian bank brought by a company owned by tribal members because neither of the exceptions applied.[33] The court's opinion focuses on the tribe's authority to regulate the bank's sale of fee land it owned within the reservation rather than addressing whether the tribal court had authority to hear the discriminatory lending claim under the consensual relationship exception. However, some private companies believe that this decision may not eliminate all of the uncertainty as to the nature and extent of tribal court jurisdiction that makes off-reservation businesses reluctant to trade on Indian reservations or with tribal members who live on reservations. For example, the brief filed by a railroad association asked the court to adopt a brightline rule that tribal courts may not exercise jurisdiction over claims against nonmembers absent clear and unequivocal consent to tribal court jurisdiction. The association argued that such a rule would ensure that litigation against nontribal members will be addressed by a forum that the nonmember has agreed affords acceptable law, procedure, and fundamental safeguards of process and fairness.

SPECIAL PROVISIONS FOR GAMING AND SMALL BUSINESS CONTRACTING

In contrast to the unique issues that can cause uncertainty or pose challenges to economic activity in Indian country, tribes can take advantage of special provisions for gaming and small business contracting. Indian gaming, a relatively new phenomenon, started in the late 1970s when a number of Indian tribes began to establish bingo operations as a supplemental means of funding tribal operations. In 1987, the U. S. Supreme Court ruled that state regulation of tribal gaming would impermissibly infringe on tribal governments, thereby barring state regulation of tribal gaming in states which did not prohibit all forms of gaming.[34] In response, the Indian Gaming Regulatory Act of 1988 was enacted, which established a regulatory framework to govern Indian gaming operations.[35] In section 2(4) of the act, Congress found that a principle goal of federal Indian policy is to promote tribal economic development, tribal self-sufficiency, and strong tribal government. To that end, the act generally requires that the net revenues from tribal gaming operations be used to (1) fund tribal government operations or programs, provide for the general welfare of the Indian tribe and its members, promote tribal economic development, (4) donate to charitable organizations, or (5) help fund operations of local government agencies. A tribe may distribute its net revenues directly to tribal members, provided that the tribe has a revenue allocation plan approved by BIA and meets certain other conditions.

According to the final report of the National Gambling Impact Study Commission,[36] gambling revenues have proven to be a critical source of funding for many tribal governments, providing much needed improvements in the health, education, and welfare of Indians living on reservations across the United States. The National Indian Gaming Commission reports that for 2009

- 233 tribes operating 419 gaming operations generated $26.5 billion in revenue (233 tribes represents about 40 percent of the 565 federally recognized tribes),
- the top 21 operations (or about 5 percent of all the operations) generated 38.7 percent of all the revenues, and
- the top 71 operations (or about 17 percent of all the operations) generated 69.5 percent of all the revenues.

In addition, in 1986, a law was enacted that allowed Alaska Native corporation (ANC)-owned businesses to participate in the Small Business Administration's (SBA) 8(a) program—one of the federal government's primary means for developing small businesses owned by socially and economically disadvantaged individuals. This program allows the government to award contracts to participating small businesses without competition below certain dollar thresholds. Since 1986, special procurement advantages have been extended to ANC firms beyond those afforded to other 8(a) businesses, such as the ability to win sole-source contracts for any dollar amount. In April 2006, we reported on the use of special procurement advantages by ANCs, and found that 8(a) obligations to firms owned by ANCs increased from $265 million in fiscal year 2000 to $1.1 billion in 2004.[37] In fiscal year 2004, obligations to ANC firms represented 13 percent of total 8(a) dollars. Sole-source awards represented about 77 percent of 8(a) ANC obligations for the six procuring agencies that accounted for the vast majority of total ANC obligations over the 5-year period.

ANCs use the 8(a) program to generate revenue with the goal of providing benefits to their shareholders, but the ANCs we reviewed did not track the benefits provided to their shareholders specifically generated from 8(a) activity. Thus, an explicit link between the revenues generated from the 8(a) program and benefits provided to shareholders is not documented. Benefits vary among corporations, but include dividend payments, scholarships, internships, burial assistance, land gifting or leasing, shareholder hire, cultural programs, and support of the subsistence lifestyle. The special procurement advantages for ANCs also generally apply to tribes and Native Hawaiian organizations (NHO). To obtain more information on the benefits these entities receive from participation in the 8(a) program, SBA recently promulgated regulations that require each 8(a) program participant owned by an ANC, tribe, or NHO to submit information showing how the ANC, tribe, or NHO has provided benefits to tribal or Native communities or tribal or Native members due to its participation in the 8(a) program.[38] The data submitted should include information relating to funding cultural programs, employment assistance, jobs, scholarships, internships, subsistence activities, and other services provided by the ANC, tribe, or NHO to the affected community. We have ongoing work looking at the use of these special procurement advantages by ANCs, tribes, and NHOs.

Chairman Lankford, Ranking Member Connolly, and Members of the Subcommittee, this concludes my prepared statement. I would be pleased to answer any questions that you may have at this time.

End Notes

[1] 75 Fed. Reg. 60810 (Oct. 1, 2010); 75 Fed. Reg. 66124 (Oct. 27, 2010).

[2] Linda A. Riley, B. Nassersharif, and J. Mullen, *Assessment of Technology Infrastructure in Native Communities*, a study based on a survey of 48 Native communities, New Mexico State University, (Las Cruces, N.Mex.: 1999), EDA project no. 99-07-13799.

[3] Act of June 18, 1934 (Indian Reorganization Act), ch. 576, 48 Stat. 984-988 (1934), *codified as amended at* 25 U.S.C. §§ 461-479.

[4] Department of the Interior regulations provide that zoning ordinances do not apply to land in trust except as permitted by the Secretary. 25 C.F.R. § 1.4.

[5] 25 C.F.R. pt. 151.

[6] The 5-million acre difference between these two figures represents the net change of Indian land in trust from 1934. In addition to Indian applicants seeking to have land converted to trust status, Indian applicants can also seek to have land already in trust status converted to fee status (which is subject to property tax) and tribes and individual Indians can also lose trust lands through a variety of means, including probate and foreclosure. These two processes result in land "coming into trust" (referred to as acquisitions) and land "going out of trust" (referred to as disposals). The regulations governing taking land out of trust are in 25 C.F.R. pt. 152. For example, for the calendar year ending December 31, 1997, BIA reported acquiring about 360,000 acres and disposing of about 260,000 acres, for a net increase in tribal and individual Indian trust acreage of about 100,000 acres.

[7] GAO, *Indian Issues: BIA's Efforts to Impose Time Frames and Collect Better Data Should Improve the Processing of Land in Trust Applications*, GAO-06-781 (Washington, D.C.: July 28, 2006).

[8] Carcieri v. Salazar, 555 U.S. 379 (2009).

[9] For additional information on BIA's administrative process for granting federal recognition and a list of newly recognized tribes see GAO, *Indian Issues: Improvements Needed in Tribal Recognition Process*, GAO-02-49

(Washington, D.C.: Nov. 2, 2001). Also see enclosure II of GAO, *Indian Issues: BLM's Program for Issuing Individual Allotments on Public Lands Is No Longer Viable*, GAO-07-23R (Washington, D.C.: Oct. 20, 2006) and appendix II of GAO, *Native American Graves Protection and Repatriation Act: After Almost 20 Years, Key Federal Agencies Still Have Not Fully Complied with the Act*, GAO-10-768 (Washington, D.C.: July 28, 2010) for updated lists of new and restored tribes. The Shinnecock Indian Nation of New York, the newest federally recognized tribe, was recognized as of October 1, 2010. 75 Fed. Reg. 66124 (Oct. 27, 2010).

[10] Patchak v. Salazar, 646 F. Supp. 2d 72 (D.D.C. 2009), *rev'd*, 632 F.3d 702 (D.C. Cir. 2011) (remanding to district court for further proceedings); Clark County v. Salazar, No. 11-002 78 (D.C. Cir. filed Jan. 31, 2011).

[11] GAO, *Indian Programs: BIA's Management of the Wapato Irrigation Project*, GAO/RCED-97-124 (Washington, D.C.: May 28, 1997); GAO, *Indian Programs: BIA Should Streamline Its Processes for Estimating Land Rental Values*, GAO/RCED-99-165 (Washington, D.C.: June 30, 1999).

[12] Under these laws, EPA may authorize states to establish their own standards and carry out a state program in lieu of the federal program. State standards must meet or exceed federal requirements.

[13] The acts generally use the term "treat as states." EPA and most Indian tribes prefer to use the term "treatment in the same manner as a state."

[14] GAO, *Indian Tribes: EPA Should Reduce the Review Time for Tribal Requests to Manage Environmental Programs*, GAO-06-95 (Washington, D.C.: Oct. 31, 2005).

[15] 97 F.3d 415 (10th Cir. 1996), *cert. denied*, 522 U.S. 965 (1997).

[16] Pub. L. No. 109-59, § 10211, 119 Stat. 1144, 1937 (2005).

[17] GAO, *Federal Tax Policy: Information on Selected Capital Facilities Related to the Essential Governmental Function Test*, GAO-06-1082 (Washington, D.C.: Sept. 13, 2006).

[18] Indian Tribal Government Tax Status Act, Pub. L. No. 97-473, § 202, 96 Stat. 2605 (1983), *codified as amended at* 26 U.S.C. § 7871(c).

[19] On August 9, 2006, the Internal Revenue Service published an advanced notice of proposed rulemaking regarding the definition of essential government function and solicited comments on a definition. 71 Fed. Reg. 45474 (Aug. 9, 2006).

[20] Pub. L. No. 111-5, § 1402, 123 Stat. 115, 351 (2009).

[21] 75 Fed. Reg. 39730 (July 12, 2010).

[22] 26 U.S.C. § 168(j). Indian reservation is defined as (1) Indian reservations; (2) public domain Indian allotments; (3) former Indian reservations in Oklahoma which are within the jurisdictional area of an Oklahoma Indian tribe as determined by the Secretary of the Interior and are recognized by the Secretary as eligible for trust land status under applicable regulations in effect on the day of the provision's enactment; (4) land held by incorporated Native groups, regional corporations, and village corporations; (5) all land within the limits of any Indian reservation under the jurisdiction of the United States Government; (6) all dependent Indian communities; (7) all Indian allotments, the Indian titles to which have not been extinguished; and (8) any lands not within the limits of an Indian reservation, part of a dependent Indian community, nor an allotment which is either held by the United States in trust or held by any Indian tribe or individual subject to a restriction by the United States against alienation.

[23] GAO, *Tax Expenditures: Available Data Are Insufficient to Determine the Use and Impact of Indian Reservation Depreciation*, GAO-08-731 (Washington, D.C.: June 26, 2008).

[24] GAO, *Telecommunications: Challenges to Assessing and Improving Telecommunications For Native Americans on Tribal Lands*, GAO-06-189 (Washington, D.C.: Jan. 11, 2006).

[25] The Indian Self-Determination and Education Assistance Act, as amended, directs Interior, at the request of a tribe, to contract with Indian tribes or tribal organizations to carry out the services and programs the federal government provides to Indians. Therefore, as authorized by the act, regional nonprofit corporations or tribal entities can assume management of the realty function from BIA to perform realty services for Indian lands. 25 U.S.C. § 450f.

[26] 25 C.F.R. § 169.3.

[27] GAO, *Alaska Native Allotments: Conflicts with Utility Rights-of-way Have Not Been Resolved through Existing Remedies*, GAO-04-923 (Washington, D.C.: Sept. 7, 2004).

[28] Act of May 17, 1906 (Alaska Allotment Act), ch. 2469, 34 Stat. 197 (1906), *repealed by* Alaska Native Claims Settlement Act, Pub. L. No. 92-203, § 18(a), 85 Stat. 688, 710 (1971).

[29] Lands allotted in severalty to Indians may be condemned for any public purpose under the laws of the State or Territory where they are located in the same manner as land owned in fee may be condemned, and the money awarded as damages shall be paid to the allottee (25 U.S.C. § 357). Under Alaska state law a public utility may exercise the power of eminent domain for public utility uses (Alaska Stat. § 42.05.631).

[30] Pub. L. No. 109-58, § 1813, 119 Stat. 594, 1127 (2005). Tribal land is defined as any land or interests in land owned by any Indian tribe, title to which is held in trust by the United States, or is subject to a restriction against alienation under laws of the United States.

[31] GAO, *Indian Country Criminal Justice: Departments of the Interior and Justice Should Strengthen Coordination to Support Tribal Courts*, GAO-11-252 (Washington, D.C.: Feb. 14, 2011).

[32] Montana v. United States, 450 U.S. 544 (1981).

[33] Plains Commerce Bank v. Long Family Land and Cattle Company, 554 U.S. 316 (2008). The non-Indian bank made operating loans to the company owned by tribal members and accepted the deed to the company's fee land inside the reservation but leased the land back to the company, with an option to purchase it at the end of the lease. The company did not exercise its option and the bank subsequently sold the property to non-Indians. The company then sued the bank in tribal court on a variety of claims, including claiming that the bank discriminated against the company because it had sold the company's land to non- tribal members on terms more favorable than those offered to the company. The tribal court awarded the company an option to purchase some of the land at issue, which effectively nullified the bank's previous sale of that land to non-Indians.

[34] California v. Cabazon Band of Mission Indians, 480 U.S. 202 (1987).

[35] Pub. L. No. 100-497, 102 Stat. 2467 (1988), *codified at* 25 U.S.C. §§ 2701-2721.

[36] The National Gambling Impact Study Commission, Final Report (Washington, D.C.: June 18, 1999). The National Gambling Impact Study Commission Act created the commission and required it to produce this report. Pub. L. No. 104-169, 110 Stat. 1482 (1996).

[37] GAO, *Contract Management: Increased Use of Alaska Native Corporations' Special 8(a) Provisions Calls for Tailored Oversight*, GAO-06-399 (Washington, D.C.: Apr. 27, 2006).

[38] 76 Fed. Reg. 8222, 8264 (Feb. 11, 2011). Although the regulation, 13 C.F.R. § 124.604, requires reporting by each participant in the 8(a) program, the preamble to the regulation states that only parent corporations and not the individual subsidiary 8(a) participants will be required to submit this information. Generally, the new regulation became effective on March 14, 2011. However, SBA decided to delay the benefits reporting requirement to further study how the requirement could best be implemented without imposing an undue burden on ANCs, tribes, and NHOs. SBA has delayed the implementation for at least 6 months and noted that further delay may be necessary if the refinements to the requirement take longer than 6 months. 76 Fed. Reg. 8222, 8236 (Feb. 11, 2011).

In: American Indians. Volume 1
Editors: Albert O. Hughes and Eric A. Sanders

ISBN: 978-1-61122-351-4
© 2012 Nova Science Publishers, Inc.

Chapter 6

INDIAN GAMING REGULATORY ACT (IGRA): GAMING ON NEWLY ACQUIRED LANDS[*]

M. Maureen Murphy

SUMMARY

The Indian Gaming Regulatory Act (IGRA) (P.L. 100-497) generally prohibits gaming on lands acquired for Indians in trust by the Secretary of the Interior (SOI or Secretary) after October 17, 1988. The exceptions, however, raise the possibility of Indian gaming proposals for locations presently unconnected with an Indian tribe. Among the exceptions are land: (1) acquired after the SOI determines acquisition to be in the best interest of the tribe and not detrimental to the local community and the governor of the state concurs; (2) acquired for tribes that had no reservation on the date of enactment of IGRA; (3) acquired as part of a land claim settlement; (4) acquired as part of an initial reservation for a newly recognized tribe; and (5) acquired as part of the restoration of lands for a tribe restored to federal recognition.

During the latter half of 2010, the Department of the Interior (DOI) conducted a series of consultation sessions with Indian tribes focusing on whether the implementing regulation should be revised. The regulation was issued on May 20, 2008; it specifies the standards to be satisfied by tribes seeking to conduct gaming on lands acquired after October 17, 1988. The regulation includes limiting definitions of some of the statutory terms and considerable specificity in the documentation required for tribal applications. On June 13, 2011, DOI determined the regulation to be satisfactory and withdrew earlier departmental guidance, which had been issued before the regulation had become final. The guidance addressed how DOI handled tribal applications for off-reservation land acquisitions for gaming. It had elaborate requirements for a tribe to satisfy with respect to applications for gaming facilities not within commutable distances from the tribe's reservation.

In the 111th Congress, two bills were enacted with gaming prohibitions in connection with land-into-trust acquisitions: (1) Section 2601 (h)(4)(A) of P.L. 111-11, which prohibits

---

[*] This is an edited, reformatted and augmented version of the Congressional Research Service Publication, CRS Report for Congress RL34325, dated January 26, 2012.

class II and class III gaming on land which the provision transfers to be held in trust for the Washoe Tribe; and (2) P.L. 111-323, which prohibits gaming on federal land transferred to the Hoh Tribe.

Legislation in the 112th Congress includes S. 771, the Tribal Gaming Eligibility Act, which requires tribes to satisfy new standards before newly acquired lands may be found to be eligible for IGRA gaming on the basis of a land claim settlement, an initial reservation, or restoration of lands. There is also a bill, S. 1424, which would set new standards for taking off-reservation land into trust for gaming. Other bills providing for federal recognition of tribal status or taking land into trust include explicit provisions relating to gaming. Among them are S. 121 8/H.R. 27, the Lumbee Recognition Act; H.R. 475, the Fountainhead Property Land Transfer Act; H.R. 783/S. 379, the Thomasina E. Jordan Indian Tribes of Virginia Recognition Act; S. 675/H.R. 1250, the Native Hawaiian Government Reorganization Act; H.R. 1991, the Cocopah Lands Act; S. 617, the Elko Motocross and Tribal Conveyance Act, which transfers land into trust for the Te-moak Tribe of Western Shoshone Indians of Nevada; S. 908, which provides for the addition of certain real property to the reservation of the Siletz Tribe; and H.R. 2938, the Gila Bend Indian Lands Replacement Clarification Act.

REQUIREMENTS FOR GAMING ON "INDIAN LANDS"

The Indian Gaming Regulatory Act (IGRA)[1] provides a framework for gaming on "Indian lands,"[2] according to which Indian tribes may conduct gaming that need not conform to state law. The three classes of gaming authorized by IGRA progress from class I social gaming, through class II bingo and non-banking card games, to class III casino gaming.[3] One of the requirements for class II and class III gaming is that the gaming be "located in a State that permits such gaming for any purpose by any person, organization or entity."[4] The federal courts have interpreted this to permit tribes to conduct types of gaming permitted in the state without state limits or conditions. For example, tribes in states that permit "Las Vegas" nights for charitable purposes may seek a tribal-state compact for class III casino gaming.[5] On the other hand, the fact that state law permits some form of lottery or authorizes a state lottery is not, in itself, sufficient to permit a tribal-state compact permitting all forms of casino gaming.[6]

GEOGRAPHIC EXTENT OF IGRA GAMING

A key concept of IGRA is its territorial component. Gaming under IGRA may only take place on "Indian lands." That term has two meanings: (1) "all lands within the limits of any Indian reservation"; and (2) "any lands title to which is either held in trust by the United States for the benefit of any Indian tribe or individual or held by any Indian tribe or individual subject to restriction by the United States against alienation and over which an Indian tribe exercises governmental power."[7] Under the first alternative, gaming under IGRA may take place on any land within an Indian reservation, whether or not the tribe or a tribal member owns the land and whether or not the land is held in trust. Determining the applicable boundaries of a reservation is a matter of congressional intent and may entail a detailed analysis of the language of statutes ceding tribal reservation land, and the circumstances surrounding their enactment as well the subsequent jurisdictional history of the land in question.[8]

The second alternative has two prongs: (a) the land must be in trust or restricted[9] status, and (b) the tribe must exercise governmental authority over it. Determining trust or restricted status involves Department of the Interior (DOI or Department) records. Determining whether a tribe exercises governmental authority may be a simple factual matter involving, for example, whether the tribe has a governmental organization that performs traditional governmental functions such as imposing taxes.[10] On the other hand, it could be a matter requiring judicial construction of federal statutes.[11]

HOW LAND IS TAKEN INTO TRUST

Congress has the power to determine whether to take tribal land into trust.[12] There are many statutes that require DOI to take land into trust for a tribe or an individual Indian.[13] An array of statutes grant the Secretary of the Interior (SOI) the discretion to acquire land in trust for individual Indian tribes; principal among them is the Wheeler-Howard, or Indian Reorganization Act of 1934 (IRA).[14] Procedures for land acquisition are specified in 25 C.F.R., Part 151. By this process Indian owners of fee land, that is, land owned outright and unencumbered by liens that impair marketability, may apply to have their fee title conveyed to SOI to be held in trust for their benefit. Among the effects of this process are the removal of the land from state and local tax rolls and the inability of the Indian owners to sell the land or have it taken from them by legal process to collect on a debt or for foreclosure of a mortgage. In determining whether to approve an application to take land into trust under this statute, the SOI is required to consider a number of factors[15] and to inform "state and local governments having regulatory jurisdiction over the land to be acquired," giving them "30 days in which to provide written comments as to the acquisition's potential impacts on regulatory jurisdiction, real property taxes and special assessments."[16]

SECRETARIAL TWO-PART DETERMINATION EXCEPTION TO IGRA'S PROHIBITION OF GAMING ON LANDS ACQUIRED IN TRUST AFTER ENACTMENT OF IGRA

Lands acquired in trust after IGRA's enactment are generally not eligible for gaming if they are outside of and not contiguous to the boundaries of a tribe's reservation. There are exceptions to this policy, however, that allow gaming on certain "after acquired" or "newly acquired" land. One exception, sometimes referred to as a two-part determination, permits gaming on lands newly taken into trust with the consent of the governor of the state in which the land is located after the SOI: (1) consults with state and local officials, including officials of other tribes; (2) determines "that a gaming establishment on the newly acquired lands would be in the best interest of the Indian tribe and its members"; and (3) determines that gaming "would not be detrimental to the surrounding community."[17]

OTHER EXCEPTIONS

Other exceptions permit gaming on after-acquired land and do not require gubernatorial consent, consultation with local officials, or SOI determination as to tribal best interest and effect upon local community. They relate to any of five circumstances:

1. Any tribe without a reservation on October 17, 1988, is allowed to have gaming on newly acquired lands in Oklahoma that are either within the boundaries of the tribe's former reservation or contiguous to other land held in trust or restricted status by SOI for the tribe.[18]
2. If a tribe had no reservation on October 17, 1988, and is "presently" located in a state other than Oklahoma, it may have gaming on newly acquired lands in that state that are "within the Indian tribe's last recognized reservation within the State."[19]
3. A tribe may have gaming on lands taken into trust as a land claim settlement.[20]
4. A tribe may have gaming on lands taken into trust as the initial reservation of a tribe newly recognized under the Bureau of Indian Affairs' process for recognizing groups as Indian tribes;[21]
5. A tribe may have gaming on lands representing "the restoration of lands for an Indian tribe that is restored to Federal recognition."[22]

FINAL RULE FOR GAMING ON NEWLY ACQUIRED TRUST LANDS

The Bureau of Indian Affairs (BIA) of the Department of the Interior (DOI) issued a final rule for gaming on newly acquired trust lands, 25 C.F.R., Part 292, on May 20, 2008.[23] The rule applies to all requests under 25 U.S.C. §2719 on which there has not been final agency action prior to June 19, 2008, the effective date of the regulation. There is an exception to this for DOI or National Indian Gaming Commission (NIGC)[24] opinions issued previously, which reserve "full discretion to qualify, withdraw or modify such opinions."[25]

In addition to specifying procedures for securing determinations as to whether land may qualify for one of IGRA's exceptions to its prohibition on gaming on newly acquired trust lands, the rule specifies factors that will be considered in making determinations under the statute. The rule covers both the two-part Secretarial Determination that gaming would benefit the tribe and not be detrimental to the surrounding community and the other exceptions to IGRA's ban on gaming on lands acquired after October 17, 1988: lands contiguous to the reservation boundaries; lands taken into trust on the basis of land claims settlements; initial reservations for newly acknowledged tribes; and lands restored to newly restored tribes. Requests for Secretarial Determinations must be directed to the SOI. Land-into-trust applications or applications requiring a determination of reservation status are to be directed to the BIA's Office of Indian Gaming; requests for opinions on whether a particular parcel meets one of the other exceptions may be directed either to the BIA's Office of Indian Gaming or the NIGC.[26]

Secretarial Determination

The rule specifies both procedures and application requirements for Secretarial Determinations that gaming on newly acquired lands would be in the best interest of the tribe and not detrimental to the surrounding community.[27] The information to be included in consultation letters sent to state and local governments is specified.[28] The rule specifies that a tribal application for a Secretarial Determination may be submitted at the same time as the application to have the land taken into trust.[29] The regulation includes (1) a definition of "surrounding community" that covers local governments and tribes within a 25-mile radius;[30] (2) detailed requirements as to projections that must accompany the application respecting benefits to the tribe and local community, potential detrimental effects, and proposals to mitigate any detrimental impacts.[31] In addition to projected benefits and detrimental impacts, the application for the Secretarial Determination must include (1) proof of present ownership and title status of the land; (2) any approved gaming ordinance, tribal organic documents, or gaming management contract; (3) distance of the land from any tribal reservation or trust lands and from the tribal governmental headquarters; and (4) the class III gaming compact, if one has been negotiated, otherwise, the proposed scope, including size, of the gaming operation.[32]

Among the detailed information which an application must contain on the projected benefits of the proposed gaming establishment are projections about income; tribal employment; benefits to the relationship with the non-Indian community; distance from the tribal government's location; and evidence of "significant historical connections, if any, to the land."[33] The rule also specifies that the following types of information may be included to "provide a basis for a Secretarial Determination": consulting agreements, financial and loan agreements, and any other agreements relating to the gaming establishment or the land on which it will be located.[34]

For evaluating the potential detrimental impact on the surrounding community, the rule requires submission of information to satisfy requirements of the National Environmental Policy Act.[35] It also details a variety of factors that must be addressed as aspects of the potential impact on the social and economic life of the surrounding community. For example, the application must address anticipated impacts on the community's character, land use patterns, economic development, and compulsive gambling within the community. Costs and potential sources of revenue to mitigate these effects must be identified. There is also a provision that requires an assessment of the impact on the "traditional cultural connection to the land" of any other tribe which has a significant historical connection to the land.[36]

Upon determining that gaming on the new lands would be in the best interest of the tribe and not detrimental to the local community, SOI must notify the state's governor. For the application to be approved, the governor must affirmatively concur in the determination within one year, with a possible one-time 1 80-day extension. If the governor does not affirmatively concur within the required time, the SOI will inform the applicant tribe that the application is no longer under consideration.[37]

Contiguous Lands

IGRA exempts newly acquired trust lands "within and contiguous to the boundaries of the reservation of the Indian tribe on October 17, 1988."[38] The rule defines "contiguous" to mean "two parcels of land having a common boundary notwithstanding the existence of non-navigable waters or a public road or right-of-way and includes parcels that touch at a point."[39]

Land Claim Settlement

IGRA includes an exception to its prohibition of gaming on after-acquired lands for "land ... taken into trust as part of ... a settlement of a land claim."[40] The rule elaborates on this by setting forth three methods by which land resulting from a land claim may qualify for this exception: (1) the land may have been the subject of land claim settlement legislation;[41] (2) the land may have been acquired under the settlement of a land claim executed by the parties, including the United States, which returns some land to the tribe and "extinguishes or resolves with finality the claims regarding the land returned";[42] or (3) the land may have been acquired under the settlement of a land claim not executed by the United States but entered into as a final court order or "is an enforceable agreement that in either case predates October 17, 1988 and resolves or extinguishes with finality the land claim at issue."[43]

Initial Reservation for a Newly Acknowledged Tribe

IGRA provides an exception to its prohibition on gaming on after-acquired lands for "lands ... taken into trust as part of ... the initial reservation of an Indian tribe acknowledged by the Secretary under the Federal acknowledgment process."[44] To satisfy this exception, the rule requires that (1) the tribe must have been acknowledged through the administrative acknowledgment process under 25 C.F.R., Part 83; (2) the tribe must have no gaming facility under the newly restored lands exception under IGRA; and (3) the land must be the first proclaimed reservation after acknowledgment.[45] If the tribe has no proclaimed reservation, the tribe must demonstrate its governmental presence and tribal population in the state and its significant historical connections with the area within the state, as well as a modern connection.[46]

Restored Lands

IGRA provides an exception to its prohibition of gaming on after-acquired lands for "lands ... taken into trust as part of ... the restoration of lands for an Indian tribe that is restored to Federal recognition."[47] The rule specifies that the tribe must satisfy three requirements before the restored lands exception may be invoked: (1) the tribe must have been federally recognized at one time;[48] (2) it must have lost its government-to-government relationship with the federal government;[49] and (3) it must have been restored to federal recognition.[50] The lands must meet certain criteria.[51] Trust acquisition of the lands may have been mandated by restoration legislation.[52] If trust acquisition is authorized but not mandated by restoration legislation and the legislation does not specify a particular geographic area, the rule requires that (1) the lands must be in the state where the tribe's government or population is located; (2) the tribe must demonstrate one or more modern connections to the land;[53] (3) it must show significant historical connection to the land; and (4) there must be a temporal connection between the date of acquisition of the land and the date of the tribe's restoration.[54] Similar requirements apply to tribes acknowledged under the administrative process, provided they have not had an initial reservation proclaimed after October 17, 1988. Tribes recognized by judicial determination or settlement agreement to which the United States is a party are also subject to similar requirements.[55]

BUREAU OF INDIAN AFFAIRS (BIA) RESCINDED GUIDANCE

On January 3, 2008, less than five months before promulgating the final rule applicable to gaming on newly acquired lands, DOI issued departmental "Guidance on taking off-reservation land into trust for gaming purposes"[56] (Guidance), which it rescinded on June 13, 2011.[57] Virtually simultaneously with issuing the Guidance and based on the criteria in the Guidance, the department sent letters to approximately 22 tribes either rejecting their applications to take off- reservation land into trust for Indian gaming or returning them as incomplete.[58] The Obama administration subjected the guidance to scrutiny[59] and withdrew it on June 13, 2011, following government-to-government consultations with tribal leaders and a review of BIA's land acquisition regulations[60] and those applicable to gaming on lands taken into trust after October 17, 1988.[61]

The rescinded Guidance was premised on an interpretation of the Indian Reorganization Act of 1934 (IRA),[62] which often provides the statutory basis for BIA to take land into trust for an Indian tribe, as primarily intended to be a means for tribes to consolidate reservation lands that were lost through the earlier allotment policy, which the IRA repudiated.[63] The 2008 Guidance, emphasized the criteria set forth in 25 C.F.R. § 151.11(b) requiring BIA to scrutinize anticipated benefits from off-reservation acquisitions. A key element of the Guidance was an assessment of how much negative effect there would be on reservation life if proposed gaming facilities are located farther than "a commutable distance from the reservation," including (1) how the on-reservation unemployment rate will be affected; (2) the effect of any exodus of tribal members from the reservation on reservation life; (3) if tribal members leave the reservation, the impact on their descendants in terms of tribal membership and identification with the tribe; and (4) specific on-reservation benefits of the proposal, including whether jobs will be created. The Guidance presumed that state and local governments at a distance from a reservation would be unfamiliar with Indian trust land jurisdictional issues and that distance from the reservation will hamper the efficiency of tribal government operations. It virtually required intergovernmental cooperative agreements and compatibility with state and local zoning and land use requirements.

DOI REVIEW OF THE STANDARDS FOR TAKING LAND INTO TRUST FOR GAMING AND DETERMINATION TO RESCIND THE GUIDANCE

DOI conducted consultation sessions with tribal leaders throughout the United States focusing on the need for the Guidance; whether any of the provisions of the regulation on qualifying newly acquired land for gaming, 25 C.F.R., Part 292, Subparts A and C, as previously promulgated, should be revised; and whether compliance with the land acquisition regulation, 25 C.F.R., Part 151, should come prior to the two-part determination for taking off-reservation land into trust.[64]

The result of the review was a determination that both regulations were fully sufficient and that the Guidance should be withdrawn. The Guidance was found to be unnecessary for processing applications to qualify "off-reservation" land for gaming under 25 C.F.R., Part 292, and potentially confusing with respect to processing applications to take land into trust, under 25 C.F.R., Part 151, in situations where gaming was contemplated. There was no change recommended with respect to the question of whether the application for gaming should accompany the application for taking land into trust. The current rule permits this but does not require it.[65]

The review and consultation process was the result of a June 18, 2010, memorandum issued by the Secretary of the Interior, Ken Salazar, directing the Assistant Secretary of the Interior for Indian Affairs to review DOI's decision-making guidance and regulatory standards with respect to handling applications to take land into trust for gaming.[66] In the memorandum, the Secretary required DOI, in connection with this process, to "engage in government-to-government consultations ... to obtain input from Indian tribes." The review covered both land-into-trust acquisitions on an off-reservation basis under the two-part determination and "reservation and equal footing exceptions."[67] The latter category covers acquisitions on-reservation or under the exceptions for settlement of a land claim, part of an initial reservation, or restoration of lands.

In ordering the consultation, the Secretary noted that, as of the date of the memorandum, there were nine applications requiring a two-part determination, and that consultation was likely to mean a delay in processing those application, but that "given the Department's discretion in this area, it is appropriate that we take the necessary time to identify and adopt principled and transparent criteria regarding such gaming determinations," and "deliberate government-to-government consultations will lead us to the implementation of a sound policy in this area."[68] The Secretary noted that, since IGRA's enactment, only 36 applications have been approved as settlements of land claims, initial reservations, or restoration of lands; and that, at the time of the memorandum, 24 such applications were pending before the Department. He also stated that decisions on these applications "largely depends upon a legal determination" and recommended that the DOI Solicitor's Office provide a determination on such applications.[69]

DOI conducted six government-to-government consultations and elicited the following input on the issue of whether the Guidance should be modified, rescinded, or become part of 25 C.F.R., Part 292:

> Many tribes recommended that the Department rescind the Guidance Memorandum because it was not subject to tribal consultation and because it was, in their view,

inconsistent with broader Federal Indian policy. Other tribes contended that the Guidance Memorandum was unreasonable because it makes inappropriate judgments regarding what is in the 'best interests' of tribes, assumes that a tribe will experience a reduced benefit if its gaming facility is located at a certain distance from its reservation, and equates 'reduced benefit' with a harm to the tribe. Other tribes maintained that the Guidance Memorandum unfairly prejudices tribes with reservations located at great distances from population centers and ignores historical facts regarding the locations where the Federal Government created reservations. Some tribal leaders expressed support for the primary objective of the Guidance Memorandum, which is to limit off-reservation gaming to areas close to existing reservations.[70]

Assistant Secretary for Indian Affairs, Larry Echo Hawk, in a June 13, 2011, memorandum, set forth the statutory and regulatory requirements which tribes must satisfy in order to gain approval for a gaming facility on land acquired in trust after IGRA's enactment under the "off-reservation" exception.[71] He noted that decisions on gaming involve particularized facts varying with each tribe, and that the January 2008 Guidance failed to fully provide a means for considering, on a case-by-case basis, the array of factors which should be considered in each decision. According to his analysis, the Guidance established a virtually inflexible approach that assumes that a distant casino will have a deleterious effect on tribal life. His final conclusion was that the existing regulation governing gaming on after-acquired lands provides "comprehensive and rigorous standards that set forth the Department's authority and duties when considering applications for off-reservation gaming.... [and] adequately provide standards for evaluating such acquisitions ...."[72] He characterized the regulation as offering "strict and transparent standards for evaluating tribal applications to conduct off-reservation gaming."[73] With respect to the general land acquisition regulation under 25 C.F.R., Part 151, the conclusion was that the Guidance was unnecessary and that it might "unnecessarily constrain the Department's decision making process." Under the regulation, according to Assistant Secretary Echo Hawk's memorandum, the Secretary must weigh the impact of the trust acquisition on specified aspects of state and local jurisdiction in a manner that considers all the factors in the regulation, and, unlike the Guidance, the regulation does not mandate disapproval of an application on a single issue.

LEGISLATION

111th Congress

Several bills providing federal recognition or authorizing the placement of land into federal trust status contained provisions aimed at precluding gaming. Two of these bills were enacted:

- Section 2601(h)(4)(A) of P.L. 111-11, 123 Stat. 991, 1115, transfers certain federal land to the SOI to be held in trust for the benefit of the Washoe Tribe and states that such land "shall not be eligible, or considered to have been taken into trust, for class

II or class III gaming (as those terms are defined in section 4 of the Indian Gaming Regulatory Act (25 U.S.C. § 2701)."
- P.L. 111-323 prohibits gaming on federal land transferred to the Hoh Tribe.

Other 111th Congress legislation which did not become law:

- S. 338 would have amended Section 819 of P.L. 106-568, 114 Stat. 2867, 2919, to eliminate the provision that specifies that land taken into trust for the Lytton Rancheria of California under Section 819 is deemed to have been taken into trust prior to enactment of IGRA and to require the SOI to treat land taken into trust under Section 819 "as if the land was acquired on October 9, 2003, the date on which the Secretary took the land into trust." The legislation also would have authorized class II gaming on land taken into trust pursuant to Section 819 and precluded the Lytton Rancheria from expanding "the exterior physical measurement of any facility ... in use for class II gaming activities."
- H.R. 2973 would have required that any tribe which subsequently obtains federal recognition satisfy a requirement of 25 continuous years of federal recognition before IGRA applies to it.
- Various bills would have provided federal recognition for particular tribes. These included S. 1011 and H.R. 2314 (establishing a process for recognizing a Native Hawaiian governing entity); S. 1735 and H.R. 31 (providing federal recognition for the Lumbee Tribe); S. 1178 and H.R. 1385 (providing federal recognition for specified Indian tribes of Virginia); H.R. 326 (taking land into trust for the benefit of the Cocopah Tribe of Arizona); and H.R. 2040 (providing for the taking of land into federal trust status for the benefit of the Samish Indian Nation).

112th Congress

S. 771

S. 771,[74] the Tribal Gaming Eligibility Act, requires tribes to satisfy new standards before newly acquired lands may be found to be eligible for IGRA gaming. It applies to three of the exceptions to IGRA's general prohibition of gaming on lands acquired after IGRA's enactment. The only exceptions to which it applies are those under 25 U.S.C.§27 19(b)(1)(B): land claim settlement, initial reservation for a newly acknowledged tribe, or restoration of lands for a newly restored tribe. Under this bill, for a tribe to rely on one of these exceptions for gaming on newly acquired trust land, before the land is taken into trust, the tribe must have "received a written determination from the Secretary that the land is eligible for gaming" that includes findings that the tribe has "a substantial, direct, modern connection to the land" and "a substantial, direct, aboriginal connection to the land."[75]

For a tribe with a reservation to establish a modern connection to the land, the tribe must show both geographic and temporal connections to the land. The land must be within a 25-mile radius of either the tribal headquarters (for tribes with a reservation) or the residence of "a significant number" of tribal members (for tribes without a reservation). A tribe which has a reservation must show both modern and aboriginal connections to the land and wait five years after restoration or recognition to be eligible for one of these exceptions. A tribe without a reservation must show modern and aboriginal connections to the land, and (1) the land must be part of its first request for newly acquired land after being recognized or restored; (2) the application to take the land into trust must be received by the Secretary within five years of recognition or restoration; and (3) the tribe may not be conducting gaming on any other land. The modern connection to the land requirement means that any tribe seeking one of these exemptions must demonstrate "a temporal connection to, or routine presence on, the land" during the period from October 17, 1988, to the date of the Secretary's determination. To determine whether a tribe satisfies the requirement for an aboriginal connection to the land, the legislation contains a list of factors which the Secretary may consider, including historical presence on the land; lineal descent or cultural affiliation of members based on 43 C.F.R. §10.14;[76] whether the land is in an area where the tribe's language has been used; whether the land is near tribal "culturally significant sites"; whether the tribe was officially removed from the land; and other factors showing tribal presence on the land antedating the presence of "nonnative individuals, the Federal Government, or any other sovereign entity."[77]

S. 1424

S. 1424, the Off-Reservation Land Acquisition Guidance Act, requires that, before taking "off-reservation"[78] land into trust for gaming, the SOI must prepare reports assessing (1) the benefits to the tribe and (2) the concerns of state and local governments. The evaluation of tribal benefits must address on-reservation employment, impact on reservation life, specific on-reservation benefits, and "whether the tribal government can efficiently exercise the governmental and regulatory responsibilities of the tribal government if a gaming facility is constructed on the off-reservation land."[79] The report on state and local concerns must assess whether transfer of jurisdiction will disrupt the operations of local governments; impacts on real property taxes; whether there are agreements with the tribe and the state addressing state and local government concerns; negative effects of the anticipated use of the land; and potential incompatible use of the land with uses and zoning of adjacent or contiguous lands.[80] The bill requires the tribe to submit documentation of the plans for the use of the land, including contracts and agreement, and to obtain an opinion from DOI that the land is eligible for gaming. Under the legislation, the SOI may not take off-reservation land into trust under the IRA without determining, among other things, that the proposed use of the land is compatible with state and local zoning and public health and safety requirements. The bill requires applications pending at the date it is enacted as well as all future applications to comply with this act and not to be approved until implementing regulations are promulgated.

Other Bills

There are other bills which provide federal recognition of tribal status or taking land into trust for a tribe that include explicit provisions relating to gaming. Among them are the following:

- S. 379/H.R. 783, the Thomasina E. Jordan Indian Tribes of Virginia Recognition Act. This legislation provides federal recognition for six Virginia Indian Tribes: the Chickahominy Indian Tribe; the Chickahominy Indian Tribe-Eastern Division; the Upper Mattaponi Tribe; the Rappahannock Tribe, Inc.; the Monacan Indian Nation;

and the Nansemond Indian Tribe. It includes provisions prohibiting each of these tribes from "conducting gaming activities as a matter of claimed inherent authority or under the authority of any Federal law, including the Indian Gaming Regulatory Act (25 U.S.C. 2701 et seq.) or under any regulations thereunder promulgated by the Secretary or the National Indian Gaming Commission."[81]

- S. 675/H.R. 1250, the Native Hawaiian Government Reorganization Act. This legislation provides a process for federal recognition of a Native Hawaiian governing entity. It includes a provision which states that "[t]he Native Hawaiian governing entity and Native Hawaiians may not conduct gaming activities as a matter of claimed inherent authority or under the authority of any Federal law, including the Indian Gaming Regulatory Act (25 U.S.C. 2701 et seq.) or under any regulations thereunder promulgated by the Secretary or the National Indian Gaming Commission." It further states that "[t]he prohibition ... regarding the use of Indian Gaming Regulatory Act (25 U.S.C. 2701 et seq.) and inherent authority to game applies regardless of whether gaming by Native Hawaiians or the Native Hawaiian governing entity would be located on land within the State of Hawaii or within any other State or territory of the United States."[82]

- S. 617,[83] the Elko Motocross and Tribal Conveyance Act. This legislation includes a provision transferring approximately 373 acres of Bureau of Land Management land to be held in trust for the Te-moak Tribe of Western Shoshone Indians of Nevada for certain specified purposes. The legislation includes a provision which states that the land "shall not be eligible, or considered to have been taken into trust, for class II gaming or class III gaming (as those terms are defined in section 4 of the Indian Gaming Regulatory Act (25 U.S.C. 2703))."[84]

- S. 908,[85] an amendment to the Siletz Tribe Indian Restoration Act.[86] This legislation authorizes the Secretary to take land into trust for the Siletz Indian Tribe, subject to specified conditions, provided that the land is within the boundaries of the original 1855 Siletz Coast Reservation. A provision of this legislation states that "[a]ny real property taken into trust under [S. 908] shall not be eligible, or used, for any gaming activity carried out under the Indian Gaming Regulatory Act...."[87]

- S. 1218/H.R. 27,[88] the Lumbee Recognition Act. This legislation provides for federal recognition of the Lumbee Tribe of North Carolina and authorizes the Secretary to take land into trust for the Tribe. It includes a provision prohibiting the Tribe from conducting "gaming activities as a matter of claimed inherent authority or under the authority of any Federal law, including the Indian Gaming Regulatory Act ... or under any regulations thereunder promulgated by the Secretary of the Interior or the National Indian Gaming Commission."[89]

- H.R. 475,[90] the Fountainhead Property Land Transfer Act. This legislation authorizes the transfer from the Department of the Army to the Secretary of the Interior, of 18 acres of federal land in McIntosh County, OK, to be held in trust for the benefit of the Muscogee (Creek) Nation. It includes a provision prohibiting the Muscogee (Creek) Nation from conducting on this land any "gaming activities ... as a matter of claimed inherent authority or ... under any Federal law, including the Indian Gaming Regulatory Act (25 U.S.C. 2701 et seq.) and any regulations promulgated by the Secretary or the National Indian Gaming Commission pursuant to that Act."[91]

- H.R. 1991, the Cocopah Lands Act. This legislation mandates the trust acquisition of certain lands, provided certain standards are met, for the benefit of the Cocopah Tribe of Arizona. It includes a provision precluding gaming under IGRA on these lands.[92]
- H.R. 2938, the Gila Bend Indian Reservation Lands Replacement Clarification Act, would prohibit IGRA class II and class III gaming on lands acquired for the Tohono O'odham Nation pursuant to the Gila Bend Indian Reservation Lands Replacement Act, P.L. 99-503.

End Notes

[1] P.L. 100-497, 102 *Stat.* 2467, 25 U.S.C. §§2701 - 2721; 18 U.S.C. §§1166 - 1168.

[2] 25 U.S.C. §2703(4).

[3] 25 U.S.C. §§2703(6) - (8), and 2710.

[4] 25 U.S.C. §§2710(b)(1)(A), and 2710(d)(1)(B).

[5] Mashantucket Pequot Tribe v. State of Connecticut, 737 F. Supp. 169 (D. Conn. 1990), *aff'd*, 913 F.2d 1024 (2nd Cir. 1990), *cert. denied*, 499 U.S. 975 (1991). Compacts may prescribe, with exacting detail, the specifics of each game permitted. See, e.g., the compact between New York State and the Seneca Nation, Appendix A, listing 26 permitted games and the specifications for each, available at http://www.sni.org/node/22.

[6] Rumsey Indian Rancheria of Wintun Indians v. Wilson, 64 F. 3d 1250 (9th Cir. 1994), *opinion amended on denial of rehearing*, 99 F. 3d. 321 (9th Cir. 1996), *cert. denied sub nom* Sycuan Band of Mission Indians v. Wilson, 521 U.S. 1118 (1997); State ex rel. Clark v. Johnson, 120 N.M. 562; 904 P. 2d 11 (1995).

[7] 25 U.S.C. §2703(4).

[8] See, e.g., South Dakota v. Yankton Sioux Tribe, 522 U.S. 329 (1998); Solem v. Bartlett, 465 U.S. 463 (1984).

[9] "Restricted fee land" is defined to mean "land the title to which is held by an individual Indian or tribe and which can only be alienated or encumbered by the owner with the approval of the SOI because of limitations in the conveyance instrument pursuant to federal law." 25 C.F.R. § 151.2 If restricted land is involved, it may only be considered "Indian lands," for IGRA purposes if the tribe "exercises governmental power" over it. *Kansas v. United States*, 249 F. 3d 1213 (10th Cir. 2001), held that a tribe could not accept governmental authority by consent from owners of restricted land whom the tribe had accepted into membership.

[10] See, e.g., Indian Country U.S.A., Inc. v. Oklahoma, 829 F. 2d 967 (10th Cir. 1987), involving a tribe that exercised taxing authority.

[11] See, e.g., Rhode Island v. Narragansett Tribe of Indians, 816 F. Supp 796 (D. R.I. 1993), *aff'd, modified,* 19 F. 3d 685 (1st Cir. 1994), *cert. denied* 513 U.S. 919 (1994). This case held that, despite the fact that a federal statute conveyed civil and criminal jurisdiction over a tribe's reservation to a state, the criterion of exercising governmental power was satisfied by various factors including federal recognition of a government-to-government relationship, judicial confirmation of sovereign immunity, and a federal agency's treatment of the tribe as a state for purposes of administering an environmental law.

[12] U.S. Const. art. I, §8, cl. 3 (Indian Commerce Clause), and *id.*, art. IV, §3, cl. 2 (Property Clause).

[13] See, e.g., §606 of the Omnibus Indian Advancement Act, P.L. 106-568, 114 Stat. 2868, 2909, 25 U.S.C. §1778d, mandating that the SOI take into trust any land acquired by the Torres-Martinez Desert Cahuilla Indians within certain defined areas.

[14] Act of June 18, 1934, ch. 57, 48 *Stat.* 985, 25 U.S.C. §465. This statute specifies that such land is to be exempt from state and local taxation. For a discussion of a recent Supreme Court case confining the authority of DOI to take land into trust pursuant to this statute to those tribes which were "under Federal jurisdiction" when the Wheeler-Howard Act was enacted in 1934, *see* CRS Report RL34521, *Carcieri v. Salazar: The Secretary of the Interior May Not Acquire Trust Land for the Narragansett Indian Tribe Under 25 U.S. C. § 465 Because That Statute Applies to Tribes "Under Federal Jurisdiction" in 1934*, by M. Maureen Murphy.

[15] The factors are listed in 25 C.F.R. §§151.10 (on-reservation acquisitions) and 151. 11 (off-reservation acquisitions). For off-reservation acquisitions by tribes, in addition to the criteria applicable to on-reservation acquisitions, there are additional requirements. An application from a tribe seeking to have any land taken into trust must show (1) statutory authority; (2) purposed land use; (3) impact of removal of land from state and local tax base; (4) potential jurisdictional and land use problems; (5) BIA's capacity to handle the new responsibilities; and, (6) information for the SOI to meet environmental law responsibilities. 25 C.F.R. § 151.10. In addition, a tribe seeking an off-reservation acquisition of land-into-trust will be subjected to the following criteria: (1) greater scrutiny as the distance from the reservation increases; (2) preparation of a business plan specifying potential economic benefits, if a business enterprise is contemplated; and (3) a

requirement that the SOI give greater weight to concerns raised by the relevant state and local governments with respect to potential impacts on "regulatory jurisdiction, real property taxes and special assessments." 25 C.F.R. §151.11.

[16] 25 C.F.R. § 151.10. The factors which the Secretary of the Interior (SOI) must weigh in considering an application for an on-reservation acquisition include the need for the land; its proposed use; "the impact on the State and its political subdivisions resulting from the removal of the land from the tax rolls"; "[j]urisdictional problems and potential conflicts of land use which may arise." 25 C.F.R. §§151.10(b), (c), (d), (e), and (f). In addition to these factors, the SOI must consider other factors and give greater weight to state and local concerns when an off-reservation acquisition is at issue. The regulation reads:

The Secretary shall consider the following requirements in evaluating tribal requests for the acquisition of lands in trust status, when the land is located outside of and noncontiguous to the tribe's reservation, and the acquisition is not mandated:

(a) The criteria listed in § 151.10....

(b) The location of the land relative to state boundaries, and its distance from the boundaries of the tribe's reservation, shall be considered as follows: as the distance between the tribe's reservation and the land to be acquired increases, the Secretary shall give greater scrutiny to the tribe's justification of anticipated benefits from the acquisition. The Secretary shall give greater weight to the concerns raised pursuant to paragraph (d) of this section.

(c) Where land is being acquired for business purposes, the tribe shall provide a plan with specifies the anticipated economic benefits associated with the proposed use.

(d) Contact with state and local governments pursuant to § 151.10 (e) and (f) shall be completed as follows: Upon receipt of a tribe's written request to have land taken in trust, the Secretary shall notify the state and local governments having regulatory jurisdiction over the land to be acquired. The notice shall inform the state and local government that each will be given 30 days in which to provide written comment as to the acquisition's potential impacts on regulatory jurisdiction, real property taxes and special assessments. 25 C.F.R. § 151.11.

[17] 25 U.S.C. §2719(b)(1). For recent SOI two-part determination decisions see U.S. Department of the Interior, News Release, "Echo Hawk Issues Two Decisions on Tribal Gaming Applications" (December 20, 2011) (Keweenaw Bay Indian Community and Cayuga Nation of New York), and U.S. Department of the Interior, News Release, "Assistant Secretary Echo Hawk Issues Four Decisions on Tribal Gaming Applications" (September 2, 2011) (Enterprise Rancheria of Maidu Indians, North Fork Rancheria of Mono Indians, Guidiville Band of Pomo Indians, and Pueblo of Jemez). Available at http://www.bia.gov/idc/groups/public/documents/text/idc015848.pdf;http://www.bia.gov/idc/groups/public/ documents/text/idc015000.pdf.

[18] 25 U.S.C. §2719(a)(2)(A)(i) and 2719(a)(2)(A)(ii).

[19] 25 U.S.C. §2719(a)(A)(2)(B). There are other specific exceptions for certain lands involved in a federal court action involving the St. Croix Chippewa Indians of Wisconsin and the Miccosukee Tribe of Indians of Florida. 25 U.S.C. §2719(b)(2).

[20] Under this provision SOI took into trust a convention center in Niagara Falls, N.Y, now being used for casino gaming by the Seneca Nation, on the basis of legislation settling disputes over the renewal of 99-year leases in Salamanca, N.Y., 25 U.S.C. §§1174, et seq.

[21] See CRS Report RS21 109, *The Bureau of Indian Affairs's Process for Recognizing Groups as Indian Tribes*, by M. Maureen Murphy. In an opinion on "Trust Acquisition for the Huron Potawatomi, Inc.," the DOI Solicitor General's office stated that "the first time a reservation is proclaimed ..., it constitutes the 'initial reservation' under 25 U.S.C. § 2719(b)(1)(B), and the ... [tribe] may avoid the ban on gaming on 'newly acquired land' for any lands taken into trust as part of the initial reservation—those placed in trust before or at the time of the initial proclamation. Land acquired after the initial proclamation of the reservation will not fall within the exception." Memorandum to the Regional Director, Midwest Regional Office, Bureau of Indian Affairs 2 (December 13, 2000). http://www.nigc.gov/ LinkClick. aspx?link=NIGC+Uploads%2findianlands% 2f33_ nottawaseppihuronpotawatomibnd.pdf&tabid=120&mid= 957.

[22] 25 U.S.C. §2719(b)(1) (B)(iii).

[23] 73 *Federal Register* 29354. On October 5, 2006, the Bureau of Indian Affairs (BIA) issued a proposed regulation setting standards for determining whether class II or class III gaming may take place on after-acquired lands. 71 *Federal Register* 58769. The comment period was extended to February 1, 2007, 71 *Federal Register* 70335 (December 4, 2006); 71 *Federal Register* 70335 (January 17, 2007), and corrections issued. 71 *Federal Register* 70335. There were earlier proposed regulations that never became effective, 65 *Federal Register* 55471 (September 14, 2000). An earlier proposal, 57 *Federal Register* 51487 (July 15, 1991) was never issued in final form.

[24] The National Indian Gaming Commission (NIGC) is a three-member Commission established by IGRA; it is composed of a Chairman, appointed by the President with the advice and consent of the Senate, and two associate members, appointed by the SOI. 25 U.S.C. §§2704 (a) and (b)(1). It is charged with certain

regulatory responsibilities with respect to gaming under IGRA. For further information, see the NIGC website at http://www.nigc.gov/.

[25] 25 C.F.R. §292.26 (this and subsequent references to 25 C.F.R. Part 292 are to the version published in 73 *Federal Register* 29354, 29375). The regulation specifies that it "shall not apply to applicable agency actions when, before the effective date ... the Department or the National Indian Gaming Commission (NIGC) issued a written opinion regarding the applicability of 25 U.S.C. § 2719 for land to be used for a particular gaming establishment, provided that the Department or the NIGC retains full discretion to qualify, withdraw or modify such opinions." 25 C.F.R. §292.26(b).

[26] 25 C.F.R. §292.3.

[27] 25 C.F.R. §§292.13 - 24.

[28] 25 C.F.R. §292.20. The letter rule stipulates topics which recipients are to be asked to address in their comments; these parallel the potential detrimental effect factors which the tribe must address in its application. 25 C.F.R. §§292.20 (b) (1) - (6) (consultation letter); 25 C.F.R. §§292.18(b)-(g) (tribal application).

[29] 25 C.F.R. §292.15.

[30] 25 C.F.R. §292.2.

[31] 25C.F.R. §§292.17 - 18.

[32] 25 C.F.R. §292.16.

[33] 25 C.F.R. §292.17. "Significant historical connection" is defined elsewhere to mean "that the land is located within the boundaries of the tribe's last reservation under a ratified or unratified treaty, or a tribe can demonstrate by historical documentation, the existence of the tribe's villages, burial grounds, occupancy or subsistence use in the vicinity of the land." 25 C.F.R. §292.2.

[34] 25 C.F.R. §292.17(j).

[35] 42 U.S.C. §432 1 et seq.

[36] 25 C.F.R. §292.18.

[37] 25 C.F.R. §292.23.

[38] 25 U.S.C. §2719(a)(1).

[39] 25 C.F.R. §292.2.

[40] 25 U.S.C. §2719(b)(1)(B)(i).

[41] 25 C.F.R. §292.5(a). The rule covers land "[a]cquired under a settlement of a land claim that resolves or extinguishes with finality the tribe's land claim in whole or in part, thereby resulting in the alienation or loss of possession of some or all of the lands claimed by the tribe in legislation enacted by Congress."

[42] 25 C.F.R. §292(5)(B)(1).

[43] 25 C.F.R. §292.5.

[44] 25 U.S.C. §2719(b)(1)(B)(ii).

[45] 25 C.F.R. §§292.6(a)(b) and (c).

[46] 25 C.F.R. §292.6(d). Two modern connections are mentioned, either of which would qualify: the land must be near where a significant number of tribal members reside; it must be within a 25-mile radius of tribal headquarters or facilities that have existed at least two years at that location.

[47] 25 U.S.C. §2719(b)(1)(B)(iii).

[48] The regulation provides a non-exclusive list of four methods by which a tribe may establish its having been federally recognized: (1) treaty negotiations with the United States; (2) the existence of a determination by DOI that the tribe could organize under the IRA or the Oklahoma Indian Welfare Act; (3) federal legislation indicating the existence of a government-to-government relationship; and (4) acquisition by the United States at one time of land for the benefit of the tribe. 25 C.F.R. §§292.8(a) - (d).

[49] Ways of establishing loss of government-to-government relationship that are specified in the rule are: termination legislation, restoration legislation, and "'[c]onsistent historical written documentation from the Federal Government effectively stating that it no longer recognized a government-to-government relationship with the tribe or its members or taking action to end the government-to-government relationship." 25 C.F.R. §292.9.

[50] 25 C.F.R. §292.7. To establish that it has been restored to federal recognition, a tribe must show: restoration legislation; recognition under the administrative process, 25 C.F.R., Part 83; or judicial determination in a settlement agreement entered into by the United States. 25 C.F.R. §292.10.

[51] 25 C.F.R. §§292.11 - 12.

[52] 25 C.F.R. §292.11(a) (requirements for trust acquisitions for tribes restored by federal legislation).

[53] Modern connections include reasonable commuting distance of tribal reservation; if tribe has no reservation, land must be near where a significant number of tribal members reside; land must be within a 25-mile radius of where the tribal governmental headquarters have been for at least two years. 25 C.F.R. §292.12(a).

[54] A temporal relationship may be evidenced by a tribe's first request for newly acquired lands since restoration or if the tribe is not gaming on other lands, a request for trust acquisition within 25 years of restoration. 25 C.F.R. §292.12(c).

[55] 25 C.F.R. §§292.1 1(b) (administrative acknowledgment); 292.11(c) (judicial determination).

[56] "Guidance on taking off-reservation land into trust for gaming purposes," Memorandum from Assistant Secretary for Indian Affairs, Carl Artman, to All Regional Directors, Bureau of Indian Affairs, and George Skibine,

Office of Indian Gaming (January 3, 2008); available at http://www.bia.gov/idc/groups/
public/documents/text/idc-001896.pdf

[57] "Guidance for Processing Applications to Acquire Land in Trust for Gaming Purposes," Memorandum from Assistant Secretary—Indian Affairs Larry Echo Hawk, to All Regional Directors, Bureau of Indian Affairs, and Director, Office of Indian Gaming (June 13, 2011).

[58] Denial letters were issued to: the Big Lagoon Rancheria, the Chemehuevi Indian Tribe, the Hannahville Indian Community, the Pueblo of Jemez, the Lac du Flambeau Band of Lake Superior Chippewa Indians of Wisconsin, the Los Coyotes Band of Cahuilla & Cupeno Indians, the Mississippi Band of Choctaw Indians, the St. Regis Mohawk Tribe, the Stockbridge Munsee Community of Wisconsin, the Seneca-Cayuga Tribe of Oklahoma, and the United Keetoowah Band of Cherokee Indians. In addition BIA notified the following tribes that their applications were incomplete and no further action would be taken on them as submitted: Ysleta del Sur Pueblo, Turtle Mountain Band of Chippewa Indians, Muckleshoot Tribe of Washington, Lower Elwha Klallam Tribe, Lac Vieux Desert Band of Lake Superior Chippewa Indians, Kickapoo Tribe and Sac and Fox Nation, Ho-Chunk Nation, Dry Creek Rancheria, Colorado River Indian Tribes, Confederated Tribes of the Colville Reservation, and the Burns Paiute Tribe. Documents may be found at http://www.indianz.com/News/2008/006500.asp.

[59] "Echo Hawk Announces Tribal Consultation on Indian Gaming Land into Trust Determinations," Office of the Assistant Secretary—Indian Affairs, U.S. Department of the Interior, News Release (August 31, 2010); available at http://www.bia.gov/idc/groups/ public/documents/text/idc010772.pdf.
According to this News Release,
Secretary Salazar issued a directive on July 18, 2010, recommending a thorough review of the "current guidance and regulatory standards" used to make decisions for off-reservation two-part determinations under Section 20 of the Indian Gaming Regulatory Act (IGRA) and its implementing regulations. In accordance with the Secretary's directive, and in keeping with the Department of Interior's commitment to government-to-government consultation, the OIG [Office of Indian Gaming] will engage with tribal governments on three major subjects: (1) the January 3, 2008 Memorandum regarding Guidance on Taking Off-reservation Land into Trust for Gaming Purposes; (2) whether there is a need to revise any of the provisions of 25 C.F.R. Part 292, Subpart A (Definitions) and Subpart C (Two-Part Determinations); and (3) whether the Department of the Interior's process of requiring compliance with 25 C.F.R. Part 151 (Land Into Trust Regulations) should come before or after the Two-Part Determination.

[60] 25 C.F.R., Part 151.

[61] 25 C.F.R., Part 292.

[62] 25 U.S.C. §§461 et seq.

[63] The specific IRA provision upon which the trust acquisitions rely, however, does not limit the BIA's power to take land into trust to lands within existing reservations. It reads as follows: "The Secretary of the Interior is hereby authorized, in his discretion, to acquire, through purchase, relinquishment, gift, exchange, or assignment lands, within or without existing reservations, including otherwise restricted allotments, whether the allottee be living or deceased, for the purpose of providing lands for Indians." 25 U.S.C. §465. There is another IRA provision, 25 U.S.C. §467, which specifically permits the SOI to proclaim "new Indian reservations on lands acquired pursuant" to various IRA provisions, including Section 465.

[64] Letter from George T. Skibine, Acting Principal Deputy Assistant Secretary—Indian Affairs, to Tribal Leaders (August 24, 2010), http://www.bia.gov/idc/groups/public/documents/text/ idc010719.pdf. A list of nine issues for consultation is appended to the letter. It reads as follows:
LIST OF ISSUES FOR CONSULTATION
1. Whether the definitions of the following terms in 25 C.F.R. 292.2 should be amended: (1) Appropriate State and local officials; (2) Nearby Indian tribe; (3) Significant historical connection; and (4) Surrounding community.
2. Whether any of the provisions in 25 C.F.R.292.19 (How must an application describe the benefits and impacts of the proposed gaming establishment to the tribe and its members) should be modified.
3. Whether any of the provisions in 25 C.F.R. 292.18 (What information must an application contain on detrimental impacts to the surrounding community) should be modified.
4. Whether the consultation process with appropriate State and local officials and officials of nearby tribes described in 25 C.F.R. 292.19 is adequate.
5. Whether the information sought from consulted parties in 25 C.F.R. 292.20 is sufficient.
6. Whether the evaluation criteria contained in 25 C.F.R. 292.21 are appropriate.
7. Whether the timeframes for a governor's concurrence contained in 25 C.F.R. 292.23(b) should be modified.
8. Whether the Memorandum issued by Assistant Secretary Carl Artman on January 3, 2008, regarding guidance on taking off-reservation land into trust for gaming purposes should be withdrawn, modified, or incorporated into the regulations in 25 C.F.R. Part 292.

9. Whether land on which an Indian tribe proposes to establish a gaming establishment should be taken into trust before or after compliance with the requirements of the two-part determination in 25 U.S.C. 2719(b)(I)(A).

[65] 25 C.F.R. §292.15.

[66] "Decisions on Indian Gaming Applications," Memorandum from Secretary Ken Salazar to Assistant Secretary—Indian Affairs (June 18, 2010), http://www.bia.gov/WhatWeDo/ ServiceOverview/Gaming/index.htm.

[67] *Id.*, at 2. The Secretary further stated that he expected the Assistant Secretary to "undertake regular and meaningful consultation and collaboration with tribal leaders to continue to develop sound federal Indian gaming policy ... [i]n addition, it is important that we keep the United States Congress fully aware of our efforts." *Id.*, at 3.

[68] *Id.*, at 2.

[69] *Id.*, at 2-3.

[70] Guidance for Processing Applications to Acquire Land in Trust for Gaming Purposes," Memorandum from Assistant Secretary—Indian Affairs Larry Echo Hawk, to All Regional Directors, Bureau of Indian Affairs, and Director, Office of Indian Gaming, 3 (June 13, 2011). (Hereinafter, June 13, Memorandum.)

[71] June 13, Memorandum, at 1. In the Memorandum, Assistant Secretary Echo Hawk states that any gaming on newly acquired land must satisfy three criteria: (1) it must have been taken into trust; (2) it must satisfy one of the exceptions to the prohibition of gaming on lands acquired in trust after IGRA's enactment; and (3) if class III gaming is involved, there must be a tribal-state compact. With respect to the second of these, Assistant Secretary Echo Hawk distinguished between "equal footing" exceptions—for Restored Lands, Settlement of a Land Claim, and Initial Reservation—and the two-part determination exception, which he characterized as the "off-reservation" exception. (He notes that because this requires several layers of review, including concurrence in a secretarial two-part determination, only five tribes have succeeded in securing a gaming facility under this exception.)

[72] June 13, 2011, Memorandum, at 5 (with reference to 25 C.F.R., Part 292).

[73] June 23, 2011, Memorandum at 7.

[74] S. 771, 112th Cong., 1st Sess. (2011).

[75] *Id.*, Sec. 2, adding 25 U.S.C. §2719(b)(2)(A).

[76] This is a regulation implementing the Native American Graves Protection and Repatriation Act of 1990. P.L. 101-601; 25 U.S.C. 3001–3013;104 Stat. 3048–3058.

[77] *Id.*, adding 25 U.S.C. §2719(b)(2)(C).

[78] Under S. 1424, "off-reservation land" is defined to mean land that is outside of and not contiguous to a tribe's reservation, "located beyond a reasonable commuting distance from the reservation," and "likely to qualify for, result in, or be associated with the development of an Indian Gaming facility." S. 1424, 112th Cong, 1st Sess., Sec.2(a).

[79] *Id.*, Sec. 2(c)(1).

[80] *Id.*, sec 2(c)(2).

[81] H.R. 783, 112th Cong., 1st Sess. (2011); S. 379, 112th Cong., 1st Sess. (2011), sections 106(d); 206(d); 306(d); 406(d); and 506(d).

[82] H.R. 1250/S. 675, 112th Cong., 1st Sess. (2011), Section 10(a).

[83] S. 617, 112th Cong., 1st Sess. (2011).

[84] *Id.*, Sec. 2(d)(1).

[85] S. 908, 112th Cong., 1st Sess. (2011).

[86] 25 U.S.C. §711e.

[87] S. 908, §1, adding 25 U.S.C. §711e(f)(4).

[88] S . 1218, 112th Cong., 1st Sess. (2011); H.R. 27, 112th Cong., 1st Sess. (2011).

[89] *Id.*, Sec. 4(b).

[90] H.R. 475, 112th Cong., 1st Sess. (2011).

[91] *Id.*, Sec. 2(f).

[92] H.R. 1991, 1 12th Cong., 1st Sess.), §4 (e) (2011).

In: American Indians. Volume 1
Editors: Albert O. Hughes and Eric A. Sanders

ISBN: 978-1-61122-351-4
© 2012 Nova Science Publishers, Inc.

Chapter 7

INDIAN RESERVED WATER RIGHTS UNDER THE WINTERS DOCTRINE: AN OVERVIEW[*]

Cynthia Brougher

SUMMARY

Although the federal government has authority to regulate water, it typically defers to the states to allocate water resources within the state. The federal government maintains certain federal water rights, though, which exist separate from state law. In particular, federal reserved water rights often arise in questions of water allocation related to federal lands, including Indian reservations. Indian reserved water rights were first recognized by the U.S. Supreme Court in *Winters v. United States* in 1908. Under the *Winters* doctrine, when Congress reserves land (i.e., for an Indian reservation), Congress also reserves water sufficient to fulfill the purpose of the reservation.

As the need for water grows with the development of new industries and growing populations, the tension arising from the allocation of scarce water resources highlights the difficulties that often surround reserved water rights, particularly in the western states. Western states generally follow some form of the prior appropriation system of water allocation. The prior appropriation system allocates water to users based on the order in which water rights were properly acquired. Because Indian reserved water rights date back to the government's reservation of the land for the Indians, these water rights often pre-date other water users' claims. Although the prior appropriation system's reliance on seniority provides a degree of certainty to water allocation, Indian reserved water rights may not have been quantified at the time of reservation. Because *Winters* did not dictate a formula to determine the quantity of water reserved, courts apply different standards to quantify tribal reserved water rights. As a result, other water users may not know whether, or the extent to which, Indian reserved water rights have priority. Because of these uncertainties, Indian reserved water rights are often litigated or negotiated in settlements and related legislation.

---

[*] This is an edited, reformatted and augmented version of the Congressional Research Service Publication, CRS Report for Congress RL32198, dated June 8, 2011.

This report will examine the creation of Indian reserved water rights under the *Winters* doctrine. It will analyze the scope of the doctrine, including the purposes for which the water right may be claimed and the sources from which the water may be drawn. It will also discuss various quantification standards that courts have used in attempting to clarify Indian reserved water rights. Finally, it will examine the effect of the McCarran Amendment, through which Congress extended jurisdiction to state courts to hear disputes involving Indian reserved water rights.

INTRODUCTION

Although allocation of water resources is generally a matter of state law, the federal government may also allocate water rights. Under the Supreme Court's 1908 *Winters v. United States* decision, when Congress creates an Indian reservation, the water necessary to fulfill the reservation's purposes is reserved implicitly.[1] Although this doctrine appears to be fairly straightforward, the scarcity of sufficient water in more arid parts of the country has resulted in contentious debate over the requirements of *Winters* and its impact on competing water rights. Because federal reserved water rights under the *Winters* doctrine often have not been quantified but are generally senior to other water rights, the rights of more junior water users can be affected significantly, when these federal rights are exercised.

This report provides background on Indian reserved water rights under *Winters*. It analyzes the scope of these rights, including the water sources that may be used to fulfill the rights and the quantification standards courts commonly use to clarify the rights. The report also examines the effect of the McCarran Amendment, through which Congress authorized state courts to adjudicate Indian reserved water rights.

THE *WINTERS* DOCTRINE OF RESERVED WATER RIGHTS

In *Winters,* the Supreme Court examined tribal rights to water associated with the Fort Belknap Reservation located in what would later become Montana.[2] The Fort Belknap Reservation was created by an agreement in 1888 between tribal parties and the U.S. government. At the time, the government had a policy seeking to transform Native Americans from "a nomadic and uncivilized people ... to become a pastoral and civilized people" by providing them lands to develop for such purposes.[3]

By 1905, the area experienced water shortages that ultimately resulted in the *Winters* lawsuit being filed to enforce tribal rights to water against non-Indian water users who had been diverting water from the region.[4] In announcing its decision, the Court explained that the lands provided under the agreement for the purpose of developing an agrarian society "were arid and, without irrigation, were practically valueless."[5] The Court also noted that ambiguities in the agreement, such as the status of the water rights related to the land, are to be "resolved from the standpoint of the Indians," as a rule of interpretation.[6] The Court held that:

The power of the Government to reserve the waters and exempt them from appropriation under the state laws is not denied, and could not be. That the Government did reserve them we have decided, and for a use which would be necessarily continued through the years.[7]

The Court has continued to recognize the principle derived from *Winters* in both Indian and non- Indian contexts. In 1976, the Court noted that it "has long held that when the Federal Government withdraws its land from the public domain and reserves it for a federal purpose, the Government, by implication, reserves appurtenant water then unappropriated to the extent needed to accomplish the purpose of the reservation."[8]

SCOPE OF *WINTERS* RIGHTS

Under the *Winters* doctrine, the priority and extent of Indian reserved water rights is affected by the purposes of the Indian reservation, the date when the Indian reservation was created, the quantification of water sufficient to accomplish those purposes, and the sources of water that may be used to fulfill the particular water rights.

Effect on State Water Allocation

Although the federal government may act under a number of constitutional authorities to regulate water, in most instances it has deferred to the states. States either adhere to a riparian or prior appropriation system of water allocation. In a riparian system, landowners adjacent to a waterway share a common right to use the water, with a limitation of reasonableness.[9] In times of water shortages, all riparian rights holders must share the burden of the shortage proportionally.

Other states, typically the drier western states, use a prior appropriation system of water rights. Under prior appropriation, water users who make beneficial use of a water supply, regardless of their location relative to it, obtain a right to that water under a seniority system that reflects the order in which the right was obtained.[10] The date that the user put the water to beneficial use is known as the priority date. Some states incorporate elements of both the riparian and appropriation doctrines.

Because riparian rights' holders must share the burden of any water shortage proportionally, Indian reserved water rights generally do not have a noticeable impact in riparian jurisdictions. In prior appropriation systems, recognition of a tribe's water rights is often times more contentious because, in times of shortage, junior users may receive none of their allocations after a tribe with senior takes its share under the *Winters* doctrine. Tribes often have seniority because the laws, treaties, executive orders, and other legal agreements that created the Indian reservations (and thus the priority date for purposes of seniority) predate other settlement of the area.[11] Allocation of scarce water is further complicated by the fact that a tribe's reserved water rights under the *Winters* doctrine are not lost if the tribe does not maintain continuous use of the rights. As a result, junior rights holders may be unaware that a tribe has senior reserved rights, leaving the junior rights holder with little or no allocated water in some instances.[12]

Tribes may also acquire water rights under state law. That is, if water is available under the state water allocation system and a tribe requires water beyond what it receives under its federal reserved water rights, it may seek to acquire state water rights to supplement its federal reserved rights.

Purposes of Reserved Water Rights

Under *Winters*, the reserved water rights are tied to the purpose (and in some cases, purposes) of the reservation, as embodied in the particular law, treaty, agreement, or executive order that created the reservation. It is unclear, however, whether the primary purpose standard the Supreme Court adopted when applying Winters in non-Indian reserved water rights cases governs Indian reserved water rights. Under the primary purpose standard, reserved water rights may be applied only for the primary purposes of reservations, not for secondary purposes.[13] In *Cappaert*, the Supreme Court held that water rights are limited to the "amount of water necessary to fulfill the purpose of the reservation, no more."[14] In *United States v. New Mexico*, the Supreme Court further clarified that the test is whether "the purposes of the reservation would be entirely defeated" without that water.[15]

Lower courts generally define Indian reservation purposes broadly, which reflects the reasoning in *Winters* that Indian reservations were created in order to transform and sustain a new lifestyle for the tribe. In one case, the Arizona Supreme Court refused to limit Indian reserved rights to only the primary purpose of a reservation.[16] The court noted the importance of providing the Indians with "a permanent home and abiding place," as well as the need for "broader interpretation [of the purposes of Indian reserved rights] in order to further the federal goal of Indian self-sufficiency."[17] The court emphasized the need for a broad interpretation of the purposes of the reservation, recognizing that it is difficult to ascertain "the true reasons for which Indian reservations were created."[18] Similarly, the U.S. Court of Appeals for the Ninth Circuit interpreted the primary purpose of a reservation to encompass a number of related purposes.[19] It found that the primary purpose of a reservation was to create a homeland for the tribe, which included water rights that could be used not only for irrigation but also for fishing.[20] Other courts have rejected such broad interpretations, noting the inherent risks in placing no limits on the water rights associated with a reservation and accordingly limiting water rights only to purposes that were specifically contemplated when the reservation was created.[21]

Changes in Water Use

Although state law generally restricts changes in water use from the originally designated purpose of the water right, Indian reserved water rights are not subject to such restrictions. As discussed later in this report, courts quantify the amount of Indian reserved water rights based on the purposes of the reservation. Once quantified, some decisions have allowed Indian reserved water rights to be used for purposes other than those considered in the quantification of the right.[22] Other courts, however, have refused to allow tribes to change their water use from the purpose contemplated when the reservation was created. For example, the Wyoming Supreme Court refused to permit tribes to apply their reserved rights to instream flows.[23]

Water Sources

Finding the water to fulfill a water right is often the most controversial element of water rights claims, particularly in times of shortage. The question of which water sources may be used to fulfill reserved rights is not clearly resolved. Although Indian reserved rights generally attach to whatever water sources may be within or adjacent to the reserved lands, it is generally understood that reserved rights do not necessarily require that the water source be encompassed within the reserved lands.[24] Rather, courts have allowed tribes to draw water from various sources as necessary to fulfill the reservation purpose, limiting the potential sources only to the extent that the waters must be unappropriated at the time the reservation was created.[25] In other words, an Indian reserved water right cannot trump senior rights that existed at the time of reservation.

One question on which courts have disagreed is whether the reserved water right may draw from groundwater, or if it is limited to surface water. In *In re Big Horn*, the Wyoming Supreme Court rejected applying the *Winters* doctrine to groundwater.[26] While acknowledging that groundwater and surface water sources are often connected, the court held that there was no precedent for applying the *Winters* doctrine to groundwater.[27]

On the other hand, the Arizona Supreme Court has held that reserved rights may include claims to groundwater, if the groundwater is necessary to fulfill the purpose of the reservation.[28] Finding that the government's reservation must have contemplated water "from whatever particular sources each reservation had at hand,"[29] the court explained that the "significant question for the purpose of the reserved rights doctrine is not whether the water runs above or below the ground but whether it is necessary to accomplish the purpose of the reservation."[30] Although the court recognized that many possible water sources could be used to fulfill reserved rights claims, it also noted that groundwater should only be claimed if other sources were insufficient to accomplish the purpose of the reservation.[31]

Water Quality

When degradation of water quality would undermine the water's use for reservation purposes, courts have recognized water quality as another element of Indian reserved water rights. Federal courts have ruled that reserved water rights holders can seek legal protection from water quality degradation by other water users. Specifically in *United States v. Gila Valley Irrigation District*, the Ninth Circuit approved a district court's finding that a reserved water right was impaired when other users' actions increased the salinity of water used by a tribe for irrigation of agricultural crops.[32]

QUANTIFICATION

While the Supreme Court recognized Indian reserved water rights in *Winters*, it only provided that the extent of such rights were those necessary to fulfill the purpose of the reservation. Quantification of reserved rights was left for later judicial interpretation.

Practicably Irrigable Acreage Standard

In 1963, the Supreme Court approved a special master's decision on Indian reserved water rights that used a quantification standard based on agricultural water requirements in *Arizona v. California*.[33] Faced with a choice between a subjective standard favored by states seeking flexibility and an objective standard that would fix the amount of water reserved, the special master in the interstate water dispute endorsed the latter, using what is known as the practicably irrigable acreage standard (PIA). The PIA reflects the agricultural purposes of creating reservations under the *Winters* doctrine, basing the quantification of reserved water rights on the amount of lands that can be feasibly and reasonably irrigated. In reviewing the special master's decision, the Supreme Court rejected a proposed quantification "measured by the Indians' 'reasonably foreseeable needs,' which, the Court pointed out, means by the number of Indians."[34] The Court explained that such a basis was unworkable as it could only be guessed.[35] The Court held that "the only feasible and fair way by which reserved water for the reservations can be measured is irrigable acreage."[36] The Court's reasoning in *Arizona* emphasized the importance of the water right to the land reservation. Finding it "impossible" that Congress and the Executive branch would reserve land that was mostly desert without providing water as well, the Court noted that "water from the river would be essential to the life of the Indian people and to the animals they hunted and the crops they raised."[37]

The Court's approval of the special master's decision, however, did not require adoption of the PIA standard as a matter of law and other courts have interpreted quantification of *Winters* rights differently.[38] The Wyoming Supreme Court has applied the PIA using a two-part test to determine which lands would qualify for purposes of quantification of the water right.[39] Under the test, those lands include 1) those physically capable of sustained irrigation and 2) those which are irrigable at a reasonable cost.[40] The U.S. Supreme Court reviewed the decision but because the Court was evenly divided in its decision, no definitive ruling was issued.[41] Rather, without a majority of the Court agreeing on an outcome for the case, the Wyoming Supreme Court's opinion was affirmed.[42]

Other Quantification Standards

The PIA standard has not been applied by all courts, however. The Arizona Supreme Court rejected the standard because it had the potential to treat tribes inequitably based on their geographic location; because it imposed an agricultural lifestyle that was not necessarily productive in the current times; and because it posed a risk that accounting for every potentially irrigable acre would in some cases result in "an overabundance of water."[43] The court explained that creating "a permanent homeland requires water for multiple uses, which may or may not include agriculture."[44] The court further explained that "the PIA standard, however, forces tribes to prove economic feasibility for a kind of enterprise that, judging from the evidence of both federal and private willingness to invest money, is simply no longer economically feasible in the West."[45] The court instead offered a number of potential factors for consideration in the quantification: 1) the tribe's history of and cultural need for water; 2) the nature of the land and associated resources of the reservation; 3) the tribe's economic status and the proposed economic development to the extent that they involve a need for water; 4) historic reliance of the tribe on water for the proposed purpose; and 5) the tribe's current and projected population.[46]

ADJUDICATION OF INDIAN RESERVED WATER RIGHTS

Indian reserved water rights are subject to adjudication by federal and state courts. Federal courts have historically been authorized via federal question jurisdiction to determine Indian reserved water rights under the *Winters* doctrine. In 1952, however, Congress enacted an appropriations rider known as the McCarran Amendment that waived federal sovereign immunity in specified forms of water adjudications. Although the language does not explicitly mention Indian water rights, the McCarran Amendment gives consent to join the federal government in state lawsuits regarding adjudication of water rights in river systems and the administration of those rights.[47]

The Supreme Court has held that the McCarran Amendment allows state courts to adjudicate Indian reserved water rights.[48] As a result, the McCarran Amendment has had a significant effect on Indian water law. As evidenced in the varying outcomes of decisions related to the scope and quantification of Indian reserved water rights, the states have not interpreted the requirements of *Winters* uniformly, adding to the complexity of determining a tribe's reserved water rights.

The grant of state jurisdiction over the adjudication of Indian reserved water rights has resulted in a contentious debate over the appropriate forum for such claims.[49] The Court has explained that Congress' enactment of the McCarran Amendment indicated a policy supporting "the availability of comprehensive state systems for adjudication of water rights" and noted that concurrent federal proceedings may lead to duplicative and possibly contradictory judgments.[50] However, concerns exist regarding the expansion of jurisdiction over federal water rights to state courts. Tribes have long considered state courts to be hostile, and the prospect of having those same courts adjudicate Indian reserved water rights has been one of the primary motivations for pursuing negotiated settlements.[51] Also, some have questioned the ability of state trial courts to adjudicate Indian water law issues, which often involve complicated federal legal issues.[52]

End Notes

[1] Winters v. United States, 207 U.S. 564, 575-77 (1908). Reserved water rights established under the *Winters* doctrine are only one form of Indian water rights and will be the focus of this report. Other forms of Indian water rights include rights commonly referred to as *Winans* rights and Pueblo Indian rights, but these are beyond the scope of this report.

[2] *Id.*

[3] *Id.* at 576.

[4] Cohen's Handbook of Federal Indian Law § 19.02, LexisNexis/Matthew Bender 2009.

[5] *Winters*, 207 U.S. at 576.

[6] *Id. See also* CRS Report 97-589, *Statutory Interpretation: General Principles and Recent Trends*, by Larry M. Eig.

[7] *Winters*, 207 U.S. at 577 (citations omitted).

[8] *See* Cappaert v. United States, 426 U.S. 128, 138 (1976).

[9] *See generally* A. Dan Tarlock, Law of Water Rights and Water Resources, ch. 3 "Common Law of Riparian Rights" (2008).

[10] *See generally id.* at ch. 5 "Prior Appropriation Doctrine."

[11] *See, e.g., Winters*, 207 U.S. 564 (statute); United States v. Adair, 723 F.2d 1394 (9th Cir. 1983) (treaty); Arizona v. California, 373 U.S. 546 (1963) (executive order).

[12] *See Winters*, 207 U.S. 564. *See also* Cohen's Handbook of Federal Indian Law § 19.03[1].

[13] *Id.* at 702 ("Where water is necessary to fulfill the very purposes for which a federal reservation was created, it is reasonable to conclude ... that the United States intended to reserve the necessary water. Where water is only valuable for a secondary use on the reservation, ... Congress intended ... that the United States would acquire water in the same manner as any other public or private appropriator.").

[14] *Cappaert*, 426 U.S. at 141. Although the *Winters* doctrine has generally been extended to non-Indian reservations, certain aspects of the reserved right may be treated differently in Indian rights contexts as compared to non-Indian rights contexts.

[15] United States v. New Mexico, 438 U.S. 696, 700 (1978).

[16] *In re* General Adjudication of All Rights to Use Water in the Gila River System and Source, 35 P.3d 68, 74-75 (Ariz. 2001).

[17] *Id.* at 74 (internal quotations and citations omitted).

[18] *Id.* at 75.

[19] Colville Confederated Tribes v. Walton, 647 F.2d 42, 47 (9th Cir. 1981).

[20] *Id.*

[21] *See, e.g., In re* General Adjudication of All Rights to Use Water in the Big Horn River System, 753 P.2d 76, 96-99 (Wyo. 1988) (finding that the sole purpose of the treaty creating a reservation at issue was agriculture, even though the treaty also implied that the tribe may engage in a number of other activities).

[22] The Supreme Court approved a special master's decision noting that a quantification based on a standard measured by agriculture purposes did not prohibit the tribe from putting the water to use for other purposes. See Arizona v. California, 1960 Term, No. 8 Orig. Report of Simon H. Rifkind, Special Master 254-66 at 265-66 (Dec. 5, 1960); Arizona v. California, 439 U.S. 419 (1979).

[23] *In re* General Adjudication of All Rights to Use Water in Big Horn River System, 835 P.2d 273, 279 (Wyo. 1992). Instream flows generally refer to water that remains in the river.

[24] *See Cappaert*, 426 U.S. at 138-39; *Arizona v. California*, 373 U.S. at 598-99; *Winters*, 207 U.S. at 565. *See also* United States v. Ahtanum Irrigation Dist., 236 F.2d 321, 325 (9th Cir. 1956).

[25] *See* Arizona v. California, 373 U.S. 546 (1963).

[26] *In re Big Horn*, 753 P.2d at 99-100.

[27] *Id.*

[28] *In re* General Adjudication of All Rights to Use Water in the Gila River System and Source, 989 P.2d 739, 745-48 (Ariz. 1999).

[29] *Id.* at 747.

[30] *Id.*

[31] *Id.* at 748.

[32] United States v. Gila Valley Irrigation District, 117 F.3d 425 (9th Cir. 1997), *aff'g* 920 F. Supp. 1444 (D. Ariz. 1996).

[33] 373 U.S. 546.

[34] *Id.* at 600-01.

[35] *Id.*

[36] *Id.* at 601. The quantification approved by the Court called for about one million acre-feet of water for about 135,000 irrigable acres of land. *Id.* at 595-96.

[37] *Id.* at 598-99.

[38] The special master's decision approved in Arizona v. California specifically noted that applying the PIA standard did not mean "that water reserved for Indian Reservations may not be used for purposes other than agriculture and related uses." Arizona v. California, 1960 Term, No. 8 Orig. Report of Simon H. Rifkind, Special Master 254-66 at 265-66 (Dec. 5, 1960). The Court approved application of the PIA standard in that case because the parties had agreed that reserved rights could be used for purposes other than agriculture. *See* Arizona v. California, 439 U.S. 419 (1979).

[39] *In re Big Horn*, 753 P.2d at 100-01.

[40] *Id.* at 101.

[41] Wyoming v. United States, 492 U.S. 406 (1989).

[42] *Id.*

[43] *In re Gila River*, 35 P.3d at 77-79.

[44] *Id.* at 78 (internal quotations omitted).

[45] *Id.*

[46] *Id.* at 79-81.

[47] 43 U.S.C. § 666.

[48] Colorado River Water Conservation District v. United States, 424 U.S. 800, 809-11 (1976). *See also* Arizona v. San Carlos Apache Tribe of Arizona, 463 U.S. 545, 566-69 (1983).

[49] *See* Stephen M. Feldman, *The Supreme Court's New Sovereign Immunity Doctrine and the McCarran Amendment: Toward Ending State Adjudication of Indian Water Rights*, 18 Harv. Envtl. L. Rev. 433 (1994).

[50] *Colorado River Water Conservation District*, 424 U.S. at 819.

[51] *See* Daniel McCool, Native Waters: Contemporary Indian Water Settlements and the Second Treaty Era 75-76 (2002).

[52] *See* Feldman, *supra* note 49.

INDEX

C

D

E

I

J

K

L

M

N

O

S